# Teaching English as an International Language

# NEW PERSPECTIVES ON LANGUAGE AND EDUCATION
**Series Editor:** Professor Viv Edwards, *University of Reading, Reading, Great Britain*
**Series Advisor:** Professor Allan Luke, *Queensland University of Technology, Brisbane, Australia*

Two decades of research and development in language and literacy education have yielded a broad, multidisciplinary focus. Yet education systems face constant economic and technological change, with attendant issues of identity and power, community and culture. This series will feature critical and interpretive, disciplinary and multidisciplinary perspectives on teaching and learning, language and literacy in new times.

**Recent Books in the Series**
Distance Education and Languages: Evolution and Change
    *Börje Holmberg, Monica Shelley and Cynthia White (eds)*
Ebonics: The Urban Education Debate (2nd edn)
    *J.D. Ramirez, T.G. Wiley, G. de Klerk, E. Lee and W.E. Wright (eds)*
Decolonisation, Globalisation: Language-in-Education Policy and Practice
    *Angel M.Y. Lin and Peter W. Martin (eds)*
Travel Notes from the New Literacy Studies: Instances of Practice
    *Kate Pahl and Jennifer Rowsell (eds)*
Social Context and Fluency in L2 Learners: The Case of Wales
    *Lynda Pritchard Newcombe*
Social Actions for Classroom Language Learning
    *John Hellermann*

**Other Books of Interest**
Cross-linguistic Similarity in Foreign Language Learning
    *Håkan Ringbom*
Developing Minority Language Resources
    *Guadalupe Valdés, Joshua A. Fishman, Rebecca Chávez and William Pérez*
Deep Culture: The Hidden Challenges of Global Living
    *Joseph Shaules*
Education for Intercultural Citizenship: Concepts and Comparisons
    *Geof Alred, Mike Byram and Mike Fleming (eds)*
Language and Identity in a Dual Immersion School
    *Kim Potowski*
Language Learning and Teacher Education: A Sociocultural Approach
    *Margaret R. Hawkins (ed.)*
Language, Space and Power: A Critical Look at Bilingual Education
    *Samina Hadi-Tabassum*
Living and Studying Abroad: Research and Practice
    *Michael Byram and Anwei Feng (eds)*
Online Intercultural Exchange: An Introduction for Foreign Language Teachers
    *Robert O'Dowd (ed.)*
Understanding Deaf Culture: In Search of Deafhood
    *Paddy Ladd*

**For more details of these or any other of our publications, please contact:**
**Multilingual Matters, Frankfurt Lodge, Clevedon Hall,**
**Victoria Road, Clevedon, BS21 7HH, England**
**http://www.multilingual-matters.com**

**NEW PERSPECTIVES ON LANGUAGE AND EDUCATION**
Series Editor: Viv Edwards

# Teaching English as an International Language
## Identity, Resistance and Negotiation

Phan Le Ha

**MULTILINGUAL MATTERS LTD**
Clevedon • Buffalo • Toronto

**Library of Congress Cataloging in Publication Data**
Phan, Le Ha
Teaching English as an International Language: Identity, Resistance and Negotiation
Phan Le Ha.
New Perspectives on Language and Education
Includes bibliographical references and index.
1. English language–Study and teaching–Foreign speakers. 2. English language–
Globalization. 3. Language teachers. 4. Language and culture. 5. Second language
acquisition. I. Title.
PE1128.A2P49 2008
428.007–dc22                    2007040061

**British Library Cataloguing in Publication Data**
A catalogue entry for this book is available from the British Library.

ISBN-13: 978-1-84769-049-4 (hbk)
ISBN-13: 978-1-84769-048-7 (pbk)

**Multilingual Matters Ltd**
*UK*: Frankfurt Lodge, Clevedon Hall, Victoria Road, Clevedon BS21 7HH.
*USA*: UTP, 2250 Military Road, Tonawanda, NY 14150, USA.
*Canada*: UTP, 5201 Dufferin Street, North York, Ontario M3H 5T8, Canada.

The policy of Multilingual Matters/Channel View Publications is to use papers that
are natural, renewable and recyclable products, made from wood grown in
sustainable forests. In the manufacturing process of our books, and to further support
our policy, preference is given to printers that have FSC and PEFC Chain of Custody
certification. The FSC and/or PEFC logos will appear on those books where full
certification has been granted to the printer concerned.

Typeset by Bookcraft Ltd.
Printed and bound in Great Britain by the Cromwell Press Ltd.

# Contents

# Foreword

The emergence of English as a global language has given rise to many interesting and important debates. Who, if anyone, owns the language – the relatively smaller numbers of native speakers or the much larger numbers of speakers who use it for an ever-growing range of functions? Does International English offer opportunities for neutrality that mitigate the colonial imperialism of the British or the cultural imperialism of the USA? Alternatively, is what we are witnessing best understood in terms of appropriation, as international users harness English for their own purposes?

The meteoric rise of English is closely mirrored, of course, by the growth in the teaching of the language. Given the millions of consumers and the thousands of teachers and support staff, references to the English language *industry* are by no means overplayed. Initially, native speakers dominated English language teaching and they remain in high demand. Growing numbers of English teachers are, however, multilingual, non-native speakers of English. But how do they position themselves in relation to the debates about English? Do they see themselves as international servants or mediators of English? How are they perceived within their own societies? How do they reconcile their own cultural assumptions about teaching with those which underpin the pedagogies associated with teaching English as an international language?

In the pages which follow, Phan Le Ha addresses these and many other related issues. Her arguments and evidence challenge conventional wisdom and nudge our thinking forward. At the same time, and most unusually, she melds Western and Eastern perspectives on similar themes. She sets about this task with a highly distinctive, often lyrical, voice.

Many writers alert us to the dangers associated with the post-colonial dimension of TESOL and ownership of English as an international language. Phan Le Ha, however, demonstrates that this is not a black-and-white issue by drawing attention to both advantages for international teachers of English and to the ways in which they negotiate and resist.

She communicates the tensions for Western-trained teachers using the wonderful metaphor of the 'daughter-in-law of a hundred families'.

There are different messages for different audiences: for native speakers she challenges many assumptions; for non-native speakers she offers strength through introspection.

Viv Edwards

# Acknowledgements

Writing is my identity. Writing this book has shaped my identity as much as my identity has shaped what and how I have written.

When I was very little, I always saw my parents reading and writing, and that captured my attention and generated my love for writing. One day, after coming home from school, I told my parents that I was selected to participate in a competition for gifted literature students in Hanoi, and that I was expected to attend a preparatory course held by the Department of Education and Training of Hanoi. Right from that moment, I could feel that my parents would give me everything they could afford for my dream to be fulfilled. And today I am writing my own book.

I am most grateful to my parents for nurturing my dream and for their ceaseless encouragement and confidence in me. The support and love I have received from my husband, Phan Luong Dang, cannot be expressed in words. I thank my little twins, Ha Le and Ha Chi, for understanding my worries, anxiety and determination. All these supports have given me strength to work hard and make my dream come true.

I deeply and sincerely thank Lesley Farrell and Rosemary Viete, my very first 'writing' lecturers in Australia, for their generous comments and support of me having my own voice in writing. Their appreciation for my ideas and voice has been so important in building self-confidence in my writing journey. I thank Marie-Therese Jensen and Margaret Gearon, my lecturers, whose classes were the initial catalyst for my increasing interest in teacher identity. I would like to pay tribute to the useful guidance and valuable comments of Viv Edwards, editor of the *New Perspectives on Language and Education* series. My gratitude is also extended to the Multi-lingual Matters staff, especially Marjukka Grover and Tommi Grover, who have always been friendly, supportive and available whenever needed. Roby Marlina, my dear friend, student and colleague, has always shared with me how he feels, as a teacher, when reading my work. His reflective eye on my writing is invaluably meaningful.

I am grateful to Fazal Rizvi for having challenged me with his extensive knowledge of postcolonial theories and accordingly advising me to incorporate the works of postcolonial writers in this book. I thank scholars whose philosophies have inspired me and served as grounds for me to shape, extend, challenge, question and enrich my ideas, especially Phan Ngoc, Tran Ngoc Them, Tran Quoc Vuong, Duong Thieu Tong, Robert Phillipson, Alastair Pennycook, Stuart Hall, Henry Widdowson, Adrian Holliday, Suresh Canagarajah, Claire Kramsch and Gay Garland Reed. I thank all other scholars whom I have referred to throughout the book.

I thank my colleagues Farzad Sharifian, Simon Marginson and Matthew Piscioneri for their generosity in sharing their knowledge with me and spending time commenting on my work. Farzad, in particular, offered detailed feedback on my book proposal and recommended it be sent to Multilingual Matters. Coming from a philosophy background, Matthew's taking the devil's advocate role in relation to my ideas has helped me clarify many important arguments. I thank the staff in the Faculty of Education, Monash University, and my friends and students for their encouragement over the years. In particular, Ying (Faith) Wen's kindness in offering to go through all the references helped make the book ready at the very final stage.

I thank all the teachers who have kindly agreed to be part of this project and shared with me their identity formation journeys as Western-trained Vietnamese teachers of English. They are the very ones who have kept my research interest alive and helped it to be carried out. They deserve my final words of gratitude.

I have made every effort to ensure careful interpretations and presentation of all references. However, if I misinterpret any point discussed in these references, I would like to apologise to the authors in advance. Should there be any errors or omissions in referencing or citation, I hope to be advised so as to be able to fix it. I would like to acknowledge that several sections of this book are drawn from my previous publications: Phan Le Ha (2004); Phan Le Ha (2005); Phan Le Ha (2006); Phan Le Ha (2007); Phan Le Ha (forthcoming); and Phan Le Ha and Phan Van Que (2006).

Phan Le Ha
*Monash University, Australia, May 2007*

Chapter 1
# Introduction

*Teachers of the English word,*
*we are tossed about,*
*defined by others,*
*insecure*
*yet whole.*
*We are special,*
*knowledge experts, moral guides*
*and yet the public's tails.*
*We have access to the world,*
*we belong,*
*yet seem foreignised,*
*unselectively*
*Westernised.*
*We are not allowed to be human,*
*to fall in love*
*(with students),*
*yet we need to live, to change.*
*We are nobody in this world of Others*
*yet not the shadow of native English teachers*
*we light the way for our own.*
*We are the daughter-in-law of a hundred families*
*And proudly ourselves,*
*growing.*

## The Need to Investigate Teacher Identity in the Context of English as an International Language

The recent tendency to treat English as an international language (EIL) has suggested the possibility of forming a new group of EIL teachers (Llurda, 2004; McKay, 2002). Those who support this tendency have argued that much of the communication in English nowadays is between non-native speakers, and speakers of English tend to be multilingual. Nevertheless, how to teach EIL and how teachers of English negotiate their identities and reconceptualise their pedagogies remain under-discussed. In other words, while attention has been given to the development of EIL and EIL methodologies, the question of EIL teacher identity formation has hardly been addressed. In addition, within the limited existing literature on teacher identity in bilingual and second language education (Block, 2005; Morgan, 2004; Varghese, 2004; Varghese *et al.*, 2005), identity is not a central concern. Neither is teacher identity in these works explored in close relationship with local teaching contexts and English as an international language.

Various aspects of teacher identity are assumed and imagined rather than proved in current literature on the ownership of EIL, such as whether teachers of English see themselves as ambassadors/international mediators or 'servants' of English, whether they negotiate their identities according to the romanticising prospects of EIL and how being teachers of English is seen by their societies. While globalisation heavily relies on English, and English language teaching (ELT) solely relies on English teachers and English teaching, what happens to English teachers and their teaching is an important question that needs to be explored, particularly in the context of mobility and transnationality. Moreover, understanding what teachers want, how they perceive themselves and how they are often represented is crucial to the success of ELT teacher training courses and EIL pedagogy in global and local contexts.

This book discusses in particular the identity formation of Western-trained Vietnamese teachers of English, whose identity formation processes respond to all of the above concerns. These EIL teachers see themselves as 'the daughter-in-law of a hundred families', a figurative translation of the Vietnamese expression 'lam dau tram ho'. It is assumed in Vietnamese society that being a daughter-in-law is very demanding, since a girl has to try hard to please her in-law family, particularly the mother-in-law. She will have to distribute her attention everywhere so as not to be judged as bad. She has to 'please' many parties. So when being a teacher is compared with being a daughter-in-law, it suggests that being a teacher is already hard, but being a daughter-in-law of a hundred families is a hundred times more difficult. How can a teacher satisfy all expectations from multiple parties? This expression indicates how difficult it is to play the teacher role in Vietnamese society, where whatever a teacher does is being judged by the whole society. At the global and transnational level, specifically given the literature surrounding EIL and these teachers' movement in space and time between Vietnam and the English-speaking

West, the identity formation processes of these 'daughters-in-law of a hundred families' undergo complexity, contradictions, tensions, negotiations, sophistication yet fluidity, connectedness and continuity at all these interlinked mobile domains, personal, local, global and transnational.

In particular, this book examines how Western-trained Vietnamese teachers of EIL see themselves as professionals and as individuals in relation to their work practices. It reveals the often invisible sides of their identity, which are the tensions, compromises, negotiations and contradictions in their enactment of different roles and selves. Furthermore, very importantly, as Holliday (2005) consistently demonstrates in his book, native-speakerism (his term) is dominant in almost every teaching setting, and heavily influences EIL teachers' perceptions and practices. This book on the one hand examines in what ways and aspects native-speakerism applies to these Vietnamese teachers and on the other shows that they often do not identify themselves in relation to it and offer us alternatives that are healthy for critical EIL pedagogy.

## 'Daughter-in-Law of a Hundred Families': Western-trained Vietnamese Teachers of EIL

As a result of historical and political circumstances, Vietnam has only recently opened its doors to the world. English language education, though enjoying a long history in Vietnam (Phan Van Que *et al.*, forthcoming), has only started to boom over the last 20 or so years. This boom has created opportunities for teachers of English to go overseas for further professional training. Australia has appeared to serve as the second 'former Soviet Union' in terms of training tertiary teachers and scholars for Vietnam since then. In addition, other English-speaking countries have also contributed to this teacher training and/or professional development process. There is now a large group of so-called 'Western-trained Vietnamese teachers of English' working at universities in Vietnam.

The last 20 years have witnessed the heyday of Vietnamese teachers of English. Their identities have been coupled with how English has been seen. Being a teacher of English has become desirable and fashionable, and it is attached to opportunities, wealth and advanced education. Teachers of English have also been seen as being more 'Westernised', in that their enactment of their teacher roles has been assumed to be more or less influenced by English and associated values. Those teachers who are trained in English-speaking countries are seen even more critically by Vietnamese society. They are, again, labelled with additional identities because of their physical exposure to the West.

Unlike its neighbouring countries, such as China, Japan, Korea and Thailand, where much of the English language teaching is done by native-English-speaking teachers (for example, Han, 2004; Sakui, 2004), in Vietnam most of this teaching is undertaken by local teachers. I see this as being healthy and playing an important role in the ways Vietnamese teachers of English perceive their identities, as they rarely face the native–non-native dichotomy directly in their working environments. This may give them certain self-images as teachers of English. And this, again, largely influences how their professional identity formation takes place, and hence goes far beyond the native-speakerism discussed in Holliday (2005). Native-speakerism is not necessarily the factor that defines English teachers.

The Western-trained EIL Vietnamese teachers referred to in this book have been all lecturers or hold adjunct lecturing positions at universities in different regions of Vietnam. Most of what is reported in this book was based on a case study research project (from 2000 to 2004), with the data obtained from seven Vietnamese teachers who, at the time of this study, were doing their Master of Education degree, specialising in TESOL, at different universities in Australia. Follow-up email exchanges and phone conversations with them continued after they had completed their courses and returned to Vietnam. To understand their identity formation, intensive use of in-depth interviews, reflective writing and email correspondence was adopted over the research period. A similar study, but on a less intensive scale, was conducted over 2005 and 2006 with another nine Vietnamese teachers who had finished their postgraduate studies in TESOL-related areas in the UK, US, Australia and New Zealand. Conversation-style interviews, phone conversations and email exchanges were employed for data collection.

All these 16 teacher participants had had teaching experience at either teacher training colleges/universities or universities where English was the major subject in different parts of Vietnam before they commenced their courses in Australia, the UK, US and New Zealand. There were 12 female and four male participants. Their ages ranged from mid-twenties to mid-forties. Their teaching experience ranged from three to over 20 years. Before going to Australia, the UK, US and New Zealand, these teachers had not been overseas for any training in TESOL. In Vietnam, they taught various subjects, for example general English, grammar, theories of language, teaching methodology and English literature. I gave them the pseudonyms Kien, Trung, Minh and Vinh (the male participants), Linh, Vy, Thu, Chi, Lien, Trang, An, Binh, Van, Thanh, Thao and Huong (the female ones).

I am in the same position as these Vietnamese teachers, and thus my personal accounts are interwoven with theirs.

## Morality in Teacher Development and the Teaching Profession in Vietnam

Morality plays a significant and indispensable role in all processes of teacher identity formation and the teaching profession in Vietnam. For this reason, I want to highlight why morality and demonstrating morality is important to teachers in Vietnam, and why the notion of teacher-as-moral-guide influences how teachers see themselves and are seen by others. Given the cultural politics associated with EIL and ELT (Pennycook, 1994, 1998) and their physical exposure to the English-speaking West, teacher-as-moral-guide appears even more important as a dominant 'core' identity that defines EIL Western-trained Vietnamese teachers. Their teacher morality seems to be challenged, especially when the language they teach, no matter how international it has become, is associated with problems of ethics and politics (Pennycook, 1994, 1998; Phillipson, 1992).

Baurain (2004b: 35) draws on a Vietnamese saying 'first learn the behaviour, then learn the lesson' (tien hoc le, hau hoc van) to acknowledge the essential role of morality and values in teaching, particularly in the field of ELT. He regards 'teaching as a moral enterprise' (p. 35) and suggests Bill Johnston's (2003) *Values in English Language Teaching* as a 'classic in the field' (Baurain, 2004a: 2). Johnston's discussion of the role of teachers as moral agents is in part similar to the role of teachers as perceived in Vietnam. Like Miller (2003), I find Johnston's arguments on the role of morality in what it means to be a teacher significant. In particular, he teases out the complex and often contradictory moral dimensions of the language classroom when teachers must make moral decision as they interact with students, showing how teachers' beliefs influence their moral choices. Edge (2003) and Pennycook and Coutand-Marin (2004) also strongly argue for the role of morality and ethics in ELT, urging teachers of English to take morality and ethics into serious consideration in their teaching.

Before discussing the role of morality in teacher development and the teaching profession in Vietnam, I acknowledge that morality is a complex and not a unified concept. Although I use the term 'morality' throughout the book, I by no means treat it as a unified notion on which all Vietnamese agree. Rather, I regard it, in many cases, as socially acceptable and proper behaviour and manner, and in other cases, as dominant ethical values which are generally shared by the society.

The aim of education in Vietnam is to help people to become good citizens in terms of both knowledge and morality. Teachers themselves are accordingly assumed to be moral guides or role models (Duong Thieu Tong, 2002; Constitution of Vietnam; Education Law of Vietnam). It is often believed that teachers tend to develop themselves both in knowledge and morality to meet the social, cultural and educational expectations of themselves as the moral guides. Moreover, since being a teacher is largely governed by the norms and values of morality, the personal of the teacher is often shaped by and acts according to the professional. On the surface, the professional and the personal seem to permeate one another, and the former seems to dominate.

Being a teacher in Vietnam involves demonstrating morality in every way. Teachers are expected to be moral guides, and Vietnamese society and culture expect that they themselves will lead a morally acceptable life. Evidence for this significant role of morality can be found in Vietnamese history and folklore and in empirical studies related to education in Vietnam.

Historically, according to Duong Thieu Tong (2002), ancient Vietnamese philosophies of education (Lac Viet, around 2000 BC to AD 1), highlighted and advocated caring for and supporting each other and living in harmony with others as well as nature. These philosophies aimed at nurturing individuals who are moral, ethical and live for others. Duong argues that ancient Vietnamese education was developed on the basis of 'realistic humanism' (p. 66), which focused on the representation and appreciation of values held by individuals, families and the society. These philosophies also offered teachers a very high and noble status in society. Since Lac Viet education was the education of the people, by the people and for the people, which placed emphasis on moral education and took responsibility for educating morally good individuals, teachers in this society were expected to demonstrate morality in all aspects of their lives. This educational emphasis on morality was maintained among Vietnamese villages and communal societies during the thousand years of Chinese colonisation (from approximately 111 BC to AD 938). Duong demonstrates that the Lac Viet educational philosophies had been developed and practised in Vietnam for at least a thousand years before Vietnam had contact with China. Consequently, the influence of Confucianism on Vietnamese education should not be seen as the only source of underlying philosophical ideals. Duong shows that Confucianism has been Vietnamised and served Vietnamese people's educational purposes. This point is supported by Phan Ngoc (1998) and Tran Quoc Vuong (2000).

Duong strongly emphasises that Confucian education was never the only education in Vietnam during Chinese colonisation. Neither was it implemented everywhere in the country. Taoism and Buddhism had entered and influenced the local philosophies before Confucianism. Importantly, both Taoism and Buddhism blossomed in ancient Vietnam because these philosophies complemented the local philosophies and culture. Buddhist education was also considered the 'national education' during that time, and it had significant influence on Vietnamese cultural identity (Duong Thieu Tong, 2002: 62). While Confucian education was for the 'elites', those who worked for the colonial government, Buddhist education was for everyone. Both Duong and Phan Ngoc (1998) argue that monks and Buddhist devotees played a vital role in educating the people. The social status of these Buddhist teachers was very high, and through them Lac Viet educational philosophies and Buddhism were maintained and enhanced, and the role of morality in education was consistently strengthened. Since Confucianism also put great emphasis on moral education, particularly highlighting the moral role of the teacher and the learner, it was not in conflict with Lac Viet and Buddhist education in ancient Vietnam. Rather, these philosophies enhanced one another. They all melded together to contribute to the values and morality of Vietnamese education. This integrated educational philosophy continued to be maintained during the feudal times (938–1945).

Duong indicates that teachers in feudal Vietnamese society did not differentiate between their responsibilities for the education of their students, the education of their families and the education of society. All of these responsibilities were part of educating individuals with knowledge and morality. The teachers in those days also presented themselves as morally good examples for students and for society in every way. Duong demonstrates that since the 15th century, the requirement that intellectuals also be moral exemplars in Vietnamese society was formalised in Vietnamese feudal law, known as the Hong Duc law. The law also clearly identified their rights and responsibilities regarding their personal life, family life and social life. This put pressures on teachers to behave, as well as encouraging them to live morally if they chose to be teachers.

Le Xuan Hy *et al.* (2005) discuss the 'care orientation' in Vietnamese culture, and claim that human relationships are at the core of the care orientation (p. 4). They highlight the three significant aspects of the strong human relationships in Vietnamese culture, namely '(1) human relationships as the foundation of ethics; (2) a strong emphasis on respect for the other; and (3) responsibility for the other to the point of self sacrifice' (p. 4).

The focus on human relationships in Vietnamese philosophy has been woven into educational ideals in Vietnam, and is manifested in traditional as well as modern teachings. This philosophy supports morality and ethics education. One reason why teachers in Vietnam see the need and will to demonstrate morality is that 'respect toward the other is one of the most crucial ethical teachings in the Vietnamese society' (p. 5). In Vietnamese philosophy, 'the teaching "kinh tren, nhuong duoi" or "respect the older, and yield to the younger" has become one of the most important ethical codes for mutual relationships among the Vietnamese' (p. 5). This philosophy has been practised in education as well. Both teachers and students need to respect each other and mutual respect is expected between the two. Teachers' respect for students is manifested in the exercise of their responsibilities and willingness to care for students and educate them in terms of both knowledge and morality.

In modern times, being a teacher in Vietnam involves demonstrating morality by both behaving morally and ethically as individuals and giving students moral education. Teacher morality and roles regarding moral education are encoded in rules and regulations. For example, the Constitution of Vietnam clearly states that:

> the aim of education is to form and nurture the personality, moral qualities ... to imbue [people] with ... good morality ... (Article 35)

The Education Law clearly identifies the role, tasks and rights of the teacher in Articles 14, 61 and 63, in which the teacher:

> must constantly learn and train in order to set a good example for the learners

> ... discharge[s] their task, preserve[s] and develop[s] the tradition of respecting the teacher and glorifying the teaching job

> must have good moral qualities, ethics and ideology

> [is] 1. to educate and teach according to the objective, principles and programs of education; 2. to be exemplary in fulfilling the citizen's duties, and observing the regulations of law and the statute of the school; 3. to preserve the quality, prestige and honor of the teacher, respect the dignity of the learners, to behave justly with learners, and protect their legitimate rights and interests; 4. to constantly study and train in order to raise their quality, ethics, professional and specialty standard and set good examples to the learners.

'Every teacher should be a model for the students' (Moi thay co giao la tam guong cho hoc sinh noi theo) is a motto at Vietnamese schools (Nguyen & McInnis, 2002: 152). So, in addition to social and cultural expectations of the teachers, legal rules and regulations strengthen and formalise the role of the teacher in demonstrating moral education.

In terms of folklore and popular culture, this moral role of teachers in Vietnamese educational philosophies is reflected in Vietnamese proverbs, sayings, expressions and quotations (Breach, 2004, 2005; Duong Ky Duc, 2000; Mai Xuan Huy, 1999) and music and poetry. Breach's findings on the Vietnamese notion of 'a good teacher' capture and reflect quite thoughtfully the culturally situated notions of the teacher embedded in Vietnamese society. Below are the original and translated versions of the 10 most commonly listed proverbs about teachers and teaching Breach culled from lists suggested by her students in Vietnam (Breach, 2004: 32).

> Without teachers, one can't do anything. (Khong thay do may lam nen.)
>
> He who teaches you one word is a teacher, he who teaches you half a word is also a teacher. (Nhat tu vi su, ban tu vi su.)
>
> If one wants to cross the water, build a bridge. If one wants his child to be educated, respect the teacher. (Muon sang thi bac cau Kieu, muon con hay chu thi yeu lay thay.)
>
> The first day of the Tet [Lunar New Year] holiday celebrates the father, the second day the mother, the third day the teacher. (Mong mot Tet cha, mong hai Tet me, mong ba Tet thay.)
>
> A teacher is like a fond mother. (Co giao nhu me hien.)
>
> Like teacher, like student. (Thay nao tro nay.)
>
> Respect teachers, respect morality. (Ton su trong dao.)
>
> Rice father, clothes mother, knowledge teacher. (Com cha, ao me, chu thay.)
>
> Teaching is the most noble profession among other noble professions. (Day hoc la nghe cao quy nhat trong nhung nghe cao quy.)
>
> A teacher is an engineer of the soul. (Giao vien la ky su tam hon.)

These proverbs show that teachers in Vietnamese society are regarded as 'a source of productive activity', 'providers of knowledge', 'moral role models', 'moral or spiritual guides (shapers of character)' (p. 32). They emphasise 'the respect [one] should have towards someone who has taught [one] even a small thing' and 'the respect that must be shown to the teacher by the entire family' (p. 32). They also show society's respect for teachers and the honour due to them and the teaching profession. Honouring the teacher comes immediately after the honouring of one's own parents, and the teacher's role is compared to the role of a loving parent (p. 32).

Teachers are respected and loved for being role models of knowledge and morality in every sense. Vietnam has produced great teachers, whose knowledge and morality sparkle and inspire people generation after generation. Chu Van An, Nguyen Binh Khiem, Nguyen Dinh Chieu and Ho Chi Minh are among those who represent the ideal image of Vietnamese teachers, devoting their entire life to humanity's development.

In addition to the love, respect and care the whole society always gives teachers and the teaching profession, one particular day is set aside for teachers in Vietnam, Vietnamese Teachers' Day, 20 November. Society celebrates and pays honour to teachers in various ways. Songs and poems about teachers and teaching are sung and recited everywhere and in the mass media. Flowers and gifts are given to teachers to show the respect, love, gratitude and sincerity one has for them. Several days prior to Teachers' Day and on the day itself, different generations of students visit their teachers (at all levels) with their best wishes, flowers and affection. These practices contribute to the maintenance and promotion of the respected role of teachers in Vietnamese society and culture. This encourages and requires teachers, however hard their life is, to dedicate themselves to the aims of education.

> My teacher is as kind as Tam [female character representing kindness, love and ethics in Vietnamese fairy tales]
>
> Her voice is as soft and warm as my mother singing lullabies ...
>> (My translation of part of a poem students learn at primary schools in Vietnam.)
>
> When my teacher writes on the blackboard ... some chalkdust falls onto the ground and some falls onto his hair. I love this very moment when my teacher's hair seems greyer and greyer because of his dedication to teaching us ... Never in my life, shall I forget my teacher ...
>> (My translation of lines from a song about teachers.)

Besides historical and folklore references, empirical studies of education in Vietnam also indicate the significant role of morality in teachers' perceptions and enactments of their profession (for example, Kramsch & Sullivan, 1996; Le Van Canh, 2001, 2004; Sullivan, 2000). These studies show that teachers of English in Vietnam include in their teaching of English the need to demonstrate morality or good behaviour. They enact their roles as both knowledge expert and moral guide (Kramsch & Sullivan, 1996) and harmonise the seemingly contradictory roles of a 'facilitator' in teaching English and a moral guide as expected by Vietnamese society and their professional values.

Nguyen Quoc Hung (2000) looks particularly at the role of teachers of English with a specific focus on Vietnam. He reviews different methods of teaching languages, and his discussion suggests that teachers in Vietnam always play the role of moral educator. Whether using teacher-centred or learner-centred methods, grammar-translation methods or communicative approaches, teachers are expected to guide students in terms of behaviour and good manners, either explicitly or implicitly. In this sense, Vietnamese teachers of English are not at all different from teachers of other subjects in that society. They do demonstrate moral education because they are, first of all, teachers.

## Whether We Need to Theorise Teacher Identity

With regard to teacher identity in general, Varghese *et al.* (2005) observe that very little has been done to theorise teacher identity. They, therefore, first discuss three perspectives, namely Tajfel's (1978) social identity theory, Lave and Wenger's (1991) theory of situated learning and Simon's (1995) concept of the image-text, and go on to argue for taking multiple approaches to obtain 'richer and more useful understanding of the processes and contexts of teacher identity' (p. 21). This book, on the one hand, is on the same wavelength as Varghese *et al.*'s argument, but on the other extends the argument much further by introducing other conceptual tools that not only complement and consolidate the existing perspectives but also have their own merits and function well in their own right. Importantly, on this basis, I argue that theorising teacher identity will limit our visions of and insights into the complex world of teacher identity and may create 'baskets' for certain teacher identities, and this is what critical pedagogies want to resist. Significantly, in this book, I propose understanding teacher identity by expanding the notion of the postcolonial Self and Other and through theories of identity from scholars whose experiences and discussions help make sense of the identity formation processes of the EIL Western-trained Vietnamese teachers referred to throughout the book. Writer-as-insider perspectives with me as an EIL teacher educated in Vietnam and Australia and teaching in different countries are also inter-woven to interpret these teachers' identity formation. Detailed discussions of these conceptual tools are presented in Chapters 2 and 3.

## Identity Formation and the Multiplicity of Conceptual Tools

Together with the debate about the role of English, ELT and English teachers in the world, the debate about identity has produced different, even conflicting arguments about what identity is and means. For example, those who follow essentialist views tend to look at identity in terms of wholeness, stability, a core identity, belongingness and homo-geneity, whereas those who pursue non-essentialist ideas explore iden-tity with regard to dynamic change, hybridity, fragmentation and multiplicity (Dolby, 2000; Farrell, 2000; Hall, 1997b; Hall & du Gay, 1996; Woodward, 1997). The latter argue that identities are multiple and they are constructed, instead of being available out there in the world. Iden-tity involves 'becoming' rather than 'being', and is a question of us constructing our 'routes' rather than going back to 'roots' (Hall, 1996: 4). They also argue that identities are changing, formed and transformed and never unified and defined (Dolby, 2000; Farrell, 2000; Hall, 1997a, b; Holland, 1996; Reed, 2001). In particular, theories of identities seen in light of mobility and transnationality have played a major role and offered new grounds for the understanding of identity. However, while numerous studies related to mobility and transnationality in a wide range of areas, such as workplace, commodities, technologies and migra-tion, have been published (Crang *et al.*, 2003; Koczberski & Curry, 2004; Lin, 2002; Paasi, 2002; Smith, 2002; Willis & Yeoh, 2002), there have hardly been any published works about English teacher identity seen in light of these two notions. While Block (2005) and Holliday (2005) place language teachers in international and mobile contexts, they do not decode their identities using mobility and transnationality theories. In these works, identity is not treated as the main concern, either. This is the very missing chapter in the literature that I particularly focus on in this book, hoping to enrich studies of identity in the context of globalisation and transnationality.

Non-essentialist views have dominated the conversation about identity-related issues in the academy over the last 20 years, resulting in the tendency to neglect other ways of looking at identity, for example that identity is about a coherent growth, a sense of connectedness and a sense of wholeness (Phan Ngoc, 1998; Tran Ngoc Them, 1999, 2001a, b, c). My experiences and observations regarding identity formation have suggested that non-essentialist views alone are insufficient to understand identities. An example of a process that follows a more essentialist trend is what happened after the September 11 event. From the media shaping of the event, I have a feeling that this very event has made American people aware of the so-called 'national spirit'. Such an event makes people realise that they belong to one nation, and they need to unite under one identity to overcome and grow. Other individual identities suddenly become secondary, and one overall identity is needed to give people a sense of belonging. They need it to feel secure and united. This identity is national identity, which is something imagined, something invented, something constructed as many Western authors argue. But such an event has made it something visible, tangible and real.

This makes me think of Vietnam – my country. I wonder why we Vietnamese people often talk about and affirm our Vietnamese identity. Why do Vietnamese scholars ceaselessly argue for a Vietnamese identity, which has unique characteristics (Phan Ngoc, 1998; Tran Ngoc Them, 1999, 2001c; Tran Quoc Vuong, 2000)? Why do I, who have been influenced by Western theories of culture and identity, also feel that we have a Vietnamese national and cultural identity? Vietnam has its own identity. I myself feel this identity and it is the very thing that gives me a sense of belonging when I am here, in Australia, and far from my homeland.

However, this way of understanding identities as national identity alone also seems to silence other identities which all contribute to identity formation. When one set of ideas does not work sufficiently to understand identity formation, it is necessary to draw on multiple theories to seek a better understanding. This book hence draws on a number of Vietnamese and Western theorists' perceptions of identity, language and culture to best present the multiplicity of theories of identities and positioning. This multiplicity also helps examine how the processes of identity formation take place, and explains the meanings of different contexts which affect the identity formation of the Western-trained Vietnamese teacher of English.

This book problematises and challenges the seemingly dominant views of identity as always changing, hybrid and fragmented. It highlights the importance of the sense of belonging, connectedness, continuity and a coherent growth in identity formation. It signifies the role of national and cultural identity, the concept that is often criticised for being associated with essentialist viewpoints. In the book, I argue that this very sense of national and cultural identity serves as a platform for all other identities of the Western-trained Vietnamese teachers of English to be constructed, negotiated and reconstituted. This sense of national and cultural identity tends to take the form of cultural and professional values that are closely connected to a particular locality. Furthermore, what this book explores confirms the necessity to look at the notions of identity in close association with the sense of being and belonging. In this very sense, this book not only incorporates the notion of 'cultural continuity' strongly advocated by Holliday (2005) but also challenges this understanding by showing the vital role of culture in 'the struggle to teach English as an international language' as Holliday has quite thoroughly documented.

Given what has been expressed above and the nature of this book, in order to best understand the identity formation processes of these Vietnamese teachers, it is essential for me to draw on two bodies of knowledge, Vietnamese and Western theorists' perceptions of language, culture and identity. As the focus of the book is situated in the context of ELT with a specific focus on the politics of ELT, postcolonial notions of Self and Other are thus relevant elements in identity formation. Issues related to how English and ELT have contributed to shaping identities of teachers of English, such as what is going on in TESOL programmes and how CLT has been promoted with regard to teachers' and students roles', are also relevant to the discussion of identity formation.

## My Autoethnography: The Insider Researcher/Writer

I am writing this section as a story about my 'autoethnography' – a term I borrow from Brodkey (1994, 1996, cited in Kamler, 2001: 4–5), and which depicts my growth/development as a researcher and a scholar in reference to the topic and context addressed in this book. The nature of what is presented in this book dictates the importance of defining my positioning as the writer in relation to English, ELT, the West, Vietnam/Vietnamese and being a teacher. I first need to define myself in the jungle of varied and even conflicting viewpoints regarding these issues. Since the book discusses the identity formation of Western-trained Vietnamese teachers of English, I find myself one of them. I am thus both the writer and the insider.

Autoethnography, the genre suggested by Lionnet, 'opens up a space of resistance between the individual (auto-) and the collective (-ethno-) where the writing (-graphy) of singularity cannot be foreclosed' (cited in Kamler, 2001: 4). Brodkey develops her metaphor of autoethnography as a research method, in which 'autoethnographies are grounded in data collected from "interviews with the self", [and] memories are treated as "data" which are discussed, analysed' (p. 4). In light of these discussions, I now write my autoethnography.

## Ha and English

After closing Pennycook's (1994, 1998) and Phillipson's (1992) books, I keep on thinking of how English has entered my world and shaped my identity. I have different stories to tell, not a story told by a person who speaks English as the mother tongue, not by a person who speaks it as a second language or not by a person who has had to use it painfully as it is the language of the coloniser. But my stories are told from myself, a person who learns and uses English as her language, and has a 'boundless' love for the English language. Thus my experience can be very different from that of hooks (1994), Ngugi wa Thiong'o (1993) and other people who come from different backgrounds. Both Ngugi wa Thiong'o and hooks write from their experiences as those who have used English as the language of the coloniser, the language that reminds them of African slavery and the entire history of British colonisation over their own people. These two authors' writing shows that they on the one hand resent the English language but on the other hand accept it as the language they have to use in order to be heard and recognised. They accept it and resent it, use it and resent it. This is like a vicious circle. They are aware of such a circle and they moan and struggle within the circle. I hear their voices, feel the sadness and a 'national spirit' in their voices but at the same time sense that their voices are overpowered by the English language and what norms English has set upon their people.

Now this is my story with English. We have had English in our family for decades. Both my parents are university lecturers in English in Vietnam. They were university classmates when they both majored in English for five years. By the time they entered university, Vietnam was at war with America, so learning English was not liked by our people since English was the language of 'the enemy', at least in the north of the country. But we still actively learned English in order to protect our country from being 'culturally' invaded, to understand our stronger enemy and above all to appreciate the language. We learned it both in Vietnam and in other countries, such as Russia. Another reason why my parents learned English at university was that they were appointed to the Faculty of English. They did not have the right to choose the language they liked at that time, Russian or Chinese or French. For historical and political reasons, these languages had high status in Vietnam in those days. It also meant that learning and teaching English then would lead people to an 'insecure' future with almost no chance for further study overseas. And going overseas in the 1970s, 1980s and early 1990s did not just bring about new knowledge but also meant 'changing one's material life' to 'wealthiness' or at least 'well-furnituredness'.

But life still went on for teachers of English in Vietnam even though they had to struggle. I still remember clearly what and how I felt when my younger brother was standing outside a neighbour's window, watching their television through a tiny hole. That neighbour was a teacher of French. So my parents invested all to buy us a television, a very old one but more than enough to satisfy their two innocent children. No matter how difficult our life was, my parents still enjoyed their profession. They went on to pursue their postgraduate studies in English. They taught English every day at university although the number of students of English was far less than that of other foreign languages. And at home they spoke English with one another when they did not want us to know what they were talking about. That really made me want to know the language they spoke. I did not want to be the outsider. They sang English songs and their students taught me some English songs, too. I imitated word for word without understanding the language at all but gradually I could sense the beauty of the words I sang. 'English must be something wonderful', I thought, and my desire to learn English was generated. I told my parents that I would study English when I grew up. They smiled happily and they knew that they had passed on to me their love of the language they taught.

I started secondary school when I was 11 years old. I went to a school for gifted students of maths, and Russian was the only foreign language there. I took Russian, naturally, and loved the language more as I studied it. Four years of studying Russian made me appreciate it, but at the same time my love for English was also increasing. I was very proud of the fact that I could sing some English songs to my friends whenever we had a gathering, and that my parents were teachers of English while most of my friends' parents did not know English. My unconditional love for the English football (soccer) team was another reason why I loved English then. I watched as many international football matches broadcast on TV as possible. My parents and the majority of our people supported the former Soviet Union team while I myself was stubbornly in favour of the English team. I patiently tried to persuade my parents and friends to be for my favourite team and now all of my family cheer 'my team'.

Surprisingly, I did not know English but I could identify whether a person spoke English or other languages, and the sound of English fascinated me. I wanted to learn it, to learn it well and to be completely fluent in it. My chance came when I successfully passed the national exams to the Specialised High School for Foreign Languages in 1991. Without any hesitation, I picked English. Compared with the time my parents first started learning English, things changed dramatically when I had the opportunity to learn the language. The Russian language was losing its 'privileged' status after the collapse of the Soviet Union and the Communist bloc in Eastern Europe. Chinese had already been 'hated' on account of the tension between Vietnam and China since 1978. French started to 'keep silent' and 'watch out' for the 'right moment' to 'expand'. The government's 'open-door' policy from late 1986 had enabled the expansion of English in Vietnam, with the emergence of foreign companies, services and tourism throughout the country. Hence, it was just the right moment to study English. In addition to my high achievement in English, my attachment to English was strengthened by romantic English songs. These songs, either sent to me in a sealed envelope or placed inside my notebooks, helped my male friends express their admiration to me. This touched the 'young and emotional' heart of a 17-year-old girl like me. This was so sweet and unforgettable. Even now whenever I listen to those songs, I still feel my heart beat as it used to. My love for English has increased and increased as I use it more.

Now one can see that I study English because I wanted to learn it, because I like it and also because of my family's influence. Maybe the reason why people learn English now is different from mine, since their motives are determined by their job constraints and/or opportunities in a globalised and internationalised world. I have multiple relationships with English, from a very personal level to a family level, from a local level to a national level, and from a national level to an international level. One can also see that, whether in my parents' time or in my time, our people choose to learn English and take control of it. We do not learn it just because it is the language of the powerful, but because we want to use it to strengthen and protect our proud, rich and old culture. We are not forced to learn it. We have the right over which language we choose to learn.

### Ha as a writer of English

My love for English and my academic achievement gave me the opportunity to do my TESOL Master's in Australia. I started the course with high confidence, because I had always been a good student in Vietnam. But I was 'knocked down' by my lecturers' comments that my English was good but the way I wrote in English was different from theirs and was not the right way. I interpreted these comments as 'I don't know how to write in English yet.' But what was the way? I found nothing wrong with my writing. I, as a result, became determined to find the answer.

The chance came when I was exposed to the literature of critical pedagogies introduced in the Master's course. I became aware of stereotypes of Asian students studying in Australia, whose writing was described as being 'circular', 'unclear' and lacking a logical mind, as opposed to the 'linear', 'clear' and logical English writing. I felt I must do something. I wanted to disrupt these stereotypes. I thus decided to take Vietnamese and English academic writing as the focus of my Master's thesis. I used the language to argue against its norms. That was when I really started to be a 'real' writer of English.

I write English with passion. I feel that I can 'communicate' very well with the language when I write it. English seems to 'understand' what I want to write. This book is consequently like an arena where I hope I would be able to best communicate with readers through the medium of English. Again, I am using English to disrupt its associated colonial and imperial norms and decolonise the underlying dichotomy of postcolonial Self and Other. This seems to be a double-standard practice. But more than that, I am writing English naturally, as it comes from the heart. It is my language.

> *Alone*
> *Calm*
> *Quiet*
> *Interwoven in the rhythm of eternity*
> *Carrying away worries*
> *In the wings of waterlilies.*

(My poem)

## Ha as teacher of English

English is not only the language I have learned, but also the language I have taught. Learning English has actually given me a job as a teacher. So what does being a teacher mean to me? Born into an intellectual family, since I was little, I have realised how meaningful teaching is to my parents and their colleagues. I have known for sure that my parents receive much respect from their students and society. Thus, a child of a teacher is often expected to have 'good characteristics', 'proper behaviour' and 'good academic performance', as teachers are believed to raise good children compared with people having other professions. So I enjoy my own pride having two teacher parents. They are the mirrors through which I can see and judge positive and negative qualities of a teacher, so as to develop myself better. This is one factor that has influenced my self-perceptions of the teacher. When I was at school and at university in Vietnam, my image of a good teacher was also shaped by the concept of role models expected in society. If my parents were role models for their students, then some of my teachers could be my role models too. For me, a good teacher was one who was able to offer pupils both knowledge and moral development. This perception has actually grown stronger, particularly in the context of globalisation and international integration, when everything is more open and subject to change more rapidly and somehow uncontrollably. For me, this image of good teachers can be extended but needs to retain these two essential values, teacher as knowledge cultivator and moral guide. There is no doubt that what I think of a teacher has also been nurtured by this image.

Another factor that has brought me closer to the teaching profession is the tradition of 'respect for teacher and teaching' in our society. Every year, on Vietnamese Teachers' Day, 20 November, my house is full of flowers, my parents and I are deeply moved by the love, respect, gratitude and sincerity students have had for us. Yes, although we receive love and respect from students every day, on Teachers' Day our confidence is more strongly confirmed when different generations of students visit us with flowers and affection. I feel that I owe my country and my people so much for maintaining and promoting such a lovely tradition, so that we teachers, however hard our life is, are encouraged to dedicate ourselves to education.

## Ha and dilemmas

I myself have been using English for over 10 years now and recently I have used it more often than ever. It is now the main medium in my work, the language I use to communicate with the outside world. I feel comfortable using the language, as it is extremely useful and rich. I have come to love it, as it has been part of my life, a very important part that I cannot deny. Do I see it as an advantage? Yes, I must say so. This is my identity. However, I have never let myself 'overuse' English against my mother tongue, Vietnamese. This is also my identity. I am aware of how my way of thinking is shaped by the language I speak and the language I use for my study and work. But after all, what I want to be is a Vietnamese and a global citizen, who firmly connects to the cultural pulse of Vietnam and simultaneously operates globally through the medium of English. At this point, I would like to attach myself to my national identity 'Vietnamese', but at the same time I have to say that my love for English comes from my heart. However, the more I read and observe, the more I understand the political and cultural side of English as an international language and the problems of ethics and lack of appropriacy of ELT pedagogy. I also understand how painful it can be for a person when he/she speaks the language that is used to define the 'Them' (the colonised) and the 'Other' (the coloniser). My pride and consciousness of my national identity has become more obvious and stronger than ever when I think of how hard our people have been trying to construct a united Vietnamese identity.

Now the story of one of my friends from Bangladesh is apparent in my mind. His concern about his identity reveals how much the English language has deeply influenced the way he behaves, lives and thinks. He told me his story, and I have written up my notes of this as if it were his direct speech. I acknowledge my reconstruction of his story is honest.

> I'm now writing in English more than I am in Bangla, our own language. Even when I write letters to my parents I write in English. I find it easier but at the same time I feel a sense of 'shame' that I'm not writing in my own language, the language that I was brought up with, the language that makes me a Bangla person, the language that gives me an identity. I'm so ashamed because sometimes I can't find a good Bangla word to express my ideas but I can always find English words for that purpose. And even when I can find a Bangla word, I still want to use English because this gives me a sense of 'being smarter' and 'being fashionable'. Oh, how much and how deeply this language – English – has changed my ways of thinking, my ways of life and my ways of doing things. I had never thought of such political sides of English and ELT before I came to Australia and read the literature about how our ways of thinking are shaped by English. Now I try not to mix my Bangla with English whenever I speak with my students, either all English or all Bangla.

With deep consciousness, my friend cries for his own remedy to cure his loss of Bangla identity, as he spelled it out. His concern shares parts of my concern. However, I believe that this dilemma can be resolved. That is why I write this book.

### How my positioning influences what is discussed in this book

I am not only concerned about my own identity but also identities of the Western-trained Vietnamese teachers of English whom I refer to in this book. I by no means suggest that I am doing them any favours; rather, I owe them for sharing with me their journeys of identity formation. Yes, I am one of them. I am the insider. I am a Vietnamese teacher of English being trained in Australia. I am expected to bring back home optimal teaching methodologies for ELT in Vietnam. I see part of myself in their stories. Their identities embrace part of my identity. So, when I analyse their stories and explore their inner world of a teacher, I am actually defining myself and trying to picture part of my identity. Likewise, my analyses and interpretations of their experiences definitely reflect my subjective viewpoints as an insider, someone who is also defined as a Western-trained Vietnamese teacher of English.

Several years of living and studying in Australia, an English-speaking country, known as the 'Self', as defined by postcolonial theorists, has broadened and enriched my views of teaching. Being exposed to an open and 'debating' society, I have had the opportunity to revise my views through different lenses. In addition, researching into this very complicated and sophisticated topic, which requires self-engagement at the highest level, has helped define my views more clearly. However, the more I have read about the cultural politics of ELT, the more easily I fall into my own trap. That means, although my purpose is to contest the stereotypes constructed by the West about the East, in doing so I happen to reinforce such stereotypes. Why? Because the literature of colonialism is so powerful that wherever we go we crash into it. We find a way out here but we get stuck there. While we are trying to disrupt preconceptions to make the West appreciate our cultures, we subconsciously admit that we are inferior. We seem to create the decolonisation-patronisation paradigm. Why? Because many of our fellows have been made to believe that the West is better, so their voices actually reassert such perceptions. This makes my desire grow stronger. Yes, I must find a way to fight against this, as Pennycook (1994, 1998) has succeeded in proving the 'guilt' of ELT in serving imperialism and colonising the Other. But what way? Please be patient and follow me to the end of this book, and judge whether I have achieved the target.

Teaching is not merely the work of the brain. It is the work of the heart, the work of the soul, and it cannot be separated from the education of good citizens. This is my point of view. However, one should not assume that this point is fixed. It will be extended as I have said elsewhere, but the extension or variation will take place along the lines of the main points. My exposure to the world through English has made me an international TESOL lecturer, and this status is part of my identity. This identity also influences my views of teaching. The Vietnamese teacher permeates the global teacher in me, and a local teacher simultaneously shares her perceptions of teaching with other teachers at the global level while developing her cultural teaching values. This integration is thus a fluid process, and the degree to which my views are extended and changed is largely influenced by this process.

My perceptions of the teacher and teaching may also have influenced the way I interpret other teachers' perceptions, whether we had shared views or whether they had different views, or even conflicting views to my own. I hence may have been tempted to judge their views through my lenses, and have convinced them to see the world the way I do. I may also have eagerly intruded and judged where I should not have. For example, when we discussed English and ELT in Vietnam in one group interview, I was so enthusiastic that I 'gave them a long talk' on and engaged in discussion about how English was viewed in the literature with indirect reference to Pennycook's (1998) and Phillipson's (1992) views. The teacher participants then admitted that they had only looked at English from a linguistic perspective. Hence, what I had said to them was something they had never thought of. This made me realise the fact that as a researcher I should not 'feed' them and make them say what I wanted to hear. I then drew their attention to another topic. However, it should be noted that I only told them about the literature after we had already had an intensive discussion about English and ELT in Vietnam.

My engagement with the literature of English, ELT and postcolonial notions of Self and Other may have tempted me to lead the teacher participants towards what I wanted them to say. I may also have rushed to ally myself to those participants who shared my views and consequently silence those who did not. For instance, in one group interview, when the participants commented on their Master's course in Australia, they mentioned that they were not happy with the way some lecturers gave lectures in class. One participant added that before she came to Australia, she used to think that lecturers there were much better and more advanced than those in Vietnam, but what she experienced in her Master's course changed her assumption. I was so pleased to hear this comment, and I next eagerly talked about ethnocentrism and some implications about Self and Other, though not at all explicitly. After that, the participants became more open to talk about how they saw this issue in their TESOL course. However, I acknowledge that I did not lead the participants deliberately. It was they who initiated the topic and I extended their points of view.

The nature of myself as the insider researcher also makes me more aware of where I should be 'seen' in the process of data collection and data analysis and interpretation. This status makes me both engaged with and distant from the whole process. I am the insider but I am not allowed to speak for myself wherever I wish to. I have to wait until my voice is considered legitimate and valid by definitions of research. However, I must acknowledge that despite my awareness and intention to distance myself where necessary, I may still be subconsciously present in parts of the process.

## Epistemology: Ways of Knowing

I acknowledge that my positioning as a lover of English, an English teacher and a researcher is important, because knowledge varies from one to another and thus ways of knowing are shaped by many things, including culture, society and individual experiences. Understanding these ways of knowing is fundamental in understanding identity. But it is also central to an understanding of the way in which it is most useful to go about the research.

The nature of my research requires my active involvement as the researcher in all stages. Hence, my ways of knowing play a significant part in carrying out the research. My ways of knowing are determined by my personal experiences as a lover of English, an English teacher and a researcher. These ways are also shaped by the way I have been brought up, the way I have been educated to see the world and the way I have been developing myself as a scholar in the field of social and educational sciences. My perceptions of teacher and teaching, my awareness of the political side of English and ELT, my passion for English and my necessarily 'objective' role as the insider researcher all actively participate in my writing of the book. They too give weight to my interpretation of the perspectives of the teachers whom I interviewed and communicated with through emails, telephone and other written modes, in part because I too am multiply shaped.

In order to acknowledge the multiplicity of ways of knowing I draw on both Western and Vietnamese theorists' views about language, culture and identity. The way we see the world as regarded by me and the Vietnamese theorists I draw on is constructed by the society we live in. Likewise, how I see the world is also formed by my experiences as a researcher through the mode of Western thinking. As a result, when I look at the situations I am investigating, I need to understand the way in which influences, such as culture, history, education and position in the world, operate on people's perspectives. Moreover, this concept of multiplicity is becoming important in the TESOL context, in which we understand the need for a more global concept of English, that is English as an international language (McKay, 2002). This concept of language used interculturally without being the property of any one nation emphasises the need for interpretive/conceptual tools that are not products of any single culture.

The multiplicity of ways of knowing is also used for positive purposes through my employment of multiple frameworks, such as those of processes of identity formation and those of postcolonial notions of Self and Other. Different frameworks come up with different pictures of the context in which what is expressed in this book is located. Rich and multiple insights are accordingly more likely to be obtained.

Throughout the book, I use the terms native teachers of English (NET) and non-native teachers of English (NNET), Self and Other, and other dichotomies, such as Centre and Periphery, Inner Circle and Outer/ Expanding Circle, teacher and/or student, Western-trained teachers of English and/or non-Western-trained teachers of English. I acknowledge that I am fully aware of the weakness and shortcomings of these terms and dichotomies. Moreover, I use these terms and dichotomies not as a way to differentiate the world but, instead, more as a tool of inquiry, a means to interpret the identity formation processes of EIL Western-trained Vietnamese teachers rather than the meaning underlying the word(s). In this way, dichotomy/dichotomies serve as a way to understand and identify variation in identification rather than a way of characterising the world from the postcolonial writer's position.

## Chapter 2
# Language, Culture and Identity

## Introduction

This chapter discusses the relationships between language, culture and identity, as perceived and approached by a number of Western and Vietnamese scholars. Since language and culture are intimately interrelated (Hall, 1997a; Kramsch, 1998; Sharifian & Palmer, 2007), language acts as social practices (Fairclough, 1989; Farrell, 1997a; Gee, 1999; Liddicoat, 1997; Phan Le Ha, 2001) and culture is about 'shared meanings' (Hall, 1997a: 1), one's sense of identity is constructed within the relationship between language and culture (Hall, 1997a). We construct identity through language, as language is used about us, by us and for us. Each of us has embedded within us cultural values, and through language we communicate our culture. Language acts as a means through which identity is communicated, extended, confirmed, constructed, negotiated and reconstituted.

Before I continue with this chapter, I would like to acknowledge that I by no means essentialise the West/Western and Vietnam/Vietnamese. So at times when what I present seems so, it might just be that I discuss these notions without constantly referring back to my acknowledgement of the limitations associated with them.

It has been long argued that language and culture are closely interlinked. Whether in the 'East' or 'West', the relationship between language and culture has been explored and consolidated by theories and well-argued studies. While defining this relationship, scholars of different cultures have come up with different approaches to the notions of language and culture, demonstrating the complexity and interconnectedness of such notions. Although the arguments about language, culture and identity developed and pursued by many Western and Vietnamese scholars are from two almost completely different traditions, bringing them together is helpful in understanding the identity formation of Vietnamese teachers of English who were trained in the West. On the one

25

hand, when Western theorists fail to decode why a strong sense of belonging was shared among these teachers, Vietnamese authors are able to do the job persuasively with their theory of the *'being'* and *'becoming'* of identity. On the other, while Vietnamese authors seem to ignore the notion of individual identity and thus fail to acknowledge its existence, Western theorists help by introducing their constructivist approach to identity formation. According to them, identity is constructed minute by minute, and is multiple, dynamic and hybrid. They pay attention to fragmented identities rather than one overall identity, as suggested by Vietnamese authors. Moreover, the very idea expressed by a number of Western theorists of identity presents a paradox. They argue the central formative and responsive role of culture and cultural values in identity formation, yet at the same time do not seem to consider and acknowledge the validity of views shaped by other cultures which may emphasise quite different aspects of identity. For example, Vietnamese thinkers emphasise the importance of a national identity based on the study of culturally shaped values. As a result, the introduction of Vietnamese scholars' views of identity is helpful in harmonising or resolving this paradox. Thanks to both traditions, Western and Vietnamese, the multiple identities of these teachers are acknowledged, and the issue as to why they perceived a consistent sense of being Vietnamese within these multiple identities is answered with reference to the ways in which culture can shape our sense of self. Through the lenses of both traditions, the complexity and sophistication of the identity formation of these Western-trained Vietnamese teachers of English are best revealed, understood and argued. The notion of the influence of culture is the thread that brings these two very different sets of views together, despite their apparent contradictions.

It should be noted that in this book I am not trying to invent a new coherent conceptual tool based on these two seemingly contradictory traditions. It is not possible to make a hybrid model, either. It seems important to use the range of ideas to better interpret and represent the diversity of experience and the tensions between apparently contradictory senses of self for professionals in local and global contexts. Creating a harmonious model would belie these tensions.

## Language, Culture and Identity

Many Vietnamese authors argue that language and culture are closely interlinked. Tran Ngoc Them (1993) remarks that while language and labour made human beings, they are also the sources of all cultures. Therefore, the development of both culture and language (mother tongue) is simultaneous (Do Anh, 1993). According to Nguyen Lai (1993), language is not only included in the definition of culture but it also influences culture through multiple levels of complexity. He also argues that language formation is a multifaceted premise for culture formation and development, and culture in turn enables language development. He further observes that language is considered the only means to decode all forms of arts associated with culture since language is an act of thinking. Based on this function, language has the ability to comprehensively create artistic works with words, reflecting the cultural development of a community. Therefore, in the relationship with culture, language – after 'melding' with other arts – is able to draw a lively, comprehensive picture of a community's spiritual life. Because both language and culture are interrelatedly developed and act as 'tradition inheritors', they embed in themselves the most distinctive features of a nation's spirit and appearance.

Nguyen Duc Ton (1993: 18) explores a national culture in parallel with language and language thought-patterns. He sees that characteristics of a national culture are reflected through human beings' activities, and language is a vital means and condition for the genesis, development and activities of other elements within culture. In his argument, language is one of the most distinctive features in any national culture since language best stores and represents a national culture. To emphasise this, he refers to Vereshchagin and Kostomarov's idea that 'language is a real mirror of a national culture'. Vu Ngoc Khanh (1993) shares this view by arguing that the development of a national culture can be seen through the development of its language. Language records different stages of development of a culture as well as providing a way to 'master' science. Language itself is created to represent new ideas and new concepts, and language itself in turn promotes intellectual breadth and cultural development. Vu Ngoc Khanh also links language with thinking and discusses how thinking reflects the level of development of a nation, and thus how the degree of development of a culture can also be seen through language.

Nguyen San's (1999: 2–3) discussions about language and culture seem to reflect the above authors' perspectives, presenting a comprehensive picture of this at once simple and complex relationship. He argues that despite dozens of definitions of language and hundreds of definitions of culture, they all agree on the systematic quality of both language and culture. Thanks to this quality, both language and culture have been able to maintain the stability of a particular society and community. That is to say, socially speaking, language and culture have functioned to organise a society and unite its members to gradually create a national identity generated at a certain point in history. Nguyen San emphasises that language together with other factors simultaneously fulfils the function of national culture. He suggests that the cultural distinctiveness of each people is represented through different ways of viewing and defining the world. Nguyen San proposes four theoretical points regarding the relationship between language and culture. First, language and culture are social institutions and signifying, spiritual activities. Second, language both directly and implicitly determines culture, although language is one element of culture. Third, language and culture permeate each other to develop in accordance with the principle of inheriting traditions, and hence they possess the most distinctive features of a community spirit. Fourth, language carries and promotes culture, heading towards civilisation.

These above Vietnamese authors also view language as social practices. Nguyen Lai (1993) observes that both culture and language are social organisations. In principle, both culture and language activities are spiritual activities, which are based on a process of symbolisation of psychosocial values. Culture and language embody in themselves the social norms of a particular society and this gives them a sense of the 'specific' and 'defined' in addition to common values shared by different communities. He refers to Saussure's remark that if one wants to discover the nature/truth of language, one should at first view language in terms of what it shares with other similar systems. Language and culture are thus viewed as 'signs' and this takes into account the psycho-social premise which is closely connected with the humanities. Nguyen Lai proposes the rather provocative argument that, as a means to progress from culture to civilisation, language is an 'open' act and despite this 'openness' it is not necessarily easily 'foreignised' or 'derooted' as many scholars fear. The concept of being 'foreignised' or 'derooted' here partly refers to the campaign 'For the purity of the Vietnamese language'. Every Vietnamese is asked to make efforts to preserve the cultural richness and purity of the language. This effort helps deny and minimise foreign elements, so as to protect the language from losing its cultural traits and purity. So when many scholars are afraid of the Vietnamese language being 'foreignised' or 'derooted', they actually suggest that language and culture are something visible, tangible, something 'out there', and thus can be lost. Nguyen Lai sees language and culture as interdependent and language as social practice, which means for him that language is subject to deliberate human efforts to control it.

Nguyen Duc Dan (1993) notes that language is social and a nation's cultural vision is reflected in its language. In addition to this, Nguyen

Trong Bau (1993) remarks on the role of language in clearly visualising a nation's spirit, cultural values and life. Nguyen San (1999) contends that language and culture are social institutions and signifying spiritual activities.

So far it is clear that except for Nguyen Lai (1993) and Nguyen Trong Bau (1993) there is an emphasis on 'high culture', arts, spirituality and intellectual life, but not much about values and philosophies underlying practices. All the Vietnamese scholars discussed firmly attach themselves and their arguments about language and culture to national culture and identity, in this case, Vietnamese culture and identity, which are both the means and ends in their arguments.

In the same vein, many Western scholars demonstrate their understanding of language as social and cultural practices. In reviewing Hall's works in the field of cultural studies, Grossberg (1996: 157) demonstrates that Hall views culture as 'the struggle over meaning, a struggle that takes place over and within the sign'. Culture is 'never merely a set of practices, technologies or messages, objects whose meanings and identity can be guaranteed by their origin or their intrinsic essences' (p. 157). Instead, 'culture is "the particular pattern of relations established through the social use of things and techniques"' (pp. 157–158). Grossberg goes on to state that Hall sees culture as 'the site of the struggle to define how life is lived and experienced, a struggle carried out in the discursive forms available to us' (p. 158). These arguments support the view that language operates as social practices.

Liddicoat (1997: 13) argues that 'language use in a group is a form of cultural behaviour.' This suggests that language is seen as cultural/social practices. Socially valued text types, or genres, therefore, are determined by socio-cultural norms. Hence, 'any study of a body of texts must see genre as culturally situated, culturally defined and culturally defining' and 'texts like other parts of language are cultural activities and the act of writing is an act of encoding culture as much as it is a case of encoding information' (p. 13). This results in the relationship between culture and writing (as a form of language) about which Soter (1988: 178) concludes that 'the ways in which we express thought in writing are very strongly influenced by our experiences with discourse generally and written text specifically and the related conventions that govern each of these within our own social and cultural contexts.' In addition, Fairclough (1989) contends that 'actual discourse is determined by socially constituted orders of discourse, sets of conventions associated with social institutions.' This strongly supports his perception of discourse and language as social practice 'determined by social structures' (p. 17). Also, Farrell (1994) alludes to the fact that whether elements of a text are considered to be important in an argument is determined by culture. Recognised as a substantial element of the 'cognitive apparatus' (p. 17), culture is invoked by individuals to create coherence in discourse within each particular disciplinary framework.

The above authors have clearly indicated that language is seen as social and cultural practices and thus always carries social and cultural messages and is contextualised. Language itself never stays alone and is never meaning-free. As such, language use is a way to communicate culture and social practices. Importantly, these authors, both Vietnamese and Western, acknowledge the vital role of language and culture in identity formation. The subsequent section will specifically present their views on the relationship between language, culture and identity.

Hall's (1997a) arguments about the intimate relationship between language and culture have partly asserted his approach to defining identity, which he sees as being constructed through the process of meaning production. These arguments offer grounds for the question of identity – 'who I am' – to develop and be explored in great depth. Not only that, his arguments have also opened the door to understanding the inside world of human beings, since we all construct meanings as we go on, and 'meaning is what gives us a sense of our own identity' (p. 3). With different meanings we have constructed, reconstructed and will construct as we undergo diverse experiences in life, with different contexts in which we interact with different members of different groups, different identities have also been constructed, shifted, and subjected to change. Accordingly, we may realise multiple identities within us. However, our identities do not exist separately or independently. Instead, they are 'tied up with questions of how culture is used to mark out and maintain identity within and difference between groups' (Hall, 1997a: 3). Similarly, they are contextualised and situated as Gee (1999) argues. We, consequently, need to understand peoples, things and events in their cultural contexts. That is why sharing 'cultural codes' or 'conceptual maps' is very important, since this enables us to avoid stereotyping others and their practices. Even when people share 'conceptual maps', it is not guaranteed that members of the same culture would interpret the world in exactly the same ways. This leaves room for individuals' identities to get into their big cultural 'loop' and assert their positions. Thus, meanings, which individuals construct, are not only shaped by their cultural practices, but also reflect their own identities, for example, meanings constructed from gender, religion or age perspectives. These meanings embodied in different 'selves' of the same individual are, in fact, also influenced by the culture in which the individual is surrounded. But as meaning production is a process, it will always create new concepts and signs as human life is always on the move. At the same time, it may polish, change and renew words and concepts to represent new faces and practices of culture; or it may 'delete' words or concepts that are no longer needed. As a result, vocabulary is not a 'closed' system, and neither is culture. That explains why 'language-in-action is always and everywhere an active building process' (Gee, 1999: 11), and so is culture.

Hall (1997a) argues that identity is constructed through the production of meaning, which gives us a sense of identity, of who we are, and with whom we belong. Therefore, we have multiple identities, not just one identity. Meanings hence do matter with identities: 'they define what is "normal", who belongs – and therefore, who is excluded' (p. 10). This results in their relations with power when one thinks of how one's life is shaped because meanings of the same concept may be different or act differently in different circumstances. Although there is the presence of shared cultural codes, it cannot 'guarantee that meanings will remain stable forever' (p. 10), and thus as meanings matter, identities cannot be guaranteed to be 'static' or 'unchanged'. However, one's identity is tied to a specific history and culture, which creates a 'positioned' context determining the 'self' of a person (Hall, 1997b: 51). Woodward (1997: 2) interprets 'the circuit of culture' suggested by du Gay _et al._ (1997) in such a way that 'identities are produced, consumed and regulated within culture – creating meanings through symbolic systems of representation about the identity positions which we might adopt.'

Vietnamese scholars, such as those discussed earlier and Phan Ngoc (1998), Tran Quoc Vuong (2000) and Tran Ngoc Them (2001a, b, c), also agree upon the intimate relationship between language, culture and identity, but tend to develop their perspectives from and are influenced by the national culture and national/cultural identity as one united element and a core sense of 'wholeness', which each Vietnamese should maintain and develop. In contrast, the Western scholars focus more on the individual without referring to national culture as something 'out there', but something individuals construct as they go on and interact with members in the same community. The Vietnamese scholars draw readers' attention to their arguments by proudly focusing on Vietnamese culture with its richness and senses that we – Vietnamese – and others can distinguish from non-Vietnamese cultures. These scholars strongly believe in the core values built into Vietnamese culture, which they have been brought up with, sensed and been surrounded by. It is this belief that leads its members to think and act under this national umbrella, and what each member does is to conform with and strengthen this core value. Although these scholars do acknowledge that language and culture are 'open acts', they explicitly praise the Vietnamese values, although constructed and reconstructed, attaching to the very core that is always 'out there', and which, I believe and understand, is embedded in our spirit as Vietnamese. This will be explored specifically in the discussion of identity.

## Identity

As Phan Ngoc (1998) observes, when cultural contacts take place everywhere in the world, it is crucial to understand the significance and importance of culture and identity. Moreover, 'identity is such a concept – operating "under erasure" in the interval between reversal and emergence; an idea which cannot be thought in the old way, but without which certain key questions cannot be thought at all' (Hall, 1996: 2). Culture and identity have hence become general matters of interest and brought numerous ways of understanding the world into the agenda. Here, scholars meet one another at some points, compromise at other points and undeniably, fiercely criticise each other at many remaining points.

For many scholars in the West, identity seems to have much to do with the question 'who I am', which has long haunted humans, since it is so subtle and complicated. There are times when one thinks one clearly understands and knows who one is, but there are times one gets totally lost and panics because one feels that one has lost one's self. So, does identity merely mean 'self'? No, it is more than that, it is embedded in every aspect of our lives, ranging from the individual level to the community level, from the community level to the national level, and from the national level to the international level. The 'Self' as an individual has become the 'Self' of 'Representation', symbolising a specific community or a group of people, meanwhile the 'bigger Self' represents multiple 'Selves' within it. However, this proportion between the 'bigger Self' and the individual 'Self' has been calculated differently by authors whose arguments have added depth to our understanding of identity, which I myself still struggle to define. At this point, I want to seek support from Vietnamese authors, who have their own ways of interpreting this proportion. In other words, they approach the notion of identity from different viewpoints, which on the surface may conflict with those expressed by many Western authors.

But before I elaborate in any detail these viewpoints, I would like to discuss postcolonial writings on identity, as identity has been one of the central concerns embedded in these writings. For this reason, it will be a big limitation not to acknowledge such works and locate and extend my discussions of identity both within and beyond postcolonial writers' scope. By the same token, discussing these theories offers me the opportunity to see the notions of *the West* and *Western knowledge* especially as being inherently problematic in their own right. This grounding further consolidates my introduction of non-Western perspectives, in this case Vietnamese, on the issues that both the West and the non-West share; these are language, culture and identity.

## The West, mobility, transnationality and hybridity

Western scholars' views on identity vary hugely, and among them postcolonial writings on identity greatly contribute to the debates. This is not to say that postcolonial theory is a uniform, uncontested or homogeneous scholarship. Rather, it is presented and developed from the basis of the debates among its theorists, including literary authors, such as Edward Said, psychoanalytical authors, for instance Homi Bhabha, sociological authors, for example Stuart Hall, neo-Marxist authors, such as Dirlik, and historical authors, such as Dipesh Chakrabarty. These authors are not necessarily Westerners but their theories are developed in the West and to a certain extent represent a powerful Western strand of scholarship known as postcolonial theory. Discussions of recent postcolonial theories on identity and knowledge, especially with respect to the notions of the West, mobility, transnationality and hybridity, are particularly relevant and essential to the aims of this book.

### The West and Western knowledge in postcolonial theories

'Postcolonial theory seeks to explain issues of opposition, privilege, domination, struggle, resistance and subversion as well as contradiction and ambiguity' and contests colonialism's aftermath (Hickling-Hudson *et al.*, 2004: 2). The West and/or Western knowledge has been questioned, criticised and challenged from multiple angles by postcolonial theorists, among whose ideas the hegemonic and imperialist nature of Western knowledge is most often contested. Postcolonial theorists contest the assumption that Western thought is superior and the only truth worldwide. Its assumed superiority has been constructed, sustained and presented to the world in every way.

In his famous classic *Orientalism*, Edward Said (1978) claims that Orientalism is 'a Western style for dominating, restructuring, and having authority over the Orient' (p. 3). It is 'not an airy European fantasy about the Orient, but a created body of theory and practice ... a system of knowledge about the Orient' (p. 6), in which voices of the Orient are given no space to speak for themselves. In Said's words, 'that Orientalism makes sense at all depends more on the West than on the Orient, and this sense is directly indebted to various Western techniques of representation that make the Orient visible, clear, "there" in discourse about it' (p. 22). Orientalism, the West's invention, looks as if it were developed scientifically, systematically and reliably as truths although 'there is very little consent to be found' (p. 6).

Said's *Orientalism* was revolutionary because it argues convincingly and systematically that Orientalism as Western discourse is developed and promoted as truths. It explains why Oriental people construct themselves the way the West assumes them to. The West gives itself the right to impose its ideas, beliefs and imagination on the 'man-made' discourse of the Orient (p. 5). Said's arguments imply that the Orient is seen through the Western vision with certain fixed characteristics, and this vision is so powerful that the Orient has come to believe that they are born with these built-in characteristics. This implication has been proved to be true in many contexts, such as in a series of West–non-West dichotomies (developed versus underdeveloped or developing, progressive versus. traditional, and so on).

Nevertheless, *Orientalism* has also received criticisms, among which its failure to acknowledge non-Western peoples' agency and active resistance to the theories and practices of Orientalism appears to be the most significant (Gandhi, 1998; Graversen, 2001). Bhabha (1994) and Spivak (1993, cited in Graversen, 2001: 8) criticise Said for his oversimplification of 'the division between a dominant West and a subordinate East as a relationship of active and passive, of imperial villain and unresisting victim'. Other critics also point out *Orientalism*'s contradictory nature. Said on the one hand argues that the West needs an 'Other' to define its own identity, and Orientalism is invented as a result. This to a large extent suggests essentialism, the West vs. the Orient. However, the methodological message Said wants to send through *Orientalism* is his rejection of essentialism. In trying to reject the West's essentialisation of the Orient, Said sometimes seems to essentialise the West by suggesting that it is ethnocentric and racist and enjoys a coherent self-identity which is defined in relation to the Other Orient (Windschuttle, 1999). Although *Orientalism* has flaws, as indicated by critics, its greatest success is that it nurtured and set a foundation for critical debate in the West which is later known as postcolonial theory. Said's *Orientalism* encourages other theorists to question and revisit Western knowledge, and asks for the voices of the Orient to be heard. For example, Sered (1996) argues that 'the person who has until now been known as "the Oriental" must be given a voice. Scholarship from afar and second-hand representation must take a back seat to narrative and self-representation on the part of the "Oriental".'In light of this discussion, I see the need to present the voices of Vietnamese theorists who construct and represent themselves – the so-called Orient – through their own positioning.

Both the Orient and the Occident are not 'merely there', rather they are invented by the West (Said, 1978: 3). The notion of 'the West' is what Vinay Lal (2002) and Chakrabarty (2000) question in their works, *Empire of Knowledge* and *Provincializing Europe* respectively. Vinay Lal (2002) investigates Western thought – the 'Empire of knowledge', as he calls it. Notions such as development, modernity, nation-state and Western civilisation all have to do with the politics of knowledge, which has been developed and utilised to serve the West's interest and maintain the assumed Western superiority over non-Western peoples. Lal further points out that non-Western(s) are constructed and understood in ways that maintain this arguably assumed superior West. Western civilisation and superiority are thus used as legitimate reasons for the West's 'good-willed' interference in other countries' affairs. The West's former 'civilising mission' has been transformed into the mission of democracy, freedom and human rights to bring to light the 'outlaw' peoples who go against these Western notions. Still, the West gives itself the right to enlighten, 'teach' and punish others, no matter in what forms. Colonial thinking is still active but operates in different ways, the ways that make many follow the West and look up to it as the only example of development and civilisation.

Chakrabarty (2000) criticises the European ideology of the 'first in Europe, then elsewhere' structure of global historical time (p. 7), which, for instance, implies that modernity or capitalism originated in Europe then spread outside it. Thus, Chakrabarty urges the need to see in what way 'historicism ... posited historical time as a measure of the cultural distance ... assumed' to exist between the West and the non-West' (p. 7). He also insists that postcolonial scholarship should commit itself to engaging with the universals and theory, and by the same token pay attention to cultural and historical difference at every possible moment (Chen, 2003).

Chakrabarty argues for three propositions, which are the provincialisation of Europe, the provincialisation of history and the provincialisation of time. Chakrabarty has demonstrated how the notion of the West and Western thought has always been highly contested. He problematises the assumptions that European thought can be employed to interpret and make sense of the practice of history in a non-European place. As described on the back cover of his book, Chakrabarty's work indicates that 'the mythical figure of Europe that is often taken to be the original site of the modern in many histories of capitalist transition in non-Western countries [and] this imaginary Europe … is built right into the social sciences'. However, taking India as an example, Charkrabarty shows that European thought can neither understand adequately nor explain meaningfully the political and the historical in a country like India. *Provincializing Europe* also teases out how powerful and taken-for-granted European thought is in the social sciences. Its power and the way it is presented in scholarly works have treated non-European thinking as 'truly dead' (p. 6) and at the same time made non-Western scholars accept the European way as the only 'alive' tradition (p. 5) from whose basis they can develop their knowledge. That is why 'South Asian(ist) social scientists would argue passionately with a Marx or a Weber without feeling any need to historicize them or to place them in their European intellectual contexts' (p.6), whereas few of them if any would argue seriously with their own philosophers and theorists. His argument points out that the idea of the non-West has been interpreted in binary terms in ways that have masked its colonial constructions and continuing hegemonic role. I acknowledge the likelihood of the hegemonic role of the West in the complex development of Vietnamese scholars' views on identity and knowledge formation. Nevertheless, I am relying on the argument that many other social and historical layers of meaning inhabit these Vietnamese scholars' views in addition to Western ideas. Because of this complexity of layeredness of the Vietnamese scholars' views, I feel it necessary to represent them alongside current Western thought on identity and knowledge.

Although Chakrabarty self-positions as a postcolonial scholar and attempts to resist to a large extent the universality of European thought, the way he resists it presents a paradox. Chen makes clear this paradox by showing that 'despite [Chakrabarty's] "loving grasp of detail" when it comes to Indian life-worlds, [he] relies heavily on the "philosophical" – or what he also calls "structural" – side of history writing; and for him, the inspiration for this kind of philosophical work is Western, naturally' (2003: 4). It is clear from Duong Thieu Tong (2002) and Phan Ngoc (1998), well-known scholars in Vietnam, that Vietnamese scholars also face this paradox. However, as Phan Ngoc indicates, many Vietnamese scholars actively Vietnamise foreign philosophies (for example, Chinese Confucianism, French nationalism and Marxist and Leninist Communism), and develop their own bodies of knowledge which are also grounded in their rich sources of cultural and historical heritage. These scholars not only negotiate confidently with powerful and hegemonic foreign philosophies but also hold on to the Vietnamese sense of nationalness to construct Vietnamese voices. More discussions of this are presented in the part on Vietnamese authors' views on language, culture and identity.

While postcolonial theories have helped us to question and challenge many of the universalising claims of European philosophies, to disrupt stereotypes in many fields of knowledge and to invite the voices of the non-Western others to be heard, they have also been criticised.

Ingham and Warren (2003) state that postcolonial theories have been criticised for their focus on modernity, which results in their limited scope of studies as well as scope of time. Additionally, their focus on modernity treats 'colonial "modernity" as a fact of history rather than an ideology of colonialism' (p. 2). This also 'blocks certain routes to the past, and thus maintains certain nationalist and historicist exclusions' (p.2). Ingham and Warren refer to leading classic postcolonial writers, such as Bhabha and Dirlik, to argue that these authors, despite their influential works and theories of modernity, 'do not set out to move the postcolonial beyond modernity, and might deny the validity of this interpretation of their work' (p.4). Critics also point out that postcolonial writings just focus on consequences of Western colonialism and imperialism without considering 'the specificity of particular historical processes of colonialism' (Hickling-Hudson et al., 2004: 3). By the same token, postcolonial theories pay remarkable attention to Anglocentric concerns rather than trying to cover other places (Ingham & Warren, 2003). Another critique of postcolonialism is that 'it diverts attention from the material basis of cultural difference towards generalisations and theoretical abstractions' (Hickling-Hudson et al., 2004: 3). Above all, postcolonial theories, for many years, have put tremendous emphasis on the politics of power, the one-way impact of colonisers on the colonised, and the hegemonic and imperialist imposition of the West, without taking into account sufficiently the degrees of appropriation, resistance and active reconstitution from the non-West sides, particularly the colonised. This approach seems to disregard local cultural, social and historical realities and movements of colonised countries. To make known these missing parts of postcolonial theories, the second section of this chapter presents Vietnamese scholars' perspectives of language, culture and identity. In addition, Chapter 3 draws on and engages with a number of scholars who acknowledge and develop the notions of resistance, appropriation and reconstitution. Postcolonial theories, as a field of inquiries, need to encourage more writings regarding these concepts to bring in multiple voices and to reflect and represent multiplicity in this globalising world.

Thus far it is clear that postcolonial theory is not a unitary experience. I wish to look at it from different angles and identify what theories are most relevant to and useful for my understanding of the processes of identity formation of Western-trained Vietnamese teachers of English, who would return to Vietnam to teach again. I acknowledge that by distinguishing the West and Vietnamese, I am running the risk of essentialising both, as Edward Said has been criticised for in his _Orientalism_. However, I also acknowledge that I try to avoid it whenever I can, and it is difficult to have a discussion without using this differentiation for the aims set out in the book. While I am distinguishing Western and Vietnamese views on identity and knowledge, I am also acknowledging their complex interrelations and will take them into account in my effort to investigate the questions this book undertakes.

### Mobility, transnationality, hybridity and identity formation

Mobility, transnationality and hybridity are essential concepts in postcolonial writings on identity, and they have become particularly significant conceptual tools in the understanding of identity formation in this ever globalising world. They largely contribute to the exploration of different processes of identity formation, including fragmentations, fluidity, negotiations, accommodations, mediations, contradictions, appropriation and resistance. The discussion of mobility, transnationality and hybridity below is located in the context of identity formation. Accordingly, I only focus on arguments and points which serve this purpose. Although I present the concepts separately, I acknowledge that I am well aware of the fluid and dynamic interrelationship and interdependence of these concepts.

#### Mobility

Mobility often refers to human/population movements/flows at different levels worldwide. Movements can be at local, regional, national, transnational or global levels (Crang _et al._, 2003; Koczberski & Curry, 2004; Lin, 2002; Paasi, 2002; Smith, 2002; Willis & Yeoh, 2002,). These movements necessitate identity formation to take place in multidimensional directions, resulting in different kinds of negotiations of identities. In the same vein, these also offer 'a new terrain for the articulation and interaction of identities' (Smith, 2002: 117).

Lin (2002) examines thoroughly the relationship between identity and mobility. He points out that the shift from modernity to postmodernism has supported a new way of looking at this relationship, in which migrants [I added, as well as any others who travel] 'actively constituted, negotiated, and transformed their multiple identities in their narration of development and the centrality of such identities in shaping various mobility patterns and experiences' (p. 65). Although the relationship between identity and mobility is encouraged in the literature, Lin argues that its nature remains 'highly controversial and vague' (p. 65). For example, he shows, on the one hand, how notions such as place-based identity have been proved significant in transnational identity formation of the Chinese diaspora in the context of globalisation. In reviewing other studies related to the Chinese diaspora, he remarks that 'globalisation has not in any way downplayed the role of place-based identity in the transnational movement of people and capital.' Instead, 'globalisation has propelled a return to the local and reinforced "primordial attachments" which are instrumental to the global mobility of the Chinese diaspora' (p. 66). He also indicates, on the other hand, the increasing popularity of other contrasting notions, such as 'deterritorisation, dislocation, and displacement' (p. 66), in identity formation of Chinese transnationalism. He refers to a number of researchers who argue that 'as a result of deterritorisation and spatial displacement, identities are no longer tied to cultural (national) space and mobility is not simply shaped by place-based identity but it is the other way around' (p. 66).

These researchers, according to Lin (2002), also indicate that increased mobility has in fact enabled cultural knowledge gain, offered opportunities for the generation of new spatial images and meanings and for the formation of new cultural or national identities. By the same token, increased mobility opens spaces for the social reproduction of cultural and national identities. So, instead of viewing identity as place-based or land-based, these researchers see it as 'diaspora based' (p. 66). As a result, 'identity is reinterpreted "as a politics rather than as an inheritance, as fluidity rather than as fixity, as based on mobility rather than locality, and as the playing out of these oppositions across the world"' (Ong & Nonini, 1997: 327, cited in Lin, 2002: 66). In this view, identity formation is interpreted as 'ongoing processes of construction, negotiation, and transformation' (p. 67). Identity thus, as these authors suggest, no longer operates independently from mobility. Instead, identity is 'embedded by and constantly reworked through mobility' (p. 67).

Faced by these two contradictory arguments, discussed above, of the relationship between identity and mobility, Lin attempts to find his own answers by conducting his research into how the great spatial mobility of Hong Kong sojourners affects their identity formation. His study shows that identity and mobility are mutually interrelated and that the interrelationship between spatial mobility and place-based identity is complex and multifaceted. His study also demonstrates that despite increased global mobility of diaspora and the ongoing processes of deterritorisation and displacement, locality or place of origin plays a significant role in the transnational identity formation of Hongkongers. It further states that 'the great mobility of the Chinese diaspora from Hong Kong, and the diasporic landscape they have created, have been effectively shaped by their place-based ethno-linguistic identity' (Lin, 2002: 87). This suggests that place-based identity is 'one of the many fundamental forces operating behind the scene of the great spatial mobility demonstrated by the Hong Kong sojourners' (p. 87).

Although Paasi (2002) does not seem to disagree totally with the role of place-based identity, the author does problematise the existing narratives of fixed regional identities and the closed local/national cultures. In the context of the increasing movement of people, capital and information across spatial boundaries, Paasi explores the meanings of 'region' and 'identity' and their relationships, with a specific focus on Finnish regions and the mobility of the Finns between these regions. Paasi's study contributes to questioning 'the supposition of closed local/national cultures' (p. 144), and simultaneously challenges 'the fixed links between a territory and a group of people' (p. 144). Paasi suggests viewing 'spatial identities in more dynamic ways', paying attention to 'the dynamic links between spatial contexts and cultural flows' (p. 144). Paasi also indicates that personal mobility problematises the existing narratives of fixed regional identities and suggests that the links between space, boundaries and identity have new meanings in this mobile world. She argues that Finnish people, together with having a sense of 'roots', which are typically connected to their place of birth or their areas of origins, also 'identify themselves with new home regions' (p. 144). Her study suggests that 'we have to analyse critically any discourse of "regional identity" or "our identity" that is based on roots or common heritage, since these often hide the influence of mobility' (p. 146).

The relationship between place-based identity and mobility is seen through another dimension by Koczberski and Curry (2004). Place or locality or region in their work refers to the destinations instead of the roots of those who are mobile. They look at the mobility of people in Papua New Guinea (PNG) from areas of disadvantage to regions of better services and employment opportunities to examine how the mobility affects identity shifting in migrant destination sites. The authors locate their study in two of the major palm oil producing areas of PNG, namely West New Britain Province (WNBP) and Popondetta, Oro Province, where there are land disputes and conflicts between landowners and migrants/settlers. As a result of mobility, new group identities (collective identities) emerge, particularly those of settlers and landowners. While ethno-regional identities emerge among local landowners, settlers construct their vaira/weira identities. Vaira, coming from the local language of WNBP, 'refers to strangers/ outsiders that do not belong to the same land, language or descent group' (p. 366), and it is used by customary landowners to label settlers and other migrants in WNBP and Popondetta. The authors find out that 'while the literal meaning [of vaira] implies exclusion and difference, it is increasingly being adopted as an umbrella label by the multi-ethnic settler population to forge among themselves a shared identity and collective consciousness' (p. 366). This vaira identity is subject to construction and reconstruction, based on the notion of nation-building – 'a narrative that places the "hard-working" settler at the centre of national development and advancement' (p. 367). This narrative implies by settlers that they are superior over landowners because they are 'modern, educated and engaging in the market economy' (p. 368) and because it is they (not landowners) who bring about prosperity and development for the land/the areas. Their mobility makes the difference and their vaira identity is accordingly constructed. On the one hand, their vaira identity supports the argument of 'a unified common identity' (p. 368) which is 'out there', 'available' although constructed, but on the other hand it signifies the importance of mobility, which makes this identity construction fluid and subject to being unstable and reshaped.

Taking into account these varied perspectives of identity and mobility, I acknowledge the importance of viewing identity in relation to the simultaneity of mobility and locality. Also, treating mobility and locality as *dynamic* as well as simultaneously *out there* and *unified* helps me understand how identity makes sense of mobility. In light of these arguments, the identity formation processes of the Western-trained Vietnamese teachers of English referred to in this book are better explored and understood.

*Transnationality*

Transnationalism/transnationality originated in work on transnational corporations, and then was extended to migration and various forms of movement studies, such as the work of Beaverstock (2002), Crang *et al.* (2003), Davis and Moore (1997), O'Donnell (2001) and Willis and Yeoh (2002). Over the past decade, there have been numerous perspectives on transnationalism, ranging from work on diasporic social formations and senses of identities, cultural globalisation, hybridisation, experiences and political economies of migration to work on forms of political engagement that operate transnationally (Crang *et al.*, 2003: 439). Transnationalism/ transnationality has become 'a ubiquitous term of reference for the "multiple ties and interactions linking people or institutions across the borders of nation-states"' (Vertovec, 1999: 447, cited in Crang *et al.*, 2003: 439).

Yeoh *et al.* (2003) point out how useful and potential the notion of transnationalism/transnationality is to the way we understand many key concepts, such as 'identity', 'place', 'nation', 'transgress' and 'mobility'. These authors recognise the role of transnationality in strengthening the significance of the 'national'. Transnationality, instead of treating the world in the dichotomy of the global and the local, acts as 'a bifocal ... which views the nation-state and transnational practices as "mutually constitutive"' (p. 208). In this view, 'transnationalism studies open up the possibilities and politics of simultaneity where transnational subjects, from a range of social groups, can now "think and act simultaneously at multiple scales" and fashion transnational social practices by being both "here" and "there"' (Smith, 2001: 164, cited in Yeoh *et al.*, 2003: 208). This argument is closely associated with the question of identity formation and identity politics in transnational social spaces.

Transnational identities are not only fluid, flexible, dynamic, but also attach to specificity and particularity of places and times. While transnational identities go against essentialist and fixed notions of identity, they put emphasis on 'interconnectedness across borders' (Yeoh *et al.*, 2003: 213). This way of understanding transnational identities suggests that identities are constantly constructed and reconstructed along the lines of 'simultaneous embeddedness in more than one society' (p. 213). This quality of being 'here' and 'there' and simultaneity enable the understanding of transnational identities in ways in which 'the "individual", "group", "national" and "transnational" relate to one another – whether in collusion or collision, or both – in shaping a world with increasingly, but also complexly, fluid borders' (p. 215).

Although transnationalism has been largely used as a more popular conceptual tool in scholarly work, it receives criticisms in relation to its scope, specificity and politics. Crang *et al.* (2003) argue that despite its popularity, transnationalism stays problematic since the implication and application of the term remain:

> (a) paradoxically, locked within a national geographical imaginary of culture and identity; (b) an overdrawn distinction between nationals

and transnationals; and (c) an unhelpful preoccupation with 'disciplining' transitional studies and concepts. (p. 441)

In terms of the scope of transnationalism, Crang *et al.* review a variety of work on transnationalism and comment that several authors criticise the term for being used 'too sweepingly, with too little attention to place-specific variations in the form of cross-border activities and sensibilities' (p. 441). The deployment of transnationalism needs to acknowledge different experiences of displacement and should not treat these experiences in the same way, otherwise transnationalism is no more than a 'uniform fashion' (Lavie & Swedenburg, 1996: 4, cited in Crang *et al.*, 2003: 441) which views hugely diverse experiences of mobility as one single act of movement. Transnationalism and the notion of 'a world without boundaries' are so powerful and romanticising that various discourses have enthusiastically adopted them, and this adoption seems to neglect that 'a world without boundaries' is not for everyone yet (Kaplan, 1995: 45, cited in Crang *et al.*, 2003: 442).

In relation to the question of the historical specificity of transnationalism, Crang *et al.* claim that the use of transnationalism implies that the nation-state no longer plays a significant role in social analysis. These authors argue, conversely, that in spite of general preferences of transnationalism, 'the nation state continues to play a key role in defining the terms in which transnational processes are played out' (p. 442). Transnationalism should not neglect this role and instead it needs to take into account the specificity and particularity of histories, times and places, since every identity formation process in the mobile world means little if it is separated from its origins of locality. In this regard, I find it important to present the theories discussed by Vietnamese authors who place 'the nation' and/or 'national culture' at the heart of identity formation.

Regarding the politics of transnationalism, Crang *et al.* raise the concern that the term has been applauded for its progressive and resistant nature. It is believed that transnationalism is able to destabilise fixed constructs of people and place, and reflect the dynamics and increased mobility of the globalised world. This belief supports a particular way of seeing the world in which movement, flow and boundary crossing are emphasised and make sense. This way suggests that transnationalism is 'seen as politically transgressive and resistant' (p. 442), which often denies seeing the world as 'politically constraining, conservative and hegemonic' (p. 442). Thanks to the resistant nature of transnationalism, the term has been used to explore how people worldwide resist certain forms of global cultural flows. However, drawing on Mitchell (1997a, b), Crang *et al.* (2003: 443) argue that:

> there is nothing intrinsically 'given' about the politics of transnationality, and those who make appeals to concepts of non-fixity, in-betweenness and third spaces as inherently progressive construct transnationality in equally one-dimensional terms as those who equate transnationaliy with the operations of monolithic, American-centred transnational corporations.

In order to find ways to compensate for the three criticisms made against transnationality, Mitchell addresses the need to employ transnationality in relation to actual movements of things and people across space. She argues that:

> without 'literal' empirical data related to the actual movements of things and people across space, theories of anti-essentialism, mobility, plurality and hybridity can quickly devolve into terms emptied of any potential political efficacy ... It is through the contextualisation of concepts such as hybridity and margins ... that theories of transnationalism can best serve a progressive politics of the future. (Mitchell, 1997a: 110–112, cited in Crang *et al.*, 2003: 443)

While many transnational studies remap the spaces of cultural identity and belonging in ways that 'problematise and complicate the assumption of national territories' (Crang *et al.*, 2003: 445), this approach again falls into focusing on 'bounded communities even as it redraws their location in space', as Crang *et al.* (2003: 445) observe. These authors suggest seeing transnationalism/transnationality empirically 'without fixing the transnational on identifiable transnational communities, while being open to other more fluid and multidimensional cultural geographies' (p. 446). Their work on studying commodity culture associated with British-South Asian transnationality, as they claim, enables them to utilise all the strengths of recent accounts of transnationality and at the same time avoid all the problems they have identified so far. On the one hand, their work recognises and reflects diverse connections British-South Asian communities have with their different 'homes', which are their places of residence in the UK and their real and imagined homelands in South Asia, and with other South Asian transnationals in their diaspora. On the other hand, their work also extends 'the boundaries of transnationality to include differently located groups and individuals who may or may not be members of these specific "ethnic" communities' (p. 451). Additionally, Crang *et al.* argue that their work shapes their views on transnationality, which is 'not only multiply inhabited but also *multidimensional*' (italics in the original) (p. 451). Furthermore, they suggest that transnationality needs to be looked at as both 'an abstract cultural discourse' and 'as *a lived social field*' (italics in the original) (p. 451). Importantly, these views of transnationality do not, in any ways, deny 'the continued salience of the national in a globalising world' (p. 452). Rather, as these authors contend, these views put emphasis on 'the active constitution of identities through the process of commodification across specific national spaces' (p. 452).

*Hybridity*

In the context of mobility and transnationality, hybridity has become one of the most important notions relating to identity formation of different groups of people, communities, places and nations. This notion, however, does not enjoy a unitary definition.

Homi Bhabha is perhaps one of the first scholars to develop and theorise the concept of hybridity. Hybridity, one of Bhabha's major concepts, as Hallward (2001: 24) puts it, 'is "a difference 'within'", a difference without binary terms'.

From a psychoanalytical point of view, Bhabha (1990, 1994) questions existing knowledge of nationalism, culture, representation and resistance, and encourages a rigorous rethinking of these notions. Nations, in his view, 'are "narrative" constructions that arise from the "hybrid" interaction of contending cultural constituencies' (Graves, 1998a). Bhabha's argument for the rethinking of the above notions 'stresses the "ambivalence" or "hybridity" that characterises the site of colonial contestation, a "liminal" space in which cultural differences articulate and ... actually produce imagined "constructions" of cultural and national identity' (Graves, 1998a). Bhabha claims that colonial culture is not a simple combination of the colonising and the colonised. Rather, its hybridity, its in-betweenness is the very salient characteristic of colonial culture. Bhabha (1994: 36) coins the term 'Third Space' when he argues that 'the pact of interpretation is never simply an act of communication between the I and the You designated in the statement.' Instead, 'the production of meaning requires that these two places be mobilized in the passage through a Third Space', which suggests and implies 'ambivalence in the act of interpretation' (p. 36). The intervention of the Third Space of enunciation, as Bhabha argues, 'challenges our sense of the historical identity of culture as a homogenizing, unifying force, authenticated by the originary Past, kept alive in the national tradition of the People' (p. 37). He states the significance of the productive capacities of the Third Space which embodies a colonial or postcolonial provenance. Importantly, as Bhabha (1994) claims:

> For a willingness to descend into that alien territory … may reveal that the theoretical recognition of the split-space of enunciation may open the way to conceptualizing an international culture, based not on the exoticism of multiculturalism or the diversity of cultures, but on the inscription and articulation of culture's hybridity. To that end we should remember that it is the 'inter' – the cutting edge of translation and negotiation, the in-between space – that carries the burden of the meaning of culture. It makes it possible to begin envisaging national, anti-nationalist histories of the 'people'. And by exploring this Third Space, we may elude the politics of polarity and emerge as the others of our selves. (pp. 38–39)

Bhabha's interpretation of hybridity, ambivalence and Third Space leads to the understanding of culture as 'complex Intersections of multiple places, historical temporalities, and subject positions' (Mitchell, 1995). His ideas question the tendency to essentialise colonised countries as a homogenous identity. He argues, instead, that ambivalence is always there at the site of colonial dominance. Ambivalence and hybridity, in his arguments, embrace the sense of agency and negotiation. In the interview with Mitchell (1995), Bhabha's explanation of 'the split' supports this point.

> The split doesn't fall at the same point in colonised and coloniser, it doesn't bear the same political weight or constitute the same effect, but both are dealing with that process. Actually, this allows the native or the subaltern or the colonised the strategy of attempting to disarticulate the voice of authority at that point of splitting. … For me, [the split is] much more the idea of survival/surviving in a strong sense – dealing with or living with and through contradiction and then using that process for social agency.

In light of his arguments, neither 'coloniser' nor 'colonised' can be seen as separate entities which are constructed independently from one another. In reading Bhabha (1994), Graves (1998b) remarks that the negotiation of cultural identity that Bhabha suggests 'involves the continual interface and exchange of cultural performances that in turn produce a mutual and mutable recognition (or representation) of cultural difference'. This 'liminal' space is a 'hybrid' site where the production of cultural meanings takes place.

Although Bhabha is considered one of the most influential scholars of postcolonial theories, his work has also been criticised. According to Hallward (2001: 35), Bhabha's work is challenged for 'totalis[ing] a hegemonic global ideology, neither much tainted by its conditions of production nor transformed by the pragmatics of colonial encounters and struggles'. His theories do not pay attention to specificity and particularity of the location and the moment.

Marxist or neo-Marxist critics also participate in debates regarding identity formation. They attack the central postcolonial concepts of hybridity, flexibility and mobility. Citing Lazarus, Hallward (2001: 41) remarks that for many of these critics, these central concepts 'are of practical significance only to foreign elite and indigenous comprador classes: to the overwhelming masses of local people, they merely spell out exploitation in new letters'. Postcolonialism, as Ahmad, Dirlik, Parry and San Juan point out (see Hallward, 2001), is another form of capitalism but at a global level. 'Postcolonialism coincides with the ideology of Global Capitalism', as Dirlik (1997: viii) puts it (cited in Hallward, 2001: 41). So, in this view, the concepts of hybridity, flexibility and mobility help mask the ideology of capitalism while discouraging attachment to local identity formation and local particularity.

According to Hiddleston (2004: 371–372), 'Aijaz Ahmad and Benita Parry, largely influenced by Marxism, pour scorn on the poststructuralist emphasis on the play of identity effects, suggesting that the fetishization of endlessly shifting modes of identification renders positive political contestation defunct.' On the contrary, literary and psychoanalytical authors such as Homi Bhabha argue that 'traditional power structures rely on a form of determinism that glosses over and tyrannises the true ambivalence of both coloniser and colonised' (p. 372). Hiddleston notes that neither of these two opposite ways of looking at identity are sufficiently useful conceptual tools. She suggests, instead, the work of the Algerian novelist Assia Djebar, which, she claims, 'offers a particularly innovative approach, in that it replaces the binary opposition described above with a mode of thinking that operates on several levels simultaneously' (p. 372). Djebar's work embodies conflicting aims, and these aims 'reconfigure the opposition between identity and hybridity into a tension between the specific, the singular and the plural' (p. 372). Also, Djebar's writing 'privileges unconditionally neither the concrete agency of Ahmad's thinking nor the hybridity proposed by Bhabha' (p.384). The search for identity in Djebar's work 'is coupled with reflections both on contingent singularity and on a form of plurality that resists totalization' (p. 384).

Werbner (2001) examines the limits of cultural hybridity and contested postcolonial purifications. Werbner's overall argument is that while concepts such as hybridity and transgression have been proved to be very useful tools of resistance, they can also become a source of offence because they 'play dangerously on the boundary' (p. 138). Postcolonial theorists, such as Bhabha (1994), indicate that hybridity signifies not only the colonised's active resistance to discrimination and oppression in postcolonial times but also their agency to affirm themselves to be recognised. The colonised often draw on their cultures strategically to achieve these aims. However, hybridity is two-edged knife here. In reading Werbner, I understand that hybridity can lead to either effective resistance, recognition and appreciation or offence. The essential question thus to be raised here is 'what are the creative limits of cultural hybridity' (p. 138).

Werbner helps answer this question step by step. She first argues that 'the stress on hybridity theory on the colonial encounter as the source of reflexivity and double consciousness does not engage ... with the fact that cultures produce their own indigenous forms of transgression and hence also of critical reflexivity and satire' (p. 133). Werbner states that one key criticism of the notion of cultural hybridity is that 'it assumes the prior existence of whole cultures' (p. 134). Cultures, according to the author, 'may be grasped as porous, constantly changing and borrowing, while nevertheless being able to retain at any particular historical moment the capacity to shock through deliberate conflations and subversions of sanctified orderings' (p. 134). This argument, as the author then claims, is based on 'a key distinction made by Bakhtin between "organic" and "intentional" hybridity' (p. 134).

'Organic' hybridity, according to Bakhtin (1981: 358), means 'unintentional' and 'unconscious' hybridity (cited in Werbner 2001: 135). Bakhtin (1981: 358) argues that 'unintentional, unconscious hybridization is one of the most important modes in the historical life and evolution of languages ... [and] language and languages change historically primarily by means of hybridization, by means of mixing of various "languages"' (cited in Werbner, 2001: 135). Although 'the mixture remains mute and opaque, never making use of conscious contrasts and oppositions ... such unconscious hybrids have been at the same time profoundly productive historically: they are pregnant with potential for new world views, with new "internal forms" for perceiving the world' (Bakhtin, 1981: 360, cited in Werbner, 2001: 135). According to Bakhtin (1981: 358–359), 'an intentional hybrid is first of all a conscious hybrid' which is 'an encounter, within the area of an utterance, between two different linguistic consciousnesses, separated from one another by an epoch, by social differentiation or by some other factor' (cited in Werbner, 2001: 136). In this view, intentional hybrids are 'inevitably dialogical' and 'double voiced', embedded in a single utterance (Bakhtin, 1981: 360–361, cited in Werbner, 2001: 136). Bakhtin's notions of 'organic' and 'intentional' hybridity have similarities with Bhabha's (1994) concepts of hybridity, ambivalence, liminality and Third Space, as Werbner argues and as I have discussed earlier.

Werbner (2001) contends that Bakhtin's discussion of hybridity enables the theorisation of 'the simultaneous coexistence of both cultural change and resistance to change in religious, ethnic, or migrant groups and in postcolonial nation-states' (p. 143). But what are the limits of cultural hybridity? 'When and why do hybrid postcolonial novels cease to be funny and entertaining and become deeply offensive?' (p. 143). In this global context, 'when does transgressive hybridity facilitate, and when does it destroy, communication across cultures for the sake of social renewal?' (p. 149). Given that identities are subject to dynamic change, construction, reconstruction, negotiation, hybridisation, repro- duction but hold on to continuity as well as connectedness, as my overall argument on language, culture and identity in this chapter suggests, these questions raised by Werbner regarding the limits of cultural hybridity and even hybridity in general are of essential significance. They remind researchers that together with celebrating hybridity, we need to work on a notion of hybridity that is critical and useful for recog- nition and appreciation of difference and cultural creativity, not a notion that denies the right to be different. Hybridity and/or hybrid transgres- sions must respect and retain 'a local sensibility in a globalising world' (p. 149), so as to lead to 'a double consciousness, a global cultural ecumene' not to a 'polarization of discourses' (p. 149). As Werbner (2001: 150) observes, 'the line between respect and transgression' is very easy to cross, particularly 'in postcolonial nations and the ambivalent encoun- ters they generate'.

Pieterse (2001), in many points, shares her concerns regarding hybrid- ity, identity politics and politics of difference and recognition with Werbner (2001). Pieterse questions the relationship between difference and recognition and how hybridity plays within this relationship. After all, the politics of hybridity makes sense in the context of boundaries, because hybridity 'problematizes boundaries' (p. 220). Pieterse goes through a number of criticisms of hybridity, arguing that the most common criticisms are that hybridity does not take questions of power and inequality into consideration. She particularly reviews the anti- hybridity backlash and refers to the arguments which support hybridity.

**Table 2.1** Arguments for and against hybridity

| Contra hybridity | Pro hybridity |
|---|---|
| Hybridity is meaningful only as a critique of essentialism. | There is plenty of essentialism around. |
| Were colonial times really so essentialist? | Enough for hybrids to be despised. |
| Hybridity is a dependent notion. | So are boundaries. |
| Asserting that all cultures and languages are mixed is trivial. | Claims of purity have long been dominant. |
| Hybridity matters to the extent that it is a self-identification. | Hybrid self-identification is hindered by classification boundaries. |
| Hybridity talk is a function of the decline of Western hegemony. | It also destabilises other hegemonies. |
| Hybridity talk is carried by a new cultural class of cosmopolitans. | Would this qualify an old cultural class of boundary police? |
| The lumpenproletariat real border-crossers live in constant fear of the border. | Cross-border knowledge is survival knowledge. |
| Hybridity is not parity. | Boundaries don't usually help either. |

cited in Pieterse, 2001: 225

Although hybridity has a number of flaws, as Pieterse has pointed out, she states that she does not mean to reject hybridity. Instead, what she attempts to do is 'acknowledging the contingency of boundaries and the significance and limitations of hybridity as a theme and approach' (p. 239) so as to engage with hybridity politics. She goes on to argue that 'this is where critical hybridity comes in, which involves a new awareness of and new take on the dynamics of group formation and social inequality', and 'this critical awareness is furthered by acknowledging rather than by suppressing hybridity' (p. 239).

So far I have discussed various critical notions of postcolonial writing regarding identity formation, namely the West/Western, mobility, transnationality and hybridity. Drawing on the discussion of these notions, the following sections look particularly at notions of identity discussed by a number of Western theorists (such as Dolby, 2000; Hall,

1997a, b; Holland, 1996; Reed, 2001; Wodak *et al.*, 1999; Woodward, 1997) and Vietnamese scholars (such as Phan Ngoc, 1998; Tran Ngoc Them, 1999, 2001a; Tran Quoc Vuong, 2000). Acknowledging both the usefulness and flaws of these notions of the West, mobility, transnationality and hybridity in postcolonial writing and in relation to the theories of identity enables me to critically interpret the processes of identity formation of a group of Western-trained Vietnamese teachers of English. The fact that these postcolonial notions together with the notions of identity and related notions discussed by both Western and Vietnamese authors are employed as conceptual tools, I believe, best helps the exploration of complex and diverse identity formation processes, taking into account the dynamic, fluid transnational mobility between space and time, the Vietnamese, the West, the global, the here, the there, the past, present and future.

## Western-oriented perceptions of identity

In this section, I will focus on non-essentialist Western perceptions of identity to build a framework for my discussion in subsequent chapters. The following themes, which are generated from the debate, will be explored: identity as constructed, multiple, hybrid and dynamic; identity formation and difference; identity formation as relational; and construction of national identity.

### Identity as constructed, multiple, hybrid and dynamic

This section features the debate between essentialist and non-essentialist points of view about the notion of identity. Non-essentialists view identity as constructed, multiple and dynamic as opposed to the 'notion of an integral, originary and unified identity' suggested by essentialists (Hall, 1996: 1).

Hall (1996: 3) contests the notion of the 'stable core of the self', remaining unchanged throughout history and across time. Similarly, he expands his contestation to the notion of the stable core of cultural identity, which remains fixed, identical and static over time, as essentialists argue. He goes on to suggest that there is no 'unchanging "oneness" or cultural belongingness underlying all the other superficial differences' (p. 4). Instead, cultural identity, as well as other identities, is always changing, and transformed. Identity has and makes its own history. Woodward (1997) also refers to the debate between essentialist and non-essentialist views of identity, reporting that the latter challenge the claim made by the former that 'identity can be seen as rooted in kinship and the truth of a shared history' (p. 3) and identity is 'formed in particular historical circumstances' (p. 3).

Largely influenced by Hall (1992, 1996), other writers, such as Holland (1996), Dolby (2000) and Farrell (2000), employ 'non-essentialist' notions, including fluidity, contingency, plurality and complexity, to discuss identity issues. For example, Holland (1996) criticises essentialist perspectives of identities for their power in constructing and maintaining fixed images of Aboriginals in Australia, which are often claimed as 'authentic'. These perspectives, as she emphasises, deny differences existing within Aboriginal communities. She supports Hall's (1992: 277) argument that 'identity becomes a "moveable feast": formed and transformed continuously in relation to the ways we are represented or addressed in the cultural systems which surround us' (Holland, 1996: 109). Hall's understanding of identity, as she acknowledges, allows her to speak of herself as 'having multiple identities' and 'to recognize that in different contexts and at different times [she assumes] different identities' (p. 109). Holland's interpretation of identity demonstrates that identity is multiple, constructed and dynamic.

Another example is Dolby (2000), in which she perceives identity 'as a phenomenon that is actively produced and reproduced, instead of as a stable entity that exists before the social world' (p. 900) and 'as a site that is in constant flux, responding to and recreating itself in the new contexts in which it is located' (p. 905). This view suggests that identity has no quality of stability and immutability. Rather, it is constructed, hybrid and dynamic. Also, in this argument, identity formation seems to be an active process. Farrell (2000) also argues for the nature of identities being always contested and changed, looking at how people in their work place construct their work identities.

All of the above discussions support the understanding of identity as a question of 'becoming', but not of 'being', as Hall (1996: 4) argues. In this view, identity is not about 'an all-inclusive sameness, seamless, without internal differentiation' (p. 4). Instead, it has to do with representation, using 'the resources of history, language and culture in the process of becoming' (p. 4). This non-essentialist view of identity is further addressed in Hall's later work (1997b), in which he elaborates two different ways of presenting cultural identity. He sees identity 'not as transparent or unproblematic as we think' (p. 51). Instead, it is viewed as 'a "production", which is never complete, always in process, and always constituted within, not outside, representation' (p. 51). He is persistently against the position of viewing cultural identity 'in terms of one, shared culture, a sort of collective "one true self", hiding inside the many other, more superficial or artificially imposed "selves", which people with a shared history and ancestry hold in common' (p. 51). Cultural identities in this sense 'reflect the common historical experiences and shared cultural codes which provide us, as "one people", with stable, unchanging and continuous frames of reference and meaning, beneath the shifting divisions and vicissitudes of our actual history' (Hall, 1997b: 51). The second position supported by Hall (1997b: 52) is that in addition to many points of similarity, there is other deep and significant 'difference' which presents 'what we really are, or rather, since history has intervened, what we have become'. Cultural identity, in this case, 'is a matter of "becoming" as well as of "being"'. It has both 'past' and 'future' in it. It has histories and constantly transforms. After all, 'identities are the names we give to the different ways we are positioned by, and position ourselves within, the narratives of the past' (p. 52). In Hall's (1997b) perceptions, identity concerns both 'positioned context' and 'fragmental' values. Hall's view also suggests that identity formation has much to do with history which experiences different times. This causes contradictory identities within us to pull in different directions.

Although Hall (1997b), at some point, refers to the 'being' of identity, most of his discussions suggest identity as constructed, multiple, hybrid and dynamic. The 'becoming' of identity, consequently, is over-emphasised. Because of Hall's influence on other writers over the last few decades, this way of understanding identity has overshadowed other ways, and, to a large extent, seems to suggest that all other ways are static in nature. However, this assumption will be challenged in the section of this chapter presenting Vietnamese authors' perceptions of identity.

### Identity formation and difference

Many non-essentialist Western theorists explore the question of identity in relation to difference. 'Identity gives us an idea of who we are and of how we relate to others and to the world in which we live', as Woodward (1997: 1) observes. She goes on to argue that 'identity marks the ways in which we are the same as others who share that position, and the ways in which we are different from those who do not' (p. 1–2). She suggests that identity can be marked by 'polarisation', 'inclusion or exclusion' and 'oppositions', whether we are 'insiders/outsiders', 'us/them' or 'man/woman' (p. 2). No matter how identity is understood, it 'gives us a location in the world and presents the link between us and the society in which we live' (p. 1).

Woodward (1997) argues that identity is often defined at the expense of difference because by asserting 'who I am', we simultaneously produce the image of 'who I am not'. By doing so, we have created the 'us' and 'them'. The marking of sameness and difference is done both 'symbolically through representational systems and socially through the inclusion or exclusion of certain groups of people' (p. 4), as she observes.

Self is constructed through other; or identity is constituted 'through the eye of the needle of the other', as Hall (1991: 21) argues (cited in Dolby, 2000: 901). In other words, when we define others, we indirectly define ourselves. We make selves as well as others.

Playing an important role in identity formation, and like identity, 'difference is not a static, immobile reality' either, as Dolby (2000: 902) remarks. Difference is also constructed, produced and reproduced. Thus, identity formation becomes even more complex.

### Identity formation as relational

Since identity is constructed through difference, identity and identity formation are hence perceived as relational. That is to say, one identity needs another identity to rely on and to provide the conditions for its existence (Woodward, 1997).

As individuals are positioned in multiple relationships, exposed to numerous social situations and experience changes in life, their identities are subject to being constructed within relations. Dolby and Cornbleth (2001) conceptualise this phenomenon of identity as relational. They argue that 'identity itself is a relation – or set of relations and interrelations' (p. 293). Thereby, 'we see or define ourselves in relation to various individuals and groups, specific life situations and particular contexts' (p. 293). Because these situations and relations change over time, identity is also subject to change.

Identity and identity formation are relational in the sense of geographic space as well (Reed, 2001). Movements in space and exposure to a new place influence identity formation.

### Construction of national identity

While essentialists view national identity as 'integral, originary and unified' (Hall, 1996: 1), as 'unchanging "oneness" or cultural belongingness underlying all the other superficial differences' (p. 4), and as being 'rooted in kinship and the truth of a shared history ... [and being] formed in particular historical circumstances' (Woodward, 1997: 3), non-essentialists see national identity from different perspectives. Drawing on De Cillia *et al.* (1999), I expand a number of Western authors' discussion about notions of national identity.

De Cillia _et al._ (pp. 153–154) present five basic assumptions about nations and national identities. First, they refer to Anderson's (1988: 15) definition of nations, in which nations are understood as being _'imagined political communities'_ (cited in De Cillia _et al._, 1999: 153). Second, they argue that national identities are _'discursively ... produced, reproduced, transformed_ and _destructed'_. Third, national identity can be seen as _'a sort of habitus', 'a complex of common ideas,_ [and] _concepts or perception schemes'_. Fourth, 'the discursive construction of nations and national identities always runs hand in hand with the _construction of difference/distinctiveness and uniqueness.'_ The fifth assumption is that 'there is _no such thing as the one and only national identity_ in an essentialising sense, but rather that different identities are discursively constructed according to context' (p. 154; all italics as original).

White (1997) also views national identity as imagined, since each individual can be seen through other multiple identities. Therefore, he states that to focus on national identity is not simply to send an underlying message that that is the only significant identity, or that the many other individual identities constructed by people for themselves are irrelevant.

Turner (1986: 110) argues that 'definitions of national identity are sites of struggle', and 'the definitions are never static or fixed' (cited in Stratton, 1998: 107). Hence, as Hall (1997b: 53) argues, 'there is always a politics of identity, a politics of position, which has no absolute guarantee in an unproblematic, transcendental "law of origin".'

Although many Western theorists come up with different expressions of national identity, they offer ways which individuals employ to construct national identities. De Cillia _et al._ (1999) give a detailed list of these ways. To begin with, national identities are constructed on the basis of 'a common history, and history has always to do with remembrance and memory' (p. 154). Second, the construction of national identities is closely related to the role of culture. Third, national identities have much to do with 'internalised structuring impetus which more or less strongly influences social practices' (p. 156).

De Cillia _et al._ (1999: 160) also identify four strategies used by individuals in Austria to construct their national identities, namely constructive strategies, perpetuation and justification strategies, transformation strategies and dismantling or destructive strategies. Constructive strategies aim at building and establishing a particular national identity, using linguistic acts such as 'we-group' in statements like 'we Austrians' or 'Austrians' (p. 160). Perpetuation and justification strategies 'attempt to maintain, support and reproduce national identity' (pp. 160–161). These strategies can be seen in discussions where individuals 'construct immigrants as a threat to national identity' (p. 161). Transformation strategies involve transforming 'the meaning of a relatively well-established aspect of national identity into another' (p. 161). For example, 'some Austrian politicians have been pretending that it would be possible to re-define the Austrian neutrality in a way which would integrate modified geo-political conditions, without abandoning neutrality altogether' (p. 161). Dismantling or destructive strategies are used to 'de-mythologise or demolish existing national identities or elements of them' (p. 161). For example, some Austrians observe that it is not worth arguing for Austria's neutrality because it is 'not traceable to an autonomous "national" decision' (p. 161).

I have so far discussed a number of Western-oriented perceptions of identity. The subsequent sections explore those of influential Vietnamese authors in contemporary Vietnam.

## Vietnamese authors' perceptions of identity

Identity, as perceived by many Vietnamese authors, is often related to national and/or cultural identity. When looking at Vietnamese authors' discussions of identity, it is often tempting to judge that their views reflect and are very much the same as essentialists' perceptions of identity. However, their viewpoints are positioned within their personal and national discourses and informed by the sense of Vietnamese nationalism, all of which signal differences, similarities as well as uniqueness as compared with those belonging to other discourses. But this is not to say that their Vietnamese and personal discourses are static. Rather, these are changing over time but cohere to maintain the sense of connectedness and continuity.

### Identity as both 'being' and 'becoming'

Many Vietnamese authors argue that identity is about both 'being' and 'becoming'. This suggests stability within changes or changes that take place along the lines of continuity.

The *'being'* of identity is understood as the constituents of Vietnamese national and cultural identity. National identity, as Tran Ngoc Them (1999: 2–3) observes, is distinctive values transferred and sustained in history and their sustainable best. He acknowledges the universal truth that every people in the world loves their nation, loves their family and works hard, etc. However, this does not mean that they are all the same. Neither do his arguments about Vietnamese distinctive values suggest that Vietnamese people are better than others, or they have values that others do not have. What he tries to suggest is that Vietnamese cultural identity is affected by its structure and by the environment where its people have been living. He offers a number of Vietnamese cultural constants, which determine the feature and development of the culture. For example, in terms of natural conditions: *high level of rain and humidity*; in terms of geographical location: *Vietnam being at the crossroad of civilisations*; in terms of traditional economy: *water-based rice crops*. Let me look at Tran Ngoc Them's (1999: 3–5, 2001a, 2001c: 39–46) analysis of how the cultural constants affect the formation and becomingness of Vietnamese cultural identity.

Thanks to the high level of rain and humidity, Vietnam has *a wide range of flora*, and *complicated and uneven geology*. This results in the development of planting, and because planting depends heavily on nature, Vietnamese people have to work hard, and develop the *'sense of induction'* and *flexibility*. Flexibility enables them to easily adjust to new circumstances and learn from others. Also, planting is seasonal, so Vietnamese people have to closely unite with each other, which results in *respect for social relations* and the *sense of community* and *solidarity*. This sense of community is emotion-oriented, which is different from that of China and Japan, often thought of as more social-oriented. Because of the vitality of living within a community, Vietnamese people highly appreciate *dignity* and *personality*. The nature of planting requires people to live permanently at one place, but the complicated and uneven geology makes Vietnamese people divide into many smaller communities, resulting in the diversification of ethnic groups and languages. Therefore, in parallel with the sense of community, the *sense of self-rule* also develops. The sense of self-rule within individual communities creates the *love for home-villages*. The sense of self-rule within a broader scope creates the *love for the country* as a whole and strong *sense of national independence*. That is why the love for home-villages and the love for the Vietnamese country are interrelated and permeate each other. Interdependence in planting also leads to *emotion-biased lifestyle*, and thus *tactfulness* and *sophistication* are valued in the society. Planting requires stability as well, so the Vietnamese people tend to be a *tolerant, forgiving* and *peace-loving nation*. Thus, whenever its peace is threatened, *patriotism* and the sense of national independence are enhanced, and its people are willing to die to defend the country. Bravery hence emerges. All of these above features add the sense of harmony to the way Vietnamese people behave. That is why they often think twice before taking actions, and are optimistic in difficulty.

Tran Ngoc Them (1999, 2001a) goes on to suggest that these values had been formed before cultural contacts with China occurred, and they are still present in modern times. Nevertheless, he states that these values are not everlasting and unchanged. They change in appearance and content, but at the same time, remain relatively stable in the content, developing alongside and sticking to a common thread, which is composed of these above distinctive appearances.

Tran Ngoc Them (2001a) locates his argument within the following philosophy: in the universe, nothing is absolutely immutable and nothing is absolutely moving, either. Everything is both stable and moving, and the difference rests in the degree of stability and movement. Therefore, different concepts and notions have different degrees of movement and changes. He then defines 'cultural identity' as the everlasting existing permanence of culture. Material culture is always changing, while spiritual culture is more stable, so cultural identity is always and only spiritual values formed in history. Thus, this is the *'becoming'* of Vietnamese national and cultural identity. *'Being'* and *'becoming'* are interwoven.

In relation to cultural identity, Phan Ngoc (1998) looks at culture in terms of a series of human relations to explore his own inner life and what remains of its unchanged needs (p. 5). He argues that the way a culture chooses to represent itself is unchanged, and this thus makes different cultures (p. 15). In light of this argument, Vietnam has its own 'way' of representation, meeting its people's spiritual desire (p. 5). Yes, all human beings need to eat, somewhere to shelter/dwell, and to have some possessions, but different groups of people have different 'ways' of signifying such needs. Moreover, he argues that although human beings' forms of desires change over time and are very diverse, our spiritual/mental life remains more or less unchanged; for example, the image of a village in the mind of most Vietnamese people has always been attached to the love for the homeland. This results in the very largely unchanged way of representation.

Identity, as he argues, is the stable part within culture. However, this stable part is not a thing. It is rather a relation. It, as a result, cannot be seen with our eyes. To exemplify Vietnamese identity in cultural contact with the world, he refers to the image of a circus actor who performs on a thin rope (line) and needs to maintain balance, so that he/she will not fall. Vietnamese identity, in this view, may change unpredictably, but needs to sustain a relation similar to the importance of the balance maintained by the circus actor (p. 140). Cultural identity, similarly, refers to the unchanged part of culture in history. Culture is a system of relations, and these relations may be portrayed in different forms depending on explanations given by different times (p. 32). He argues that even the most distinctive features of Vietnamese identity are subject to change as a result of historical situations, living environment and cultural contacts. Neverthe-less, cultural identity remains more or less stable, reflecting the unchangeability of Vietnamese people's mental/spiritual desire.

Phan Ngoc (1998) views culture as a science, which has its own objects, methods and terminologies. Importantly, he makes a valuable remark that people should respect difference and live in harmony. Difference does not mean deficit. Research into the relationship between what framework man has in mind and what framework man has created is the job of culturology. On the basis of this approach and his argument that the way Vietnam chooses to represent itself is unchanged, Phan Ngoc (1998: 32–106) identifies four dominant elements portraying Vietnamese identity: Fatherland, Family, Fate and Face (Four Fs), which I interpret as the Viet-namese homeland, the Vietnamese family, the issue of status (than phan), and the issue of identity (dien mao). All of these elements are interrelated and intertwined.

*The Fatherland (Vietnamese homeland):* Phan Ngoc observes that Viet-namese people understand deeply and proudly that the Vietnamese homeland is their land, the land they have had to exchange their lives for, the land they have had to create out of nothing due to the injustice of nature (the plains in Northern Vietnam are man-made and Vietnamese people have been fighting against both natural and human enemies to sustain them). Consequently, there is nothing more important to them than their land, the land that did not come to them from nature, but was a product of their labour and struggle. This results in Vietnamese people being homeland-oriented, which means their homeland is the most signif-icant and important. They are, hence, loyal to and willing to die for their land, which belongs to all people, not to any particular families, any kings or any groups of people. This is unchanged. Different peoples have different ways of understanding and loving their countries, and this is the way Vietnamese people understand and feel about their land (p. 34). Their love for the homeland permeates and penetrates into all activities and rela-tions as much as the other way. As a result, in contact with other cultures, Vietnamese people Vietnamise every foreign value through their vision of homeland, which means they make foreign values serve the interest of their people with deep attachment to their land. For example, according to Phan Ngoc (1998), Buddhism in Vietnam is the Buddhism of patriotism, Sino-Vietnamese literature is the agenda for writers and composers to express their love for the Vietnamese country and people, and even the French-influenced Vietnamese poetry in the early 20th century expressed patriotism and the passion for peace in a combination of both a sophisti-cated and heroic voice. The notion of Vietnamese homeland has nurtured the sense of nationalism and collectivism, in which the latter is also a product of living in villages – the core image of Vietnamese culture.

Phan Ngoc lists a number of factors which are interwoven in order to form Vietnamese nationalism. For instance, first, it is the integrity and 'uniform' of ideology, and in Vietnam, it is Buddhism. Then, a myth (legend) of the Viet race was woven, saying that all Vietnamese people regardless of their living environments all over Vietnam have the same father and mother: father Dragon and mother Fairy. None the less, the most important quality of Vietnamese people is their built-in love for the homeland, the love that comes from the reality of life: solidarity is needed to fight against and live in peace with natural disasters for the sake of the water-rice agriculture, and to defend the country from human enemies. It is the very quality that holds people together and makes a core Vietnamese identity, around which other identities of Vietnam are centred.

*The Vietnamese family*: Phan Ngoc (1998) views *the Vietnamese family* in relation to Vietnamese villages, relatives, ancestor worshiping practice and, above all, *the Vietnamese homeland*. The interest of the family is harmonious with and accompanied by that of the homeland. Vietnamese family  is the very base for nurturing and maintaining the love for the homeland and the sense of nationalism (pp. 56–57). In particular, Phan Ngoc discusses generational conflicts in his own extended family as well as family conflicts in general when Vietnam experiences cultural contacts with others, whether forcedly or willingly, to prove this unchanged characteristic. Although different times may place different responsibilities on families, the core responsibility remains quite stable.

*The issue of status* (than phan*) and the issue of identity* (dien mao*)*: Phan Ngoc indicates that before the French colonisation, a single Vietnamese person had his/her status and self-identity in society. He/she was not economically and politically dependent on any powerful force. Rather, he/she enjoyed social protection, which ensured him/her a safe life if he/she lived with kindness and moral uprightness, as expected by society. Because Vietnam enjoyed a tradition of having a united political mechanism built on the basis of self-rule villages rather than a powerful bureaucratic regime, its people had to harmoniously follow two sets of relations. In either relation, Phan proves that every single Vietnamese person had a status and identity provided and protected by this dual relation.

Phan Ngoc explains why Communism was victorious in Vietnam when it was first brought in. It won people's hearts because it did care about the nation, the land, the independence and their social status and identity. He believes that if the Party can maintain and promote these values, it will have the support of the people.

It is clear that Phan Ngoc (1998) shares a number of views about culture and identity with both essentialist and non-essentialist Western authors. But instead of demonstrating identity as absolutely static and unchanging, he argues that identity (specifically Vietnamese national/cultural identity) has been changing but within a degree of stability and continuity, supported by the way Vietnamese people choose to represent themselves. He has pointed out that this way of representation appears more or less stable over time. In his arguments, identity contains both the *'being'* and the *'becoming'*, in which the *'being'* seems to dominate.

Tran Quoc Vuong is also an influential scholar of cultural studies in Vietnam, who has devoted his scholarly work and entire life to the exploration of Vietnamese culture. Tran Quoc Vuong (2000), apart from sharing his perspectives with Tran Ngoc Them (1999, 2001a, b, c) and Phan Ngoc (1998), looks at Vietnamese culture from the angle of life experiences, values and traditions. He remarks that the distinctiveness of Vietnamese culture is its non-refusing characteristic (p. 44). It only refuses forced assimilation; otherwise it is able to harmonise and integrate every cultural aspect. Moreover, he observes that Vietnamese people pay most attention to their manner of behaviour. These contribute to the formation of Vietnamese cultural identity. In his opinion, the most important factor in sustaining the on-going development of a nation is to maintain the nationalness of its cultural identity (p. 108). However, he also argues that traditions and values do change. Whether a behaviour or a cultural tradition is considered good or bad depends on historical circumstances. Tradition embodies both stability and changeability (p. 28).

Like many Western theorists, Tran Quoc Vuong (2000) emphasises the importance of exploring identity in relation to difference. Specifically, he sees the significance of juxtaposing Vietnamese culture to Chinese culture to define Vietnamese national/cultural identity. Together with other Vietnamese authors, he has indicated vital differences between the two to oppose the assumption that Vietnam is a Chinese-like culture located in South East Asia. At this very point, a strong sense of a Vietnamese cultural/national identity is significant to every Vietnamese to feel Vietnamese.

It is clear that Tran Quoc Vuong's (2000) viewpoints of culture and cultural identity also suggest that Vietnamese culture enjoys both the *'being'* and the *'becoming'*. He implies a sense of Vietnamese cultural identity, which Vietnamese people need to maintain. He also suggests that that sense of identity is continuous in the context of historical changes.

### Identity as national/cultural identity

It can be understood from the previous section that Vietnamese scholars tend to address identity in light of the notions of 'nation' and 'homeland', which have been seen in close relation to culture. They have created a comprehensive picture of 'identity', often understood as 'Vietnamese cultural identity', something very basic, fundamental and immortal regardless of time. So identity here is often referred to as 'cultural identity' or 'national identity'. This very notion of cultural identity has, as a result, established a strong tie between each individual within this identity 'loop' and the loop itself. It has also affected their behaviours and ways of doing things. In other words, it has created its own Discourse, the term used by Gee (1999), its own 'Vietnamese' uniqueness (Phan Ngoc, 1998; Tran Ngoc Them, 1999, 2001a, c). Vietnamese scholars have provided a portrayal of Vietnamese identity with widely accepted distinctive qualities of Vietnamese people within its Discourse.

Because these Vietnamese scholars strongly believe that there is a shared Vietnamese identity, they tend to believe that every Vietnamese acts, behaves and thinks with reference to this core identity. Because of this assumption, individual identities are often either neglected or underestimated. But this fact is normally compensated for by the general belief that Vietnam has a distinctive identity and each individual has the right, pride and responsibility to maintain and develop it. Let me imagine Vietnamese identity as a big umbrella, under which every individual allegedly thinks and acts in connection with it. This is to say that individuals are strongly and closely influenced by 'the shared' identity, while individual selves fade away or are put behind the scenes. Nevertheless, individuals make sacrifices for this shared identity and accept the reasons for their sacrifice. They are defined by the national identity, which takes precedence over other aspects of identity.

### Identity as the sense of belonging

Phan Ngoc (1998), Tran Quoc Vuong (2000) and Tran Ngoc Them (1999, 2001a, c) present identity as the sense of belonging. Although they have indicated that identity is about both 'being' and 'becoming', and place emphasis on Vietnamese national/cultural identity as the most important identity, what appears important in their discussion is a strong sense of continuity and connectedness, which gives one a sense of belonging.

Tran Ngoc Them (email exchange and phone conversation, 2001b, c) admits that despite his exposure to different parts of the world and

Western theories of identity and culture, he strongly feels a Vietnamese national/cultural identity. He feels a stronger sense of being a Vietnamese when he is outside Vietnam. His feelings support the argument that one defines oneself in relation to others (Dolby, 2000; Woodward, 1997). However, because he is a scholar of cultural studies who constantly argues for the existence of a shared Vietnamese identity, his feelings may present resistance to what is argued in the Western theories of identity and culture. I understand his feeling as both physical and mental. The 'being' of identity and the sense of it complement one another, and suggest a sense of belonging.

Phan Ngoc (1998) sees himself as a person experiencing major historical changes in Vietnam over the past century, and has been influenced by education in both Chinese and French in the first half of the 20th century. He has hence developed his concern about the identity of his country. Different chapters in his book, at first, aimed to answer the writer's own questions. Later, he realised that his questions are also common among his generation, those in their 70s who have been eye-witnessing the changes in Vietnam with its open-door policy. Phan Ngoc then decided to publish his book. He indicates that his book mainly reflects his own viewpoints. Phan strongly emphasises that although people like himself who have had close contacts with both Chinese (a powerful Asian culture) and French (a powerful Western culture) may have some Chinese flavour in their literary works and adopt some Western styles at work, they, most importantly, remain a Vietnamese and are able to Vietnamise a bit of Chinese and a bit of French to reflect the Vietnamese spiritual and mental life. To understand profoundly why Phan Ngoc, a highly recognised international scholar, has strongly believed in the very 'core' cultural identity of his country despite his enriched education and his mastery of various languages, it is important to note that he has a strong sense of belonging. He feels that he belongs to Vietnam.

The theory of language and culture advocated by Hall (1997a) obviously suggests that the language one speaks or uses to communicate with the world gives one a sense of identity. I thus interpret it technically as follows: the more languages you speak, the more identities you have; or the more 'independent', the more liberated and complicated your identity becomes. But this seems insufficient to explain how Phan Ngoc's identity or his view of it is presented. On the one hand, he does have a multiple and international identity, but at the same time, the more his identity is liberated, the stronger it attaches to the core Vietnamese values. Put differently, the more he contacts with the world, the more he believes in the 'out-there' cultural identity of Vietnam. He feels he has a strong sense of belonging, which many Western authors disagree with and try to argue against.

## Conclusion and main principles

So far I have discussed both Western-oriented and Vietnamese perceptions of identity.

It is clear that many contemporary Western scholars have shared a common view about identity. That is, identity is constructed, changing, hybrid and multiple. They do not agree on a 'core' and 'fixed' identity. Identity is rather transformed than unchanged. Likewise, there is no particular 'overall' identity that may always intervene in a person's behaviour or activities. Instead, a person's multiple identities will determine these acts. At one stage, one identity will come to the fore, but at another time other identities will be foregrounded while the previous one stays back. Through this process, identity will be transformed, retransformed, negotiated and renegotiated to create new aspects of identity. That is why identity, according to most of these authors, keeps moving and moving, undergoing sites of struggle. Identity is always more than just one thing.

When discussing identity-related issues, many Western writers are inclined to focus on individuals as the most important criteria to build identity. They pay most attention to fragmented aspects of identity as well. Put differently, they analyse the issue with a thorough look at every single component. In this case, they study identities of individuals, who have multiple, ever-moving and changing identities. The individual self has more space and encouragement to develop. Moreover, as there is nothing called core identity, individuals' behaviours are not determined from and towards a non-existent core identity.

While many Western theorists put an emphasis on the *'becoming'* of identity, Vietnamese authors suggest both the *'being'* and the *'becoming'*, in which the *'being'* plays an important role in maintaining a sense of belonging. Vietnamese authors argue that even though identity contains both stability and changeability, the latter occurs in a way that brings change together under a shared sense of Vietnameseness. Instead of viewing change in terms of fragmentation as some of the above Western authors argue, Vietnamese authors see it more as a fluid process of identity formation to ensure continuity and connectedness, and thus a sense of belonging. I see this view as useful, but this does not mean that Western authors' views are not useful. Identity is constructed, multiple, hybrid and dynamic, but it gives one a sense of belonging.

What Vietnamese authors suggest about the 'being' of identity and identity formation embodies a notion of 'existing' and 'persisting' values. I understand this notion as a sense of connectedness in the fluid negotiation of values, rather than entire stability as the notion may suggest. Put differently, stability is obtained through fluid movement and movement is operated through a certain degree of stability.

Both the Western and Vietnamese authors surveyed view identity in relation to difference and as relational. The former express their points more explicitly, while the latter implicitly interweave this view in their discussion. Both talk about the construction of national identity and the means used for this purpose. Although the Western authors argue that national identity is constructed and is changing over time, they seem to acknowledge that people do feel it when they identify themselves in terms of nationality, for example, as Austrian (Wodak *et al.*, 1999). As a result, I argue that there is a sense of belonging, a sense of national/ cultural identity that differentiates one people from others. Let me look at Vietnamese students studying in Australia as an example. Being positioned in an environment where their classmates come from different cultural backgrounds, they are often asked 'where are you from?' These students have to make sense of their Vietnameseness when answering 'I am from Vietnam.' Although it does not guarantee that all of them have the same perception of what it means to be Vietnamese, they at least have in mind some things to tell about it. All of these create a sense of Vietnamese cultural/national identity, which holds them together and makes them different from Chinese or Japanese, for instance.

## Other Conceptual Tools

Together with the main principles discussed above, in this section, I look at a number of notions related to the question of identity, which I employ as conceptual tools to help understand the identity formation of Western-trained Vietnamese teachers of English. They are identity fastening, unfastening and refastening; appropriation – resistance – negotiation; and identity and discourse.

### Identity fastening, unfastening and refastening

I would like to employ Reed's (2001) metaphor of identity fastening and unfastening to set the context of the Western-trained Vietnamese teachers of English who are referred to throughout the book. Identity fastening, in

Reed's definition, is referred to as 'the work that individuals do to claim insider status for themselves and for others' (p. 329). Meanwhile, 'identity unfastening often happens when individuals move from one cultural context into another where the norms and rules for membership are different' (p. 329). The latter applies to the teachers' movement from Vietnam to the English-speaking West, such as Australia, Britain and New Zealand, where their insider status is challenged. The former applies to them as they experience different sets of pedagogic performance, which governs their acts to claim insider status for themselves and others. As Reed argues, 'identities are fastened by the categories that we have available and by the ways that we submit to those categories and subject others to them' (p. 329). Reed also argues that individuals sometimes fasten identity so as to build a way to belong. This suggests that an act of identity fastening somehow secures a sense of belonging for individuals. But identities are always subject to being unfastened as individuals are in constant contact with new cultural values and norms as they move from one place to another. Consequently, identity fastening and unfastening take place side by side. In other words, they walk hand in hand and correlate. But one is also obtained at the cost of the other. As Reed asserts, they 'usually occur simultaneously and in multidimensional ways' (p. 329). Identity fastening and unfastening are part of the ongoing process of identity formation and identity negotiation. However, all of the above arguments do not suggest that identity fastening and unfastening are fixed. Rather, they are progressive processes.

Reed argues that 'identity fastening, unfastening and refastening are continuously done to us and by us' (p. 337). He gives an example that immigrants adopting a new identity often unfasten and refasten their identities. I understand his perception of refastening as reconstitution, in which refastening is not simply remaking a new identity after unfastening and fastening identities. Instead, it should be seen as part of 'the ongoing identity formation process' (p. 337), which takes into account a sense of belonging and a sense of continuity, maintained by a fluid process, despite fragmentation and/or contradiction in the course of identity formation. Fastening, unfastening and refastening are thereby better understood as processes than conditions or stages.

### Appropriation – resistance – negotiation

I now focus on three aspects that I believe contribute most to identity formation. They are the notions of 'appropriation' and 'resistance' (Pennycook, 2001), and the process of 'negotiation'.

Appropriation does not only refer to the process of 'making suitable' or 'taking possession of or making use of exclusively for oneself, often without permission' (online dictionary) or 'taking for one's own use without permission' (_Collins Compact Australian Dictionary_), but it also carries sites of resistance and reconstitution. Put differently, appropriation walks side by side with resistance and this creates 'reconstitution'. Appropriation may also include both resistance and reconstitution. Appropriation does not take place as a one-way process, rather it operates in a more complicated way, embracing the other two processes.

To explore the identity formation of these Western-trained Vietnamese teachers of English in the context of postcolonial ELT, I would like to refer to Canagarajah's (1999: 2) discussion of _resistance perspective_, which:

> provide[s] for the possibility that, in everyday life, the powerless in postcolonial communities may find ways to negotiate, alter and oppose political structures, and reconstruct their languages, cultures and identities to their advantage. The intention is not to _reject_ English, but to _reconstitute_ it in more inclusive, ethical and democratic terms.

In my understanding, this discussion actually explains the author's perception of appropriation. To simplify it, if viewing appropriation as a ruler, then negotiation will take place at every point of the ruler. Thus, although with this understanding, appropriation becomes extremely complicated, it will enable the Other to use the Self's language and norms (in this case, English and ELT) to turn against itself. Appropriation contains the possibility of change and opens up spaces for the Other to develop positively and equally compared to the Self. In the context of English and ELT as global characteristics, appropriation is specifically related to how the Other actively uses English and ELT in their tongues and for their comfort. But appropriation does not stop at an 'apolitical relativism' status (Pennycook, 2001: 71). Instead, it will assert itself by constantly creating '_third cultures_ or _third spaces_' as suggested by Kramsch (1993) (cited in Pennycook, 2001: 71).

## Identity and discourse

First of all, I must acknowledge that I am going to discuss the relationship between identity and discourse as a conceptual tool rather than as a body of knowledge. Therefore, I focus on how this relationship as a conceptual tool helps achieve the aims of this book.

I would like to employ Gee's (1999) definitions of 'Discourses' to begin the discussion of how identity is constructed within Discourse.

> *'Discourses'* with a capital 'D', that is, different ways in which we humans integrate language with non-language 'stuff,' such as different ways of thinking, acting, interacting, valuing, feeling, believing, and using symbols, tools, and objects in the right places and at the right times so as to enact and recognize different identities and activities, give the material world certain meanings, distribute social goods in a certain way, make certain sorts of meaningful connections in our experience, and privilege certain symbol systems and ways of knowing over others. (Gee, 1999: 13)

This definition suggests that 'Discourses are ways of being "people like us"' (Gee, 1996: viii). Gee also argues that 'each of us is a member of many Discourses, and each Discourse represents one of our ever-multiple identities' (p. ix). Importantly, 'these Discourses need not, and often do not, represent consistent and compatible values. There are conflicts among them, and each of us lives and breathes these conflicts as we act out our various Discourses' (p. ix). Gee observes that 'for some, these conflicts are more dramatic than for others' (p. ix).

Gee (1999: 38) treats Discourses as tools of inquiry. For him, in addition to other characteristics, Discourses involve 'situated identities' and 'ways of performing and recognizing characteristic identities and activities'.

Since we define ourselves when we speak or write (Farrell, 1994; Gee, 1999; Phan Le Ha, 1999; Viete & Phan Le Ha, 2007), language acts as a medium in and through which our identities are enacted and constructed. But as 'language makes no sense outside of Discourses' (Gee, 1996: viii), our identities are accordingly shaped in and through multiple Discourses to which we belong.

In understanding the relationship between identity and Discourses, it is important to understand cultural models and situated meanings as tools of inquiry, since 'both of these involve ways of looking at how speakers and writers give language specific meanings within specific situations' (Gee, 1999: 40). This discussion links to what Hall (1997a) means by 'meaning', in which meanings are socially constructed, multiple and subject to change. Each word is associated with both situated meanings and a cultural model.

Gee (1999: 80) defines a 'situated meaning' as 'an image or pattern that we assemble "on the spot" as we communicate in a given context, based on our construal of that context and our past experiences'. Situated meanings 'don't simply reside in individual minds; very often they are *negotiated* between people in and through communicative social interaction' (p. 80).

Gee defines 'cultural models' as '"storylines," families of connected images ... or "theories" shared by people belonging to specific social or cultural groups' (p. 81).

> Cultural models 'explain,' relative to the standards of the group, why words have the various situated meanings they do and fuel their ability to grow more. Cultural models are usually not completely stored in any one person's head. Rather, they are distributed across the different sorts of 'expertise' and viewpoints found in the group, ... much like a plot to a story or pieces of a puzzle that different people have different bits of and which they can potentially share in order to mutually develop the 'big picture'. (p. 81)

Also, 'cultural models link to each other in complex ways to create bigger and bigger storylines' (p. 81).

Farrell (2000: 21) discusses identity in connection with discourse, in which she remarks that identities 'imply sets of beliefs, values and orientation, the knowledges and the capabilities, that are available to a person in their social setting, moment by moment'. She understands 'discourse' as 'a socially recognised way of representing experience from a particular ideological point of view, ... which implies certain values, beliefs and orientations, certain identities' (p. 21). In light of Farrell's argument, identity and discourse are interrelated and one contains the other and vice versa.

As a conceptual tool, the relationship between identity and discourses discussed above is used to interpret the processes of identity formation experienced by Western-trained Vietnamese teachers of English.

## Conclusion

In this chapter, I have explored the relationship between language, culture and identity and related conceptual tools in order to understand different processes of identity formation. Also, by looking at these theories and tools, I have been able to define my positioning in the complicated discussion among scholars and theorists from the West and Vietnam.

Although some Western theorists' arguments about the relationship between language, culture and identity are both illuminating and useful, the ideas of the Vietnamese authors are equally so, as they partly spell out the sense of Vietnameseness that both I and others in my community strongly feel. Identity is multiple, dynamic and hybrid. Yet, it is also something like a 'core', a 'root' based on which new values are constructed. It is the very 'core' that unites members of a society under one identity called national identity. I argue that identity needs to be understood and studied in a specific context which has its own culture. In other words, identity needs to be contextualised. Both Western and Vietnamese scholars would support this need, despite the fact that it leads to different, sometimes contradictory, sometimes complementary points of focus. In order to understand the processes of identity formation of Western-trained Vietnamese teachers of English, the combination of these two different traditions in my analytical framework is a must.

## Chapter 3

# The Politics of English as an International Language and English Language Teaching

Before exploring the focuses of this chapter, it is important for me to acknowledge that although I draw on postcolonial theories and use many of their terms, such as Self, Other, Inner Circle, Centre/centre and Periphery/periphery, I am also aware, like many other authors such as McKay (2003), of the limitations of these terms. I use these terms mainly as conceptual tools. In other cases, these terms are employed because they are known and recognised in the literature.

## English, ELT and the Constructs of Colonialism

English: 'a language – the language – on which the sun does not set, whose users never sleep' (Quirk, 1985: 1)

'The sun never sets upon the British Empire.'

Let me start the discussion with the powerful statements that have been made about the status of English and its Mother Empire that have resulted in the tendency to assume the spread of English is inevitable and natural.

The spread of English as a world, international and global language, and the expansion of ELT to the rest of the world, have been enthusiastically discussed by many authors, such as Brutt-Griffler (2002), Crystal (1997), Kachru (1986), Krashen (2006), McArthur (1998, 2003), Melchers and Shaw (2003), Pennycook (1994, 1998), Phillipson (1992), Ronowicz and Yallop (1999), Rubdy and Saraceni (2006) and Smith (1987). Different perspectives have been expressed by authors from English-speaking countries, from countries where English is a second language or an official language, from countries where English is a foreign language of the first priority and from countries where English is one among many foreign languages to be taught. English as a global language, as these authors observe, has both positive and negative sides. On the one hand, as a lingua franca and today a global language, English has efficiently served as a bridge to connect all parts of the world, and thus made the world a village (Crystal, 1997). Through English, the world can not only hear voices of the powerless, appreciate values owned by different peoples regardless of what language they speak, what race they belong to, but also see and protest against global exploitation and inequality. Garcia and Otheguy (1989: 3) reinforce this contribution of English by indicating that English 'has facilitated political and cultural understanding across societies, as well as served as a medium to expose injustices perpetrated on powerless ethnolinguistic groups ( … by the English speaking powerful)'. Also, according to these authors, English has played the key role in understanding 'different realities of our international world' (1989: 3). On the other hand, English has been used as 'a tool for the licentious exercise of imperialist inclinations' (Verschueren, 1989: 33). Moreover, the use of English as the language of powerful nations has contributed to the superior–inferior relationships between the powerful and the powerless. The powerful play their game while the powerless are often pawns on a chessboard. As part of this dichotomy of power, Garcia and Otheguy (1989: 8) contend that 'the powerful impose communication norms and the powerless are asked to follow them.'

The explosive growth of the use of English has been accompanied by the similarly rapid expansion of ELT. The dominant status of English and ELT in almost all parts of the world is the product of colonialism, as Pennycook (1998) discussed. Phillipson (1992) sees the dominance of English and ELT as 'linguistic imperialism' when he draws readers' attention to the claim that the 'Centre' (English-speaking countries) imposes its own cultural values, military and economic power, wants and needs upon the 'Periphery' through ELT and so-called 'aid'.

To reveal how cultural constructs of colonialism adhere to English and ELT, Pennycook (1998) argues that many current ELT theories and practices embody in themselves colonial thinking and views, which strongly disadvantage learners of English as a second or foreign language. Because ELT had a long history of direct connections with colonialism, and ELT was both the product and 'weapon' of colonialism, it carries in itself many of the ways of thinking and behaving that are still part of Western cultures. If in the colonial times ELT was used to spread the empire's power and support the colonial governance, then ELT today is used to back up and strengthen the current global expansion of English and its underlying cultural values. These missions of ELT are in fact not much different since its duty is always to serve the benefit of colonialism and 'linguistic imperialism', as the title of Phillipson's book, *Linguistic Imperialism* (1992), suggests.

English – 'a superior language' – and ELT – 'a superior teaching practice' – are promoted according to these three views, known as 'capacities: English-intrinsic arguments, what English is; resources: English-extrinsic arguments, what English has; uses: English-functional arguments, what English does' (Phillipson, 1992: 271). The means used to exert linguistic power is through sticks (force), carrots (bargaining) or ideas (persuasion) (Galtung's classification, quoted in Phillipson, 1992: 283). In these days, the means of ideas (persuasion) is most appropriate and relevant to the world order and situations. Instead of using force or bargaining, the Centre has succeeded in making the Periphery peoples believe that what the Centre is doing for the Periphery is good and this is what they – the Periphery – want. This refers to Fairclough's (1989: 33) views on language and power, in which he argues that power can be maintained and exercised through '*coercion* or *consent*'. He also observes that *consent* proves to be more effective, 'less costly and less risky to rule' (p. 34). If we apply this theory to English and power, we can see clearly that the Centre has intentionally shifted the role of English and ELT from *coercion* in the old days to *consent* in recent times. In other words, if peripheral countries used to think of English and ELT as a means of actual colonisation, they have now seemed to come to believe that English and ELT have been doing more good to them.

Phillipson (1992) argues that English and ELT have helped most in gaining the success of the Centre by acting as 'a tool', 'an instrument', a 'neutral' means as the Centre calls them (English and ELT), to build a bridge between Centre and Periphery. To further his discussion, Phillipson refers to Galtung's idea that 'the "educated" in the Periphery are internalising Centre values and ways of thought to the point where the physical presence of Centre inter-state actors is no longer necessary and computers will ensure the Centre's control over the Periphery' (p. 242). This point links to the point made by Phillipson earlier in his book, that 'research by fledgling Periphery scholars could best be influenced when it was conducted and "supervised" as graduate study in Centre countries' (p. 234). In accordance with this argument, it is assumed that when scholars from Periphery countries are offered scholarships to do their research in the Centre, they are guided and influenced by the Centre and what their research aims at is to benefit the Centre. Also, these scholars are the ones who will bring Western values, ways of thought and the results of their research back to their countries. By doing so, these scholars contribute to the spread of English linguistic imperialism. They, whether unconsciously or not, are those who share common interests with the Centre's representatives. And if they are not aware of what they are doing, they then become 'harmful' forces who transmit Western values and English linguistic imperialism to their home countries. As Pattanayak comments, 'the advocacy of the norms of the Centre by "educated" persons tutored in the modes of western thinking' in language policy has had harmful effects on dominated languages and societies.

> These societies are then made permanent parasites on the developed countries for knowledge and information. By destroying interdependent self-directed societies, the elites in these countries achieve what colonialism failed to achieve through coercive occupation. (Pattanayak, 1986d: vi, cited in Phillipson, 1992. 286)

While the people of the Periphery realise the dominance of English and ELT, they are also aware of the importance and necessity of these 'effective weapons'. This has resulted in an explosive growth of English and ELT. Moreover, according to Pennycook (1994, 1998), the belief that 'the West is better' often held by both Westerners and non-Western people has also facilitated the spread of English and ELT. Non-native English teachers thus often assume that what the West provides is more advanced, and as a result, they come back and question their own ways of teaching English to their local students. These teachers, particularly those who are trained in English-speaking countries, are the ones who tend to exert an influence on language teaching policies in their countries and have at the same time been most influenced by Western pedagogical values and practices.

However, Crystal (1997) and Phillipson (1992) offer oversimplified arguments, which suggest that as the 'weapons' of the Centre, English and ELT have been carrying their missions of spreading and consolidating the Centre's values and power in the Periphery and other places, weapons so powerful that both the Centre and the Periphery have been made to believe in the advancedness, appropriateness and efficiency of ELT pedagogy as defined by the Centre. People in the Periphery, to varied extents, do resist and appropriate English and ELT (Canagarajah, 1999; Pennycook, 2001). I discuss this point in detail when I address the ownership of English. Also, concerns about the problems of ethics and inappropriateness of ELT pedagogy have been raised by authors from both the Centre and Periphery, such as Ellis (1996), Gupta (2004), Li

(1998), Liu (1998), Pennycook (1994), Phillipson (1992) and Tollefson (1991). These concerns are presented in the section on Communicative Language Teaching later in this chapter.

In light of the above discussion, those who are trained in ESL, EFL or TESOL in English-speaking countries are most closely associated with the double-sided arguments of English and ELT. Thereby, they need to be fully aware of their responsibilities for the education of younger generations in their home countries when they return home and apply to their local contexts what they have obtained through Western education. Their positioning regarding English and ELT plays an essential role in shaping their students' identity, and how the relationship between language and culture operates in the construction of identity. Hence, whether or not or to what degree they see themselves, their positioning and their images as being influenced by their exposure to the West is explored and how they construct their identities as teachers of English and individuals is examined in subsequent chapters.

## The Ownership of English as an International Language

In this section, I investigate the question 'who owns English?', and in particular English as an international language, since it is embedded in how English and ELT are perceived, practised and promoted globally.

Undoubtedly, English has gained itself the status of a world language, an international language, or a lingua franca in almost all settings (Brutt-Griffler, 2002; Crystal, 1997; Llurda, 2004; McKay, 2003; Seidlhofer, 2001, 2003). There are a number of ways to view EIL. Widdowson (1998: 399–400) suggests that EIL can be seen as 'a kind of composite lingua franca which is free of any specific allegiance to any primary variety of the [English] language'. EIL is also used interchangeably with other terms, such as English as a lingua franca, English as a global language, English as a world language and English as a medium of intercultural communication (cf. Seidlhofer, 2003: 9).

Although users of English, to various extents, have been able to appropriate the language for their own purposes (Canagarajah, 1999; Hashimoto, 2000; Phan Le Ha, 2004), this chapter argues that when the native-speaker norms are in contact with the norms of other speakers of English, it is often the case that the former are used to make judgements against the latter. Despite its international status, English in different forms of uses is still employed to exclude many of its users, to construct an inferior Other. As such, it celebrates globalisation yet limits integration, and strengthens the power of certain dominant forms of English. As long as these limitations of EIL are not acknowledged and remain unresolved, its users still face discrimination and unfair judgements.

Together with acknowledging the international status of English, I first re-examine the social, cultural and political aspects of this status so as to obtain an insight into how English is beneficial to most users yet at the same time a 'killer language' and a *'Tyrannosaurus rex'* (Pakir, 1991; Swales, 1997; both cited in Llurda, 2004: 314). Afterwards, I propose my critical notion of EIL pedagogy.

## Centre Englishes versus other Englishes

This section examines in what way EIL is still problematic and can still be used to discriminate against many of its users. Discussions are drawn on from the literature about how the Englishes in the Centre are still treated as 'better' and standard Englishes compared to other Englishes.

To begin with, although many authors have argued for the co-existence of a family of 'Englishes' (Brutt-Griffler, 2002; Kachru, 1986) given the widespread use of English and the way people have adapted it for their own uses, this family has not co-existed with equality yet. The notion of a family suggests a sense of support, love and care among its members. However, the Englishes in this family seem to enjoy a fiercely hierarchical relation, in which some members play the dominant role trying to 'support' and at the same time 'bullying' their weaker yet vulnerable 'sisters' and 'brothers'. Although there are varieties of English, such as Singaporean English, Indian English, African English, Australian English, American English and British English, it is arguable that international norms and rules of the language are not set by all these Englishes, nor even negotiated among them. Only the so-called 'native' speakers of English have a voice in the matter (Pham Hoa Hiep, 2001). We can see examples of this in the norms of English academic writing (Farrell, 1997a, b; Phan Le Ha, 2001), or in the debate about cross-cultural issues (Ballard & Clanchy, 1991, 1997; Kaplan, 1966; Liddicoat, 1997; Phan Le Ha, 2001; Viete & Phan Le Ha, 2007), or in the case of many students who have been using English since they started schooling in their countries (some African and Asian ones) but still have to take TOEFL or IELTS tests for their entrance into universities in the 'English-speaking West'.

When looking at the English languages, McArthur (1998) examines the forms of Englishes, linguistic insecurities and other related issues. His analysis suggests that Standard English has its own triumphant and decisive status, no matter how many Englishes have come into being. As one example, in the US, Black English, also known as Afro-American English, is institutionally considered inferior, with low quality, and thus those who speak it are labelled low-level achievers (p. 197).

The debate around Standard English was heated for some long time in the literature, and I would like to draw in particular on the work of Pham Hoa Hiep (2001). He argues that it is native speakers who set the norms for what is called Standard English. He clarifies his argument by drawing on definitions of 'Standard English' made by a number of authors. For example, Strevens says that Standard English is 'a particular dialect of English, being the only non-localised dialect, of global currency without significant variation, universally accepted as the appropriate educational target in teaching English, which may be spoken with an unrestricted choice of accent' (cited in Pham Hoa Hiep, 2001: 5). Pham Hoa Hiep also refers to Quirk's discussion of Standard English, which Pham expresses in his own words as 'the natural language that educated English native speakers use' (p. 5). Thus, according to Pham, it cannot be assumed that English belongs to no particular culture, or is 'culture-free' (p. 4). Indeed, he argues that the use of English does play an important part in both one's desire to communicate with the world and one's will to preserve one's identity. Put differently, English does affect identity formation, and Pham urges EFL teachers to assist students in achieving these two aims.

Native speakers of English, apart from the pride of owning the language of international communication, may see their language at risk of being 'corrupted' or 'polluted', since it has been modified and promoted every-where without any control (Marzui, 1975a; Crystal, 1988, cited in Pennycook, 1994). In order to oppose this trend, native speakers of English have found a way to protect Standard English by calling 'anything that isn't "standard" ... "dialect" if lucky and slang if not' (McArthur, 1998: 200). For example, McArthur shows that the issue of Standard English versus Black English is a matter in educational agendas in the city of Oakland in California, USA. The English Afro-Americans speak is perceived by educators as 'a distinct language spoken by the descendants of slaves' (Woo & Curtius, 1996, cited in McArthur, 1998: 198).

Let me now take a specific look at the forum on EIL initiated and sustained by Widdowson (1997, 1998) to examine in more depth what aspects of EIL are still controversial. Widdowson (1997), partly in response to authors such as Phillipson (1992), takes a provocative position in the discussion concerning 'EIL, ESL, EFL: global issues and local interests' raised in the journal *World Englishes*. Since Widdowson 'wanted to raise a number of questions for discussion' and thus made his paper 'provocative' to invite debates (p. 135), I would like to respond to several points he raises.

*First*, Widdowson makes an analogy between Englishes and Latin languages, assuming that the evolution of Englishes, such as 'Ghanaian and Nigerian [developing] out of English', parallels the development of 'French and Italian from Latin' (p. 142). Although I understand that Widdowson wants to argue for the independent status of all languages that develop out of English, I still find this assertion problematic. It obviously ignores the fact that French and Italian are separate and independent from Latin, a dead language that was mainly confined to Europe. This is far different from the story of Ghanaian and Nigerian being dependent on English, the language of developing dominance and inherent hegemony. The names Widdowson uses, 'Ghanaian and Nigerian', position these languages as other than English. They are not English, so there is only one English, and the question of whose English again comes implicitly on to the scene. I understand that Widdowson does not want his discussion to be viewed this way, but the politics associated with English denies his 'positive' assertion. Evidence suggests that within the English-speaking world, there is a dichotomy between the superior Self and the inferior Other, and the political aspect of English does play an important role in this dichotomy (Phillipson, 1992; Pennycook, 1998). Consequently, the question turns to 'power': whose English is the standard? Whose norms are to be followed? At this point, the question is no longer as simple as 'French and Italian developing from Latin'. It becomes a site of struggle between the 'centre Englishes' and the peripheral ones. For example, materials for English teaching and learning in the Periphery are mainly from the Centre (Mishan, 2007; Phan Le Ha & Truong Bach Le, 2007; Phillipson, 1992). Moreover, testing systems, such as TOEFL, IELTS and TOEIC, developed by the Centre have been used universally to assess learners' competency of English. This suggests that the centre Englishes and their related pedagogies are generally used as international standards, while other Englishes are for local uses only.

This argument of the relationship between power and English has been challenged by Widdowson (1998) in his reply to authors, such as Brutt-Griffler (1998). He clearly states that he wants to argue for English as 'a kind of composite lingua franca which is free of any specific allegiance to any primary variety of the language' (pp. 399–400) including the English from the Inner Circle. He strongly supports his view, asserting that it is because he is aware of the politics of English and its consequences that he attempts to urge English users to look at it as the language 'used internationally across communities as a means of global communication' (p. 399), but not as the language owned by the Inner

Circle. This implies that he wants to encourage others to see English as politics-free. However, many authors have pointed out that English walks hand in hand with politics, and there is always some kind of politics underlying English and ELT (Auerbach, 1995; Edge, 2003; Pennycook, 1994, 1998; Pennycook & Coutand-Marin, 2004). Moreover, as long as there are norms and requirements set by the Inner Circle in cross-cultural communication (Farrell, 1997a, b, 1998) or paradigms of nativeness/non-nativeness still function (Brutt-Griffler & Samimy, 1999; Holliday, 2005), Widdowson's position is weakened.

*Second*, in an attempt to soften the debate about Englishes, Widdowson (1997) suggests seeing EIL as a composite of registers, such as English for science and English for finance. Put differently, he argues that EIL 'is English for specific purposes' (p. 144). However, Brutt-Griffler (1998: 382) points out contradictions and unreasonableness in his suggestion, arguing that 'there are no free-standing registers.' As such, 'the question inevitably poses itself: Registers of which language?' (p. 382). Moreover, I find his use of 'register' unrealistic when he suggests taking ESP (English for Specific Purposes) away from the issues of 'community and identity' and viewing it in terms of 'communication and information' (p. 143). Furthermore, as Widdowson states in his article, it is impossible to control language once it is used. It is thus clear that ESP cannot be taken as the exception.

Although Widdowson tries to avoid Quirk's (1987) view of 'the importance of maintaining the standard language' (p. 143) by assuming that we can take a neutral view of English, he once again ignores what lies beneath ESP. Many authors have showed that English embodies political and cultural missions that have made it a non-neutral language (Brutt-Griffler, 1998; Pennycook & Coutand-Marin, 2004; Phillipson, 1992). Also, I argue that EAP (English for Academic Purposes), a register, in cross-cultural settings acts as a harsh gatekeeper to keep many non-native speakers of English out of its game, as EAP norms are based on the Self's standards (Farrell, 1997a, b; Johnston, 2003; Phan Le Ha, 2001). Johnston (2003) examines the issue of testing/assessment and values in ELT, and argues that testing is value-laden in many ways. For example, testing compares students to others, and testing in fact reflects the real world surrounding the student instead of being just about the content being tested. He claims that standardised tests, particularly TOEFL, do not consider any individual circumstances of candidates. In other words, these tests are developed based on the Self's standards and ignore the cultural, social and learning realities of those who have to sit for these tests. So EAP obviously empowers the Self and at the same time prevents the Other from participating in many academic events. Thus, even though Widdowson tries to put 'the standard' aside, it cannot stay aside without causing trouble when it is problematic in its own right.

Regarding registers, I agree with Widdowson that many native speakers of English are incompetent in a number of English registers while many non-native speakers are highly knowledgeable in these registers. However, the point here is that the former, in many cases, are still the ones who have the power to imply to the latter that 'I don't like your English because it is not the English I use', and hence 'your English is not valued'. Examples of this can be found in Farrell (1998), Phan Le Ha (2000) and Kamler (2001). These authors explore how English academic writing is assessed in Australian schools and institutions and find out that examiners value a certain way of writing, the Anglo style, and if students fail to present their writing in this style, their writing is not acknowledged and valued. At this point, neither English nor ESP could be neutral, in contrast to Widdowson's suggestion.

Thus far it is clear that although English has achieved international status and been globalised, that EIL is for all and for cross-cultural communication still has many limitations.

## Englishes in the Periphery

I now examine how beliefs about possession of English affect equality and justice within the Periphery itself. Periphery here includes both the Outer Circle and the Expanding Outer Circle.

In many Periphery countries, English is purposefully used to exclude people from power and social positions, and to create discrimination among people in their societies. Following are examples. India is a highly hierarchical society, where there are clear-cut borders among classes. According to Ramanathan (1999), Indian society is divided into an inner circle and an outer circle of power, and the classes that belong to the inner circle have more access to power and privilege. The middle class belongs to this inner circle. Ramanathan argues that the Indian middle class has used English as a tool to maintain its status and at the same time to lengthen its distance from particular groups of people in India. She finds that even in India, a country of the periphery, 'an English-related inner–outer power dichotomy appears to exist' (p. 212). This suggests that power and English adhere to each other in this country. In order to consolidate power, the Indian middle class has intentionally made English a gatekeeper, excluding those of lower income and lower caste. Institutional and educational practices with the effective assistance of

English go hand in hand to keep outer-circle students 'out of the more powerful circle' (p. 218).

Phillipson (1992) argues how discrimination and power distance have been exercised through English in Africa. He observes that although English enjoys high status in many areas of Africa, sufficient access to it still belongs only to a small group of elites. Although both the elites and the masses see the advantage of English and its connection to power and resources, English is still somehow a luxury property owned by the powerful. So English obviously accompanies inequality and injustice in many African countries.

The use of English – the language of power – in many African countries is responsible for silencing other African languages as well, as Phillipson (1992) puts it. 'The colonial language [is] still ... used in high status activities, a dominant local language ... [is] ... used for less prestigious functions, and local languages [are] used for other purposes' (p. 27). This practice suggests that English really belongs to high-status groups of people, and their achievements are more guaranteed because they have most access to English. This also suggests the belief in the superiority of English over local African languages, and thus those who have most access to English are assumed to be superior.

Gamaroff (2000) indicates that in South Africa, within the domain of ELT, there arises a major issue which is the controversial distinction between English as L1 and L2. He states that 'these notions [of L1 and L2] are so heavily value-laden that there is a danger of the distinction between these two notions being interpreted as a form of linguistic apartheid' (p. 297). He cites Young (1988: 8) who 'advocates that the "apartheid" labels "L1" and "L2" should be discarded because they imply that black "natives" are not able to assimilate western language and culture' (cited in Gamaroff, 2000: 297). Paikeday's (1985: 76) views on this matter are noteworthy.

When theoretical linguists claim an innate facility for competence in a language on behalf of the native speaker ... it seems like a white South African's claim that he [or she] can walk into a railway station in Pretoria any day, purchase a first-class ticket, get into any first-class coach, occupy a window seat, and travel all the way to Cape Town without getting thrown out at the first stop, as though a black or a coloured could not do it. (cited in Gamaroff, 2000: 297)

Gamaroff observes that many other authors, in their support of the elimination of the apartheid label of L1 and L2, argue that 'it is socially and racially discriminatory to compare levels of proficiency between L1 and L2 learners' (p. 297). Given the sociopolitical difficulties in South Africa, for these authors, this practice of ELT is inherently problematic. It suggests that this practice is power-related and implicitly used to maintain the discriminatory nature already rooted in the society.

In the case of Malaysia, according to Yin (2006), the so-called 'Standard English' or 'English' is more highly regarded and accepted by Malaysian parents when they make decisions as which English, English or Malaysian English, they want their children to learn. Yeo (2007) bitterly tells stories of Malaysians who refuse to speak Manglish or actively adopt 'standard English' as an act of being more associated with the 'English-speaking West'. Chew (2005) and a number of teachers of English in Singapore whom I met in conferences contend that Singapore is now starting to go 'backwards' in the sense that it shows its preference for Cambridge English over Singaporean English. As a result, Malaysian English and Singaporean English in Malaysia and Singapore are struggling, it seems.

The role of English and its relation to power in other periphery countries, such as Vietnam and Japan, where English is learned as a foreign language, also needs to be documented. Vietnam and Japan are selected because Vietnam is considered a developing country whereas Japan is a highly developed nation. The dominant status of English also varies in these two countries. While English is the most popular foreign language among several other ones to be taught in Vietnam, it is a must for all Japanese students in order to enter university. Moreover, English seems to have influenced Japan in a much deeper level, compared to Vietnam. For example, Japanese tend to believe that in order for them to communicate well in English and to be understood in English they have to have a concrete identity as Japanese (Kawai, 2003; Suzuki, 1999). Moreover, Japanese people's ideologies of English also reflect a deep level of influence of English in Japan (Kubota, 1998). This is discussed in the section on Japan below.

It should be noted that Vietnam has witnessed the rise and fall of a number of dominant foreign languages in its own territory (Phan Van Que *et al.*, forthcoming). Chinese, French and Russian respectively had once enjoyed dominant foreign language status in Vietnam in its modern history, but English has replaced Russian since the early 1990s, after the Vietnamese government introduced the open-door policy in 1986. The collapse of the former Soviet Union after that contributed to the welcoming of English and the decline of Russian in Vietnam. English is introduced at almost all school levels and has been present in almost every corner of urbanised areas and has rapidly reached tourist attractions in remote areas. The early 1990s witnessed the explosive growth of the English language, resulting in 'an official acknowledgement of the role and status of English' (Do, 1999: 2). The Ministry of Education and Training in Vietnam (MOET) conducted its first survey of language needs in late 1993, contributing to the formation of 'A National Strategy for Foreign Language Teaching and Learning throughout All Levels of Education' (MOET, 1994c, cited in Do, 1999: 2). The status of foreign languages, especially English, then was 'reconfirmed by an Order, signed by the Prime Minister (August 15 1994), in which government officials are required to study foreign languages, usually English' (Do, 1999: 2). Do strongly states that 'in contemporary Vietnam, there has never been a stronger, clearer decision concerning foreign language education policy and planning made at the highest-level authority' (1999: 2).

Although English in Vietnam does not seem to have anything to do with social classes, it does act as a gatekeeping tool in the society, particularly with employment and educational opportunities. Almost all jobs require a certificate in English, and proficiency in English has even started to be considered as a criterion for promotion at work (Nunan, 2003). The high status of English has thus resulted in those who do not have sufficient competency in English feeling excluded from positions which may lead to power.

The sudden replacement of Russian by English in Vietnam has caused part of the society to have negative attitudes toward Russian, and consequently made teachers of Russian struggle for their living. Phan Le Ha and Song-Ae Han (2004) have shown that English and ELT have lent a hand in creating distance and even confrontation between teachers of different languages, particularly teachers of Russian and teachers of English in Vietnam. Teaching and learning English is no longer neutral or politics-free.

Japan is a country highly regarded by the West (Pennycook, 1998). As an economic superpower, Japan does not suffer from the cultural, economic and structural disadvantages of developing countries. However, it is Japan's ideologies of English that are a matter of concern. As observed by Kubota (1998: 295):

> the dominance of English influences the Japanese language and people's views of language, culture, race, ethnicity and identity which are affected by the world view of native English speakers, and ... teaching English creates cultural and linguistic stereotypes not only of English but also of Japanese people.

Hence, 'through learning English, the Japanese have identified them-selves with Westerners while regarding non-Western peoples as the *Other*' (p. 299). This apparently has to do with who has power, and hence supports Westernisation (which is often spelt out as internationalisation) while turning a blind eye to 'global socio-linguistic perspectives' (p. 302). Power does matter and English has been inexhaustibly made use of by all parties to gain power. But within the game of power, English is not an equal property for all.

Together with creating inequalities inside a number of peripheral coun-tries, English as an international language is also used by these countries to judge each other's level of development. I remember when a group of tourists from an Asian country came to Vietnam in 1996 and they were astonished to find out that Vietnamese students could speak very good English (I was at university in Vietnam then). They commented, 'You're so intelligent. You can speak English so fluently. How come you can achieve that? We used to think in Vietnam few people could speak English or knew it, so before we came here we were afraid of facing a lot of problems.' They, perhaps, subconsciously related fluency in English with 'intelli-gence' and at the same time assumed that knowing English was more developed, and thus superior.

After all, whether learning English for good and practical concerns or for other reasons, everyone or every country wants to gain power of some kind. If the Centre sets communication norms, such as whose English counts, for the Periphery, then peripheral countries judge each other based very much on how possession of English is connected to development, representation and recognition. Not only does English have sufficient power to be regarded as a measure of ability and mentality to communi-cate with native English speakers, it also plays a key role in facilitating a country's international integration. Because English is used in regional and international conferences and forums, even Japan is afraid it will be 'under-represented in the international community' if its leaders are not able to speak English 'directly with their counterparts' (L'Estrange, 2000: 11).

From the above discussions of the ownership of English, it is clear that English is not yet a global/world property. No matter how much 'good' English has done in the world, its cultural, political and social aspects together with its continual adherence to imperialism have confirmed its guilt and intentional engagement in 'oppressing' speakers of other languages with the assistance of the ELT industry. However, I do not think the story stops here. English users may be better served by proactively taking ownership of its use and its teaching. English users, particularly non-native speakers of English, will then 'be the main agents in the ways English is used, is maintained, and changes, and who will shape the ideologies and beliefs associated with [EIL]' (Seidlhofer, 2003: 7).

## TESOL Programmes in English-speaking Countries and Criticisms

Together with spreading of English and ELT to the rest of the world, the Centre also offers TESOL programmes to train teachers of English for the Periphery and for whoever needs a TESOL qualification. TESOL programmes are normally conducted in the Centre's educational institutions, attracting an increasing number of overseas students, who tend to have better opportunities at home with a qualification from the Centre. These courses have been examined by scholars worldwide. Their nature, their contents and their operation have been brought to light, and received both compliments and criticisms. However, within the scope of this section, I look only at the criticisms of TESOL courses.

To begin with, let me take a look at Liu's (1998) study, which has raised valuable points regarding this issue. He criticises the ethnocentrism in TESOL courses in NABA (North America, Britain and Australia) as neglecting the 'needs of international TESOL students' (p. 3). First, such neglect has been seen in 'L2 acquisition theories and TESOL methodologies' (p. 4), where little consideration of other non-NABA contexts has been taken into account, and this may result in 'impractical or ineffective' (p. 4) adaptation of teaching methodologies in non-NABA countries. Accordingly, 'NABA TESOL teacher education may do international TESOL students a great disservice' (p. 6). Second, 'language improvement' (p. 7) is regarded as another area receiving insufficient attention. Few TESOL programmes pay specific attention to international TESOL students' language needs, because the focus of TESOL programmes is on 'enhancing students' explicit knowledge of the language, rather than their ability to use it', and thus it 'usually fails to meet [their] needs" (p. 7). This obviously disadvantages these students by broadening the gap between native and non-native teachers of English. Third, those students are believed not to achieve 'cultural understanding' (p. 8) in their NABA TESOL courses, since their 'exposure is often confined to campus culture' (p. 9). Liu suggests 'a systematic study of culture via a course or research project' (p. 9) should be embedded in TESOL courses. He supports this suggestion by stating that 'studying another culture does not mean embracing it or following its socio-cultural customs, nor does it mean losing one's own culture' (p. 8).

Brown (2000: 227) also explores ELT teacher training and reveals some conflicts between contemporary ELT, 'particularly but not exclusively in the "importing" of new techniques associated with communicative language teaching' and the reality of implementing such techniques in developing countries. He argues that 'cultural continuity' (p. 227) and gradual changes should be 'respected, by not losing contact with current [local] practice' (p. 227).

Edge (1996) expresses his concerns about cross-cultural paradoxes in TESOL. As a native teacher of English in Britain, Edge feels that the TESOL industry has been advocated along the lines of 'the "greed is good" governmental [British] philosophy', and hence it results in 'a cross-cultural clash, a conflict of values at the heart of society' (p. 14). The first paradox refers to the 'sociopolitical context'; Edge believes that the TESOL culture has made teachers and students heavily dependent on 'the dominant social-market perspective' (p. 14), and thus the question of value is challenged. The second paradox is called 'liberation and domination' (p. 16). Edge explains that TESOL liberates but also dominates the Other everywhere, opens doors to some yet kicks others out. 'Foundations and fundamentalism' is the third paradox (p. 20), and this refers to 'respect for the right to be different' (p. 21). Edge acknowledges that although the Centre's TESOL culture has not refused to take action to react to any challenge it may encounter, whether at home or overseas, it has still failed to respect others' values.

Chowdhury (2003) examines how relevant and useful international TESOL training is for EFL contexts. He also explores whether teachers in Bangladesh see Western ideologies as informing and/or constraining and/or legitimising their teaching practices. He finds that these teachers experienced paradoxes, in which cultural factors seem to dominate. Moreover, norms assumed by international TESOL training appear irrelevant to the Bangladeshi context, where teachers work in a very different setting.

If ELT is viewed as a commodity traded in a global market, as Pennycook (1994) contends, its products appear very narrow and fail to satisfy its customers in terms of course diversification and flexibility. If it aims to promote TESOL courses worldwide, then it should meet global demands. It offers only what it has got, not what the world needs. In the context of globalisation and internationalisation, the TESOL market needs to consider the Other's needs as well, not just those of the Self – its own needs. This narrow market has partly reflected the 'ethnocentrism' in NABA TESOL teacher education (Liu, 1998: 4). This very ethnocentrism has assumed that what the Self (NABA) offers is good and what is good for the Self is definitely good for the Other. The TESOL market and its products tend to ignore the Other's needs, obviously.

The fact that TESOL courses have insufficient subject choices may be part of what Phillipson (1992) argues, that no research has been done for the sake of the Periphery, or for questioning the contemporary ELT in action since the Centre knows well that they are in a comfortable and quite safe position to impose their ideas on others. Also, according to Phillipson (1992), this act at the same time devalues the Periphery's languages, education and traditions, and disables the Periphery's capacities of domestic educational material development. Put differently, the Periphery has been made totally dependent on the Centre, resulting in ELT being no longer non-political and acting as a 'missionary' to spread English linguistic imperialism (Pennycook, 1994, 1998; Phillipson, 1992). Many of such ELT activities are culturally inappropriate in Periphery contexts. At this point, the issue of ELT's unethical attitude and practice is invoked.

When ELT is viewed as a social good, it also embodies problems of ethics and values. Although TESOL courses act as bridges to bring different cultures closer, they carry pre-assumptions and assumptions of the Other. These stereotypes normally suggest that the Other is inferior in terms of values and culture. This accordingly urges the Other to change to adjust to what was introduced in TESOL courses. As a result, the Other finds their cultural values being disrespected and disregarded. In this sense, ELT and TESOL act as colonising forces.

The next section looks specifically at Communicative Language Teaching (CLT), since it is often referred to as the West's advanced teaching approach as opposed to other approaches practised elsewhere in the world. CLT is also known as the site where cultural and value clashes occur. As a widely promoted approach, it has caused tensions to teachers of English when they have to simultaneously consider their role as both a teacher and a culture conveyor.

## Communicative Language Teaching (CLT) as a Colonising Force

For a long time I have been questioning the fact that Communicative Language Teaching (CLT) has been introduced in many TESOL teacher training courses as 'the best', more advanced and effective than other teaching methods. At the same time, I am also well aware of many research studies which demonstrate that CLT has not emerged as 'the best' in reality. CLT has caused difficulties, problems, dissatisfaction, tensions and confusion to many language teachers and learners worldwide. More-over, I have seen many international TESOL students, particularly in Australia, doing presentations, writing essays and doing research on different aspects of CLT. Through interactions with students in class and through my research activities, I am concerned about why so many TESOL students have come to believe that CLT is better than the teaching methods they have used so far. Many of them even tend to justify their colleagues' teaching in light of how much they use CLT in teaching. Ironically, most of them (if not all) agree that CLT is not suitable for their teaching for various reasons. This observation has urged me to examine why CLT is so daunting that many TESOL professionals seem to be 'colonised' by it. I will first argue that CLT has been acting as a 'colonising' force in both theory and practice of Western TESOL. I then discuss problems associated with CLT in vast contexts in Asia, where problems seem to exist. Finally, I argue that it is not appropriate to introduce CLT as the assumed 'best' approach in language teaching in TESOL teacher training courses.

## CLT as a 'colonising' force in Western TESOL classrooms

CLT as a 'colonising' force in Western TESOL classrooms is first seen in how CLT has been presented in TESOL as 'Western superiority'. CLT is accused of supporting the discourses of colonialism in current ELT when it is represented as the Self's advanced way of teaching as opposed to the Other's traditional (backward) methods (Liu, 1998; Pennycook, 1994, 1998; Phillipson, 1992). Specifically, Liu (1998: 4) criticises current TESOL's '"methodological dogmatism" fervently promoting "new" NABA meth-odologies, particularly those entitled "communicative", while condemning tried and tested "traditional" methods still popular in many other parts of the world'. This 'superior' construct of these Western communicative approaches and the image of native-speaker teachers associated with it have resulted in many non-native teachers of English feeling less competent and even inferior in comparison with native ones (Brutt-Griffler & Samimy, 1999).

Phillipson (1992) claims that the view of professionalism (language pedagogy) of ELT clearly excludes broader societal issues, the prerequi-sites and consequences of ELT activity. He strongly criticises the issue of 'Anglocentricity' which 'devalues other languages, either explicitly or implicitly' (p. 48), and, thus, native English teachers give themselves the right to tell non-native teachers of English that their teaching methodolo-gies are 'old-fashioned' and 'should be replaced', as Pennycook (1994: 163) observes. In addition, both Phillipson (1992) and Pennycook (1994) assert that the nature of language teaching methods are generally 'Western' and hence those methods carry in themselves the 'incompatibility' potential when applied in non-Western contexts. Pennycook (1994: 159) makes this point clear when stating that:

> the dominance of the Western academy in defining concepts and practices and language teaching is leading to the ever greater incursion of such views into language teaching theory and practice around the world. The export of applied linguistic theory and of Western-trained language teachers constantly promotes inappropriate teaching approaches to diverse settings.

Therefore, these authors urge non-native English teachers to notice this question in order not to be over-influenced by the so-called 'superior' and 'advanced' Western teaching pedagogy. Teachers of English should be aware of the fact that ELT is far from neutral or natural. It is an act of cultural politics, which makes an English language classroom also a site of cultural politics (Pennycook, 1994). More seriously, by regarding Western teaching pedagogies more highly than local ones, the Other teacher and student may undervalue their own 'flourishing' initiative that could promote local strengths and linguistic realities, as Phillipson (1992) observes.

Bax's (2003) observation of how CLT is perceived by many language teachers, trainers and trainees from both Western and non-Western countries well supports Phillipson's (1992), Pennycook's (1994) and Liu's (1998) criticisms of the West's intentional promotion of its 'advanced' teaching methods. The advertisement of CLT as 'superior' has indeed implied that CLT is the best and only way of teaching and learning a language, no matter where it is used (Bax, 2003). As a result, many teachers have tended to undervalue, even look down upon, other teaching methods including their own ways of teaching. Bax argues that the CLT discourse implies two messages. The first one is that it is the teacher who generates communication, and the second one is that it is method that solves any problems in the classroom (p. 281). CLT is thus interpreted as 'the way we should teach' (p. 280), and 'the way to do it, no matter where you are, no matter what the context' (p. 281). So, CLT is operated regardless of context. These features of CLT, as Bax argues, have resulted in the 'CLT attitude' (p. 279), which assumes that 'a country without CLT is somehow backward' (p. 279). He observes that this attitude is supported by both native and non-native teachers and trainers of English.

CLT as a 'colonising' force is also seen in how international TESOL students respond to CLT itself and how they view Western TESOL lecturers in light of CLT. As clearly seen in Chowdhury (2003), Pham Hoa Hiep (2004) and Phan Le Ha (2004), international Western-trained teachers of English tend to be attracted to the principles of CLT and show a great desire to implement these principles in their teaching contexts in their home countries. These teachers seem to treat CLT as the target teaching method against which their own teaching methods are compared and justified.

A number of Western-trained Vietnamese teachers of English whom I interviewed explicitly questioned why their Australian TESOL lecturers did not demonstrate CLT at all in their lecturing, given that these Vietnamese teachers had always been encouraged by both their lecturers and their course readings to apply CLT in their teaching contexts. In their own words, they described how their Australian lecturers taught.

> They only give lectures and we listen and take notes. They sometimes ask questions, but it's mainly teacher-centred.

> She's got her PhD, so she should be really good [in terms of knowledge]. And she lectures the 'methodology' subject, which teaches others how to teach, but the way she teaches is so boring. She reads her lecture notes while students all feel sleepy. Well, she's a native speaker [of English], and she's well-trained, so you can't say that she has difficulties in communication.

> Although she reads her lecture notes from the beginning to the end, she still can't finish all, and there are always three pages left undone.

These teachers seemed to believe that CLT is a better way of teaching. This is the ethnocentrism injected in NABA TESOL teacher education, where 'methodological dogmatism' enthusiastically promotes NABA methodologies, particularly communicative approaches (Liu, 1998: 4) that has led to such a belief. ELT is not neutral at all. It, in fact, has been acting as colonising practices. This makes it clear that the complaints about 'bad teaching' are not merely 'bad teaching', but they are helpful in understanding ELT and CLT as colonising.

## Problems associated with CLT in vast contexts in Asia

### CLT in reality: Constraints and difficulties

Although CLT has often been presented as an 'advanced' teaching approach, it has also received many criticisms regarding its implementation. Specifically, many studies have demonstrated a mismatch of expectations between CLT principles and what teachers and students want to/can afford to do in their classrooms to meet their actual needs. Numerous constraints and difficulties in relation to CLT have been identified. Liu (1998: 5) observes that despite the 'attractive' features of the Western classroom, and their greater richness of resources compared to their Asian equivalents, NABA's teaching methods entitled 'communicative', materials and programmes often 'face resistance or even rejection in Asia'. One of the obvious reasons is that CLT is developed from 'different cultural and economic milieux' (Li, 1998). Also, these Western pedagogical characteristics are not seen as desirable in many other contexts.

*First,* CLT has been criticised for doing a disservice to teachers and students in the countries where success in examinations is more important and vital to students' academic advancement (Gupta, 2004; Le Van Canh, 2001; L'Estrange, 2000; Rao, 2002; Sakui, 2004). As such, being a facilitator as CLT requires may not help them to gain what the society expects. *Second,* CLT has been viewed as time-consuming, as challenging to teachers who are not confident in speaking English and as adding more work to already overloaded teachers (Li, 1998; Rao, 2002; Sakui, 2004). *Third,* many CLT principles conflict with Asian settings; for example, CLT communicative goals are unrealistic for learners, the requirement of having a variety of materials and designing communicative activities is very costly, while most Asian contexts lack funding for ELT, and group-work is not efficient in most Asian classes with at least 40 students (Gupta, 2004; Hu, 2005; Le Van Canh, 2001; Rao, 2002).

### CLT in reality: A conflict of values

When CLT is applied in reality, its pedagogical values have conflicted with a number of cultural and professional values embedded in the practice of teaching and learning in Asia; for instance, the issues of 'respect between teacher and student' and the role of the teacher in society. Edge (1996: 17) claims that by 'deliberately moving away from a teacher-centred style of teaching', the TESOL professional shows 'a lack of proper respect for teachers and, by extension, for elders in general'. The respected status of the teachers in many countries will accordingly be threatened. He is worried that other countries' futures may suffer from 'subversive and inappropriate' teaching methods offered by the Centre (p. 17). Tollefson (1991: 102) suggests that ELT practices 'must be examined for their impact upon the relationship between students and teachers, and for their ideological assumptions about the roles of teachers and students in society'.

Holliday (1994) and Ellis (1996) demonstrate that the equal teacher–student CLT principle challenges the hierarchical teacher–student relationships and the necessity to show respect to teachers in many countries, and consequently faces resistance and unwelcome attitudes in those countries.

Furthermore, Le Van Canh (2001) and Pham Hoa Hiep (2005) indicate that the Vietnamese classroom culture and discourse does not accept a number of CLT constructs. Particularly, Le Van Canh (2001) argues that the culturally and socially constructed image of the teacher in Vietnam does not generally accept the CLT teacher as a facilitator who practises error-tolerance. He articulates that because education is 'a ticket to ride' (p. 36), and success in examinations is most important, the teacher's role has more to do with ensuring their students' achievement, and hence 'corrective feedback is part of the teacher's role in the classroom' (p. 36). A study by Breach (2005) of the images of a good teacher in Vietnam also supports Le Van Canh's observation.

CLT often faces resistance from teachers and learners also because of the issue of 'expectation'. For example, many native English teachers in Vietnam notice that their students tend to think that when they [students] are having fun with communicative activities in the language classroom, they are not learning anything (Breach, 2005). The cause for this mismatch of expectation, as I understand and have experienced, is the difference between students' concept of learning and teachers' perception of teaching, in which students see learning as a serious process when solid knowledge is introduced by teachers, while many English-speaking teachers think that communicative activities including fun and relaxing ones are best. A study by Li (2004) further supports this argument. Li reports that many Asian students studying English in language schools in New Zealand found their English teachers' communicative teaching 'not serious' when their teaching was overloaded with 'group work, discussions, debates and games' (p. 8). They also found 'the "game-loving" teaching approach a waste of time and money' (p. 8), which had little to do with language learning and the preparation for their English exams. Many students even felt annoyed and humiliated when teachers treated them 'like preschool children by forcing them to play games and to engage in group work and activities that they did not find useful to their language acquisition' (p. 8).

In terms of expectation, Chowdhury (2003: 284) explains why CLT is not welcome in Bangladesh by arguing that 'students feel tempted to discard the new style and complain that the teacher is not "teaching" when tasks and activities are done in the class without meeting the "sociocultural" expectations of the students.' Students see this new style as challenging their 'sense of security and order' (p. 284) and their familiar socio-cultural status and role. Their student values, hence, seem at risk.

## My positioning in relation to CLT

Given that CLT has been presented as a 'colonising' force and embodies numerous problems as I have discussed so far, it is time to question the validity and ethics of introducing it as the assumed 'best' approach in language teaching, particularly in TESOL teacher training courses.

*First*, in light of the arguments presented above, although I acknowledge that CLT has also enhanced ELT in many settings, as a number of authors have reported elsewhere (Bruton, 2004; McDevitt, 2004; Phan Le Ha, 2004), it is clear that CLT has caused tensions for teachers who have to play the roles of the teacher of English and other teacher roles as expected by their local settings, for example, moral guide and educator.

*Second*, as a result of the presentation of CLT as signifying Western superiority, as discussed earlier, those ways of teaching that are different from CLT are often perceived as deficient. Diversity in language teaching is accordingly not acknowledged and appreciated. Other teaching cultures are not sufficiently respected either. This has resulted in general assumptions that teachers from the English-speaking West are better. Likewise, the dichotomy of native and non-native teachers of English has become an indispensable part of the ELT culture.

*Third*, as implied earlier, it seems that although every teaching method has its own merit and serves students and teachers according to their specific local needs and situations, only those entitled communicative are believed to be genuinely communicative, and all others are thought of as not for communicative purposes. As Larsen-Freeman (1986, cited in Li, 1998: 678) suggests, CLT is most obviously seen as 'almost everything that is done with a communicative intent'. However, Nunan (1989: 12) observes that 'in fact, it is difficult to find approaches which claim not to be communicative.' Thus, it is unfair not to give credit to the teaching methods/approaches that are not explicitly named as 'communicative'.

*Fourth*, meaningful communication is not necessarily achieved only through CLT principles; in the end, it depends largely on how teachers make their teaching serve particular learning aims. If students perform well in written exams, it means they communicate successfully with examiners through their writing and grammatical rules, which are also linguistic signifiers. So is 'speaking' the only desirable and effective form of communication in a language classroom?

*Finally*, after all, I find it uncomfortable to listen to teachers and students in TESOL teacher training courses discussing communicative approaches as if without such approaches students would never be able to communicate well in English. I once questioned an international TESOL student, who was highly competent in English and a great communicator, when she reported on English language teaching in her country with all negative points. I asked her 'where did you learn your English' and 'are you not a product of the teaching that you are criticising now?' The whole class suddenly realised that many of them were actually 'products' of other teaching methods (including Australian students) or the traditional language teaching styles in their home countries. But were they bad at English? Were they unable to speak it well? I am also a product of the English language teaching in Vietnam in the early 90s, and many of the scholars whose work I have referred to in this paper have similar experience with English in their home countries.

All teaching approaches are communicatively oriented in their nature (teaching itself is for communication in a broadest sense), so it is time to acknowledge and respect teachers' agency in their own teaching and their decisions on how to best serve their students. I do not suggest that we should not view teaching methods critically, but the point is that criticisms of CLT should necessitate change in both ideology and practice of interpreting difference. One way of doing it may be that different teaching methods need to be respectfully addressed in TESOL training courses, instead of just CLT itself. Also, it is necessary to listen to the voices of teachers of English from different contexts to have a comprehensive understanding of how ELT is conducted differently according to contexts. Furthermore, making TESOL practitioners aware of the values of their own teaching needs to be an essential part of TESOL courses. It is critical that TESOL lecturers in TESOL courses should not refer to CLT as the alternative for all other teaching methods and treat it as the optimal teaching approach.

I would like to quote Le Van Canh (2001: 38) to conclude this section. When examining CLT in Vietnam and Vietnamese teachers' efforts to 'reform' their teaching, he places his emphasis on what these teachers of English mean by 'reform'.

> by reform, we do not mean throwing away all traditional values and practices. Practicality and applicability to specific teaching situations are factors of success in educational reform.

At this point, Le Van Canh's (2001) thoughtful and constructive request, that we should not view teachers in training courses and/or professional development courses as 'empty vessels ... they have their own experiences, beliefs and values' (p. 38), really decolonises the whole literature of the ELT industry that assumes 'the West is better' and as a result looks down upon teachers from other parts of the world.

## The Dichotomy of Native and Non-native Teachers of English

The dichotomy between native and non-native teachers of English has been deeply rooted in ELT pedagogy and practice. Phillipson (1992) calls the tenet 'the ideal teacher of English is a native speaker' (p. 185) a fallacy. This tenet suggests that the native-speaker teacher is regarded as 'the best embodiment of the target and norm for learners' (p. 194). He strongly attacks this tenet by providing his interpretation of it.

The ideal teacher is a native speaker. Teachers are born not made. Therefore, 1) those who are not born native speakers of English cannot be ideal teachers, and 2) since teachers are born not made, native speakers do not need any training to become teachers. (p. 221)

To argue against this, Phillipson finds a solution for the image of teachers: 'teachers are made rather than born' (p. 194), and so, regardless of nationalities and races, speakers of English all have potential to become ideal teachers. Accordingly, native speakers may also prove to be 'helpless' or 'bad' teachers. This argument helps Phillipson challenge the unscientific and invalid claim of the tenet.

This dichotomy is not only insisted on by the Centre but it is also strengthened by the Periphery. Researching into the professional identity of non-native teachers of English, Brutt-Griffler and Samimy (1999) find that the literature has actually drawn the borderline between native and non-native teachers, explicitly articulating that the English language belongs to the native. This assumption suggests that the native speakers have control over the language and associated teaching methods, and hence shape 'the perceptions of language learners' (p. 417), for example: teachers' 'self-esteem', the learner's belief in 'an intrinsic connection between race and language ability' (p. 417). Seriously, these facts have caused the non-native teacher to lack confidence in their profession, as well as made non-native learners regard their own teachers as lower in competence. Accordingly, white teachers are preferred to non-white teachers, and this has added more 'colours' to the picture of native and non-native. These colours, bitterly, help the native maintain the dominant status and also consolidate the taken-for-granted truth that non-native teachers do need assistance and standards from their native counterparts (Brutt-Griffler & Samimy, 1999).

I now specifically refer to Holliday (2005) to discuss further the native–non-native paradigm in TESOL and ELT. Holliday patiently and systematically problematises past and current theories and practices of TESOL with a particular 'attack' on the native-speaker norms. In Chapter 1, he discusses comprehensively the notion of struggle in World TESOL (his term), and presents very clearly the areas that embrace this notion, particularly, 'who we think we are as ESOL educators' and how we (World TESOL people) 'behave with each other and with our students within a multicultured TESOL world' (p. 1). This chapter also goes through a number of relationships pre-existing and emerging in World TESOL and addresses these relationships as nurturing and supporting 'native-speakerism' (p. 6) in numerous ways and manners. This nature of TESOL, as a result, needs to be critically revisited and filled with *fresh contents* (my emphasis) to correspond to emerging complicated pictures in TESOL, such as English as an international language and the shift of ownership of English. As such, Holliday comes up with 'Position 2' (p. 16) as an alternative model for removing native-speakerism which is embedded in many of the World TESOL relationships and scenarios.

Chapters 1 and 2 of Holliday's book put together painful and unpleasant experiences of many TESOL professionals around the world as the meaningful and vivid beginning of the journey to contest native-speakerism. As the journey proceeds, native-speakerism, one of the products of the dominant culture of English-speaking Western TESOL as Holliday argues, is clearly teased out and well contested in a provocative and scholarly manner in Chapter 2. This is, in my opinion, one of the main strengths of the book. Holliday's criticisms of culturist perceptions of 'us' and 'them' result in his recommendation for adopting a non-essentialist viewpoint of culture, which it is hoped will minimise native-speakerism to a great extent.

In Chapter 3 Holliday addresses a number of 'conditions within which native-speakerism has developed and become such a powerful force in World TESOL' (p. 39). The discussion on 'cultural icons' is useful and interesting. Holliday's critical look at 'the four skill' approach as a cultural icon is provocative, which questions one of the most powerful taken-for-granted 'truths' with regard to theory and practice of language teaching in general and TESOL in particular. There are other ways, and 'the four skill' approach is definitely not the only one, but as Holliday points out, this cultural icon has been so deeply rooted in World TESOL that it is very hard to convince people of the presence and workability of alternatives. And this is even more dangerous when this cultural icon has been used to measure and define students and TESOL teachers from Other cultures. Together with revisiting the four skills icons, a modernistic discourse associated with TESOL is also indicated and challenged. The close connection between native-speakerism and a modernistic discourse in TESOL appears to empower and support native-speakerness and simultaneously places the Other in a much less favourable position, and worse, the real person of the student is in effect excluded from the whole picture. This becomes more serious when this connection involves 'correcting' the 'culture' of the foreign Other, and this is what Holliday tries to contest specifically. To continue, Holliday demonstrates how powerfully the residues of audiolingualism have been influencing the way an English lesson is delivered, whereby PPP or staged learning appears to play an essential role throughout. Very provocatively and firmly, he argues that many of the seemingly out-of-date audiolingualism principles in fact remain the same in current TESOL practices. What I find critical here is that his arguments imply that at the end of the day what matters is English-speaking TESOL feeling assured of their control of the Other.

Chapter 4 of Holliday's work looks at 'learner-centredness' and 'autonomy', 'two of the key concepts of English-speaking Western TESOL professionalism' (p. 63), as Holliday states. Regarding 'learner-centredness', Holliday indicates that this very concept suggests that the foreign Other of the 'non-native speaker' student needs to be trained both linguistically and culturally, and this is what consolidates, legitimises and reproduces native-speakerism. What seems problematic in this notion is 'the learner' as a pre-defined cultural type, leading to the tendency of grouping students according to national cultures and/or ethnicities, those who are assumed to lack certain abilities and have to adapt, fit in and change. Holliday further points out that 'learner-centredness' appears to be a mask which hides the intention to correct 'the behaviour and culture of the Othered "non-native speaker" students' (p. 78).

Holliday offers his own interpretation of the second key concept, 'learner autonomy', seeing it as being driven by the 'us'–'them' discourse embedded in native-speakerism and culturism, which involve 'corrective training' (p. 79). He criticises the tendency to contrast unquestionably and automatically 'passivity' (assumed to be attached to the Othered 'non-native speaker' students) with 'autonomous learners' and 'true learning' (assumed to be aligned with Western English-speaking TESOL). This tendency suggests that the Other students do not have 'autonomy' and their 'autonomy' can only be obtained by being trained through 'learning strategies' developed and advocated by the Self teacher. 'Passivity', in the mindset of the Self, seems to be a *property* (my emphasis) just owned by the Other. I find Holliday's argument on the Self's assumption of the Other's inability to be 'individualist' and 'autonomous' critical and useful in unpacking subtle but complex issues in TESOL. Interestingly, he points out that it seems very difficult not to fall into the trap of dichotomising Self and Other in TESOL regardless of how aware and critical one can be. This has made me stop and think hard about my own teacher training practice.

Chapter 5 continues the discussion on autonomy but takes a critical look beyond the ideology of TESOL professionalism to offer other ways of understanding autonomy. As such, Holliday examines 'social autonomy' and 'authenticity'. Social autonomy, in his argument, refers to 'something which students bring with them from their own worlds outside the classroom' (p. 85), and given this, autonomy is seen as coming from the same social world as social autonomy. Holliday makes a number of key suggestions in this chapter to argue for an alternative (Position 2) to native-speakerism: *appreciating* other cultures, not *beginning* with an essentialist cultural description of the Other, not *presuming* that autonomy is the domain of a Western (or any other) culture (italics in the original), *exploring* the worlds students bring with them, and *treating* people equally as people (my emphasis). Within Position 2, authenticity 'has to be *created*' (italics in the original), and 'pre-exists in the social worlds of students and teachers' (p. 105). I find Holliday's elaborations of these two key notions, social autonomy and authenticity, very useful in expanding and reshaping TESOL professionals' discourse of teaching in a manner that enriches and contributes more fruitfully to the field and general knowledge.

While the last three chapters focus on how the Other students are represented within TESOL native-speakerism, Chapters 6 and 7 pay attention to similar issues but in relation to the Other teacher. In many ways, Holliday demonstrates that native-speakerism pictures the non-native-speaker Other teacher as being deficient, needing to be trained and corrected by the native-speaker Self. Sadly, this deficit approach in viewing the non-native-speaker Other TESOL teacher is very often, if not more often, taken by these teachers themselves, as Holliday also discusses in his Chapters 1 and 2. And this mindset is even more difficult to change, I am afraid. However, thankfully, resistance and appropriation are always there and in different forms, no matter how negatively the native Self and the non-native Other see the latter.

I find Holliday's discussion on 'emergent practices' (pp. 153–154) thoughtful, but not new. These ways of teaching (namely, being one's own boss in one's way of teaching while making full use of English-speaking countries' materials, and facilitating meaningful communication with students without having an excess of oral work) occur in many places around the world (examples include my MA TESOL students' reflections on their own teaching over the past few years), but often they are deliberately ignored, unappreciated and under-researched in the literature. But Holliday makes a good point here, which is his assertion that 'communicative' and 'communication' must not be seen as '"standard" communicative tasks and groupwork' (p. 155). They operate in different forms and manners.

Although Holliday strongly argues against the 'weak version' or 'standard' version of communicative language teaching (CLT), his recommendations in relation to the 'strong version' (my interpretation) in chapter 7 appear rather vague and simplistic, which again suggest 'deficit change' to some extent.

Chapter 8, the final chapter, considers 'cultural continuity as a solution to native-speakerism' (p. 157). His suggestions include taking the 'understanding' approach to TESOL professionals instead of the 'correction' (p. 157) approach, changing professional image by removing the division native versus non-native, and changing curricula from using only native-English-speaking countries' materials to treating them as equal to other materials developed by World TESOL professionals. What I think is important in this chapter is his persistent argument for the need to see TESOL professionals and students as individuals, and this could be done through the lenses of cultural continuity. However, I have a feeling that what is reported in this chapter is rather commonsensical, superficial and known only to *scholars* (my emphasis) in the field who have access to and have contact with the literature because of their *doing research purposes* (my emphasis). Teachers, practitioners, the very ones that need to engage personally and meaningfully in these debates, appear to be *absent* (my emphasis). Again, it seems that we, scholars, give ourselves the right to speak for them, those teachers in actual classrooms worldwide, almost without them being personally present and being aware of our discussion about all the very critical issues in the field of TESOL.

In light of these above discussions, I now see that if the Self was the one to create this dichotomy, then the Other has been made a vital agent in spreading and reinforcing it. Admittedly, the construct of colonialism has proved far more powerful than its founders could imagine. Let me revisit Galtung's idea of 'persuasion' (Phillipson, 1992) and Fairclough's (1989) theory of 'consent' to reconfirm that the best solution for making anyone do what one wants is to make him/her believe that it is good and beneficial to him/her as well. Now I realise how subtle the situation has become, and I also know that the job I am doing in this book suddenly gets far more complicated because how can I say that I am 100 per cent not involved in this fallacy? I am not at all now, but at least for some periods of time I used to be.

## Concluding Points

Many authors have been investigating the tendency of English to become a world language, and suggesting the establishment of related critical literacy pedagogies (Canagarajah, 1999; Gee, 1999; McKay, 2003; Pennycook, 2001). Examples can be seen in their efforts to appreciate the role of speakers of other languages in spreading and transforming English into a world language (Brutt-Griffler, 2002; Modiano, 2001). Likewise, a critical approach to second language acquisition has been constructed to destabilise the L1 norms (Cook, 1999; Kramsch, 2000, 2001; McKay, 2003). Alternative teaching methods have been proposed to replace the problem atic Communicative Language Teaching (CLT), such as the Context Approach (Bax, 2003). Also, some TESOL courses have been redesigned to make students from non-English-speaking backgrounds aware of how their images have been constructed through English and ELT, and in what way their voices can be heard (for example, in the TESOL course for Master's students offered by the Faculty of Education, Monash University, with the unit on 'Language, society and cultural difference', students are exposed to postcolonial theories and have the chance to challenge the dichotomy of Self and Other).

Let me refer to one point raised by Widdowson (1997) to seek a solution for more 'ethical' English and ELT. I agree with Widdowson that 'as the language [in this case, English] is used it cannot be kept under your control' (p. 136). People do appropriate it. Canagarajah (1999) demonstrates that Sri Lankans have been able to appropriate English for their own purposes, taking into account local cultural and political factors. He offers an approach that resists 'linguistic imperialism in English teaching', as the title of his book suggests. Pennycook (2001: 71) also supports Canagarajah's view, suggesting change and possibilities of '*third spaces*' or '*third cultures*' (italics in the original), notions that are discussed by Kramsch (1993).

Developing her views in relation to how users of English can appropriate English, Kramsch (2001) stresses the importance of English language teachers assisting students in acquiring their own voices in using English to '*secure a profit of distinction*' (italics in the original) (Kramsch, 2001: 16). She contends that language teachers' responsibility is:

to help students not only become acceptable and listened to users of English by adopting the culturally sanctioned genres, styles, and rhetorical conventions of the English speaking world, but how to gain a profit of distinction by using English in ways that are unique to their multilingual and multicultural sensibilities. (Kramsch, 2001: 16)

The views expressed by Canagarajah (1999), Pennycook (2001) and Kramsch (2001) actually challenge and disrupt linguistic imperialism and the postcolonial dichotomy of Self and Other. However, they do not reject English. Instead, they support the use of English for one's own benefit and equality, but at the same time urge English users to work together to eliminate the discourses of colonialism active in current imperial forms. These views suggest a new and more sophisticated notion of 'appropriation', which consists of resistance and reconstitution.

Therefore, appropriation, as I would argue, necessitates the Other's awareness of resistance and conscious selection to reach reconstitution under one's own control. Hashimoto (2000) provides an example of how a country resists Western globalisation and English dominance. He argues that 'the commitment of the Japanese government to internationalisation in education actually means "Japanisation" of Japanese learners of English' (p. 39). Indeed, the use of English plays an important part in both one's desire to communicate with the world and one's will to preserve one's identity (Kubota, 1998; Pham Hoa Hiep, 2001). It also influences one's perception of one's identity (Kramsch, 2001; Lin *et al.*, 2001). Put differently, English contributes to identity formation, which constitutes both dynamics and the sense of belonging. This notion of appropriation, I believe, would somehow facilitate English to serve global citizens and at the same time would not take their sense of belonging away. However, if only the Other takes up this notion of appropriation, part of the effort is still left unsupported. The Self should also adapt its notion of the ownership of English to this idea of appropriation for the sake of all. In the context of English and ELT, facilitating appropriation by learners of English is part of the job that world English language teachers and applied linguists need to fulfil. If this could be achieved, then the issue of power and the politics of language would become less pressing in the arena of English and ELT.

I would like to add one more point to McKay's (2003) appropriate EIL pedagogy. She agrees with Brutt-Griffler (2002) that the recent worldwide spread of English is mainly due to 'macroacquisition', the term coined by Brutt-Griffler (2002), and thus this nature necessitates alternative pedagogy for EIL. McKay offers a number of features of EIL, such as many learners of English learn the language for specific purposes and use it in multilingual contexts. They also learn English to communicate their cultures and knowledge with others. She calls for a pedagogy which goes against assumptions commonly held in ELT, that the spread of English is because of linguistic imperialism, that the native speaker model is no longer valid for learning and teaching goals and that the focus on only the native speaker's culture is no longer beneficial to both teachers and learners. I agree with McKay's (2003) points; however, I want to emphasise that when it comes to academic assessment, users of English will normally lose their sense of 'owning the tongue' or at least feel insecure. Still, certain norms are employed to make judgements, and thus a certain power is exercised. So the point here is that if we all work hard for an EIL and for fairness in the teaching and learning of EIL but do not have the same attitudes towards academic assessment, then our efforts will be in vain. Likewise, as long as non-native teachers of English 'are still anchored in the old native-speaker dominated framework' and 'non-native speakers of English are not conscious of being speakers of EIL' (Llurda, 2004: 319–20), EIL will not be recognised and appreciated.

So I suggest, together with encouraging and valuing users' appropriation of English, TESOL workers also need to promote an EIL pedagogy in which the teaching and learning of EIL should involve valuing and nurturing the expression of other cultural voices in English, making explicit the values that support judgements about 'good' English and individual ability, and helping students to construct identities as owners, meaning makers and authorised users of EIL.

Before closing this chapter, I would like to draw on a number of points arising while reading Holliday (2005). This book leaves me with some thoughts. Although throughout the book Holliday demonstrates very well many issues embedded in native-speakerism and acknowledges and discusses the degree of resistance and appropriation that the non-native-speaker Other student/teacher exercises, it seems to me that there lacks an important part in this picture. Almost nowhere in the book does he talk about the Other's voices regarding how 'bad' and how 'inefficient', apart from the 'colonising' part of the discourse, the teaching/training conducted by the English-speaking TESOL West appears to be. This missing part is what I am going to address in this book. I believe incorporating the Other's voices in matters other than the Other–Self dichotomy could enrich the literature even further and thereby inform World TESOL professionals more comprehensively. In the same vein, as reported by Holliday, most, if not all, non-native TESOL teachers' experiences in relation to numerous aspects of English appear to be negative and painful as a result of native-speakerism. Non-native or the Other teachers (I use these terms with full awareness of critical debates around them) do not necessarily see their experiences as being deficient, painful or low in terms of status (Pavlenko, 2003; Setiawan, 2006). I discuss this later in this book.

Although much of the discussion in Holliday (2005) presents the native-speaker norm with a very negative eye, I do believe that many people, including myself, want to reach the level of native competence as language learners without any desires to submit ourselves to the English-speaking West and without holding an attitude that 'the West is superior'. (Here I acknowledge my full awareness of current debates around the notion of 'native speakers'). So, in my opinion, this native-speaker norm also needs to be seen as being dynamic, as much as the norm of 'culture'. Then, it might be more possible for TESOL professionals to respond to a wide range of needs and expectations from students in the world's vast contexts.

# Chapter 4
# Identity Formation: Negotiations of Apparently Contradictory Roles and Selves

## Introduction

It is now time to explore how the processes of identity formation of a group of Western-trained Vietnamese teachers of English take place. I will do this by investigating the tensions between the apparently contradictory roles and selves manifested in the two dichotomies: the professional and/or the personal; and the moral guide and/or the teacher of English. These dichotomies arose as these teachers were sharing their experiences with me.

Why are these dichotomies important and significant? The dichotomy between the professional and the personal is important to these Vietnamese teachers, since the professional is socially constructed and governed by norms and values of morality, and the personal tends to act accordingly. On the surface the personal and the professional seem to permeate each other and the latter tends to dominate. However, whether there are tensions in teachers' enactment of these roles needs to be explored.

The dichotomy the moral guide and/or the teacher of English is closely connected to the first dichotomy. It further explains the role of teachers in Vietnam and what kinds of tension teachers have in performing the Vietnamese teacher, the personal and the teacher of English. Moreover, while the first dichotomy explores these teachers' identity negotiation process in both the Western and Vietnamese contexts, this dichotomy investigates their negotiation in the Vietnamese context only. By exploring these dichotomies, I hope to capture their identity formation more fully.

## How Identity Formation Processes Take Place: The Professional and/or the Personal

The identity formation process within the professional and/or the personal particularly reveals how teacher identity is nurtured, formed, developed and reconstructed. Through discussion with the participants, I noticed a sense of being a Vietnamese teacher and its continuity throughout their professional and self development. This suggests that identity gives one a sense of belonging and connectedness (Phan Ngoc, 1998; Tran Ngoc Them, 1999, 2001a, c). This also suggests that identity is subject to reconstruction and changing but the process takes place along the lines of existing values and one's sense of self. Therefore, in this section I focus on the discussion of identity and belonging. Also, since the teachers tended to identify themselves as being teachers, they fastened their identities to claim membership status. Together with their identities defined by social norms and institutional regulations, they constructed their own identities. Arguments about identity fastening and unfastening are mainly used to support the discussion of identity and belonging.

When the teachers discussed issues of the professional and/or the personal, although I noticed two worlds, the professional and the personal, these appeared to be a unitary and integrated entity within teacher identity, but not two separate selves. These two parts were complementary in the teachers' professional self development.

What I mean by 'sense of belonging' here refers more to group membership/insider status/professional identity than merely national identity.

### Negotiating teacher identities: How teacher identities are formed

According to these Vietnamese teachers, teacher identity is mainly formed by ideologies and social norms. They govern teachers' behaviour and performance. More importantly, they define teachers and teachers tend to take on this definition to form their identity. As discussed in Chapter 1, in Vietnam it is believed that teaching is a noble job. Also, besides knowledge, teachers are respected because of their moral education role and their being good examples in the society.

In the Vietnamese moral traditions, the images of teachers are closely associated with morality and standard and decent performance. Vietnamese people also have a long tradition of respecting teachers, so I think once we've chosen to become a teacher we'll always try to achieve what the society expects from us and not to do things that have bad impact on our long tradition. (Lien)

I think my teacher self is influenced by the tradition of pedagogy in Vietnam. As teachers, we're viewed differently from others in the society. Thus, we need to be aware and conscious of whatever we do. (Trang)

[Teachers need to have many good qualities to be role models for students,] such as sense of responsibility, enthusiasm in whatever circumstance, empathy with students because we used to be students, and so on. (Thu)

I find that teacher identity is formed based on three bases. First, we look at our teachers teaching us, of course excluding bad teachers. Most of our teachers pay close attention to students' performance. I remember they always gave advice to poorly performing students, warning them that if they didn't concentrate on their study, how they could survive later. So I thought these teachers they gave moral lessons to students and I tended to copy it in my teaching later. Second, we observe our own family, how our fathers teach us and how we teach our children. Then I realise everybody needs both knowledge and morality education, and thus I bring this idea into my teacher self. And third, I think teacher identity is also based on our conscience. For example, I've observed that many kids and teenagers have become so bold/rude in their speech and I want to do something. Thus I want to educate students morally because I care for the future of Vietnam. What if they all became that rude? So, to conclude, teacher identity comes from three dimensions, family, school or teachers, and conscience. But of course it's not true that all teachers teach students morality. Some may claim that what they're paid for is only for teaching knowledge, and students' parents will teach them morality at home. But many others never care about low or high pay. What they care is students' morality because they see it as their job and what they should do. (Chi)

I think values attached to teaching are related to many things. First, for example, when I was a pupil, I observed my teachers and I wanted to learn good things from them, like a good sense of responsibility, generosity with and kindness to pupils. And second what called social norms, they also influence teacher identity formation. We should follow them and I think it's right to do so. Third, teacher values are influenced by our colleagues' performance, for example we tend to follow their positive acts. (Linh)

Now that I've been trained in the US, I've become more aware of my role as a moral guide. I can't just ignore this, simply it's part of me and makes me feel proud of. I don't want to turn down students' trust in me as a moral guide. But I do feel relaxed. Morality comes from within. (Trung)

You know, being a moral guide as a teacher is a great thing that makes me respected by my students when I was tutoring in Britain during my study there. I don't mean I explicitly 'lecture' them on their behaviour or performance, but I did guide them through with sincere belief in my heart that proper behaviour and a good morality are important. (Minh)

The above perceptions of how teacher identity was formed reminded me of what Chi said towards the end of one group interview with Thu, Lien and Trang, that 'a teacher is a daughter-in-law of a hundred families'. Teachers have to please all parties. The following sections also consolidate this metaphor of the image of teachers in Vietnam.

### The role of morality and conscience in teacher identity

Although these teachers either directly or indirectly spelt out the word 'morality' and 'conscience', they all make their arguments based on these concepts. Being a teacher always accompanies demonstrating morality. Morality here is co-constructed by the society and the tradition of pedagogy in Vietnam. It is also institutionalised by norms, regulations and disciplines set by the teaching profession. Moreover, besides commonsensical norms, morality is variably perceived and practised by teachers and it is thus constantly reconstructed and renewed. This creates the flexibility of the concept and this flexibility explains why Linh, Thu, Lien, Trang, Linh, Trung and Minh gave different perceptions of teacher identity. Also, what makes their perceptions different is what they define as 'conscience'. Conscience is not a separate entity. Instead, it is integrated with morality. Morality and its associated norms influence teachers' acts and behaviour. However, different teachers may come up with different ways of performing conscience. For example, Lien claimed that teachers should not do anything that would have a bad impact on the teaching profession. Trang argued that teachers should be aware and conscious of whatever they did, since teachers were viewed differently in the society. Chi explicitly defined what she meant by 'conscience'. She felt it was her responsibility (a teacher's responsibility) to teach morality to students. For Trung, it 'comes from within' and for Minh it needs 'a sincere belief'.

### Negotiating teacher identities: The professional and/or the personal

Although these Western-trained Vietnamese teachers of English seemed to perform their teacher roles as socially and institutionally expected, they negotiated their teacher identity as well. This was when the personal wanted to be heard and came to the foreground with the professional.

> But I think my teacher values are greatly formed by my own person-ality, my own self ... If I am a responsible and enthusiastic person, then I can do my job well ... Our teachers tend to act on standard norms in the society, but the point is whether we're willing to do it or do it unwillingly. (Linh)

> I think teacher identity is also based on our conscience. (Chi)

Linh was very clear about her perceptions of teacher values when she explicitly used 'I' and 'my' to express her viewpoints. She placed an emphasis on the personal, her own personality and her own self. Chi raised the importance of conscience, which, as I have discussed earlier, varies from one teacher to another. One's conscience and personality tended to play an important role in the teaching profession.

Vy also claimed that her personality played an important part in her teacher identity formation. She said she could not pretend to be a teacher with good qualities while in reality she was not that good. So for her she was confident that she possessed necessary qualities required by a teacher. Her profession reflected her self, more so than the other way. However, she later admitted this two-way interdependency.

It was noted in these teachers' points that the personal tended to fit in with the professional. Put differently, it seemed that to be teachers they needed certain built-in qualities, such as 'responsible' and 'enthusiastic', which were required by their profession. Although they voiced that their teacher values were partly formed by their personality, their personality happened to be constructed along the lines of their profession. Here it raises a question of what qualities/personality traits one is thought to need to be a good teacher. Again this falls into the category of morality and conscience discussed above. It seemed that these teachers did not have to negotiate their personal at the cost of the professional. The former did not go against the latter. So these teachers also constructed their teacher identity based on their personalities which served the benefit of their profession. They fastened their identities to claim their insider status.

## Negotiating teacher identities: How the professional shapes the personal

Reed (2001: 329) argues that 'identity unfastening ... might be perceived as either constructive or destructive from the standpoint of the individual.' This proves to be true when these teachers judged each other and other teachers based on how the other unfastened their identities.

### Identity unfastening as destructive

For example, Chi expressed her view of teachers and morality education.

> I find that teacher identity is formed based on three bases. First, we look at our teachers teaching us, of course excluding *bad teachers* ... But of course it's not true that all teachers teach students morality. Some may claim that what they're paid for is only for teaching knowledge, and students' parents will teach them morality at home.

'Bad teachers' implies those who have 'bad' morality and behaviour, and those teachers cannot be seen as role models or good examples for other teachers and students. They are seen as unfastening their professional identities in the wrong way.

Another example was also presented in a group interview. When Kien said he wanted to learn English swear-words, Linh and Vy were against him, asking him the rhetorical question 'is it how a teacher should be?' They seemed to assume that Kien had unfastened his teacher identities improperly. Also, they seemed to question his identity unfastening: a teacher of English needed to possess a rich vocabulary, but swear-words should not be learned, since those words represented a bad image of Vietnamese teachers, who were expected to teach students how to behave. They seemed to treat knowing swear-words and using them as one single act. I realised they viewed each other as teachers and judged each other's acts on the basis of assumed norms of being teachers. Their teacher selves appeared dominant even in such a non-academic situation. This partly helps strengthen and promote images of teachers in the society.

It was clear that those teachers who did not teach students how to behave or wanted to do something against the norms were not viewed as 'standard' teachers. In other words, they were thought of as lacking teacher morality or conscience or as 'out-of-track' teachers. Those teachers unfastened their identities and that act was seen as destructive by Linh, Vy and Chi. Together with employing morality and conscience as 'identity filters' (Reed, 2001: 330) to group themselves and exclude those who were not teachers, these teachers, Linh, Vy and Chi, also used the concepts to marginalise 'less standard' teachers.

### Identity fastening/unfastening as constructive

In contrast, these teachers' proactive act of conforming to social norms of teacher values was all agreed upon among them because this act was considered 'constructive'. Examples were found in their debate of how the professional shaped the personal.

Linh admitted that she always saw herself as a teacher, since she met her students everywhere, in markets, at airports and all other places. She clearly described how her personal was influenced by her teaching profession.

> Not only does my personal influence my profession, but also the other way around … It's like I always think that I'm a teacher so I should do this and that, and this gradually becomes part of me … Wherever I am, I feel that people look at me the way they look at a teacher … I tend to be maturer in conversations with others and behave more properly. Yes, it's like that. But I think because I'm myself already a serious person, so I don't find it's changed me into a serious one, but it certainly influences my behaviour … It's made me a calmer person, not as aggressive as I used to be. I also become more patient. Truly it's how the professional influences the personal.

Vy at first claimed that it was not because she was a teacher she had to force herself to act certain ways. However, having listened to Linh and Kien's points, she realised her behaviour was also influenced by her profession.

> Like Linh, I feel that thanks to my profession I can control myself better in dealing with people. I tend to be calmer … And I also tell

myself that I'm a teacher, I shouldn't talk without thinking. I should behave like a teacher.

Minh and Trung remarked that being a teacher in Vietnam had trained them to behave gently with others, and this was what they were loved for.

## Concluding ideas

Teaching and its underlying values have been made a tradition and this tradition is passed on from generation to generation. Moreover, the aim of education is to educate people to become good citizens in both knowledge and morality. Teachers themselves are automatically assumed to be role models. As a result, their identity is heavily formed by external factors that are powerful enough to largely silence their personal voices. But the point is that the teachers I have referred to chose to act this way because they appeared to appreciate the tradition in most cases.

One question often to be asked is whose morality should be taught to students. That is the morality constructed by the society, embedded in the tradition and manifested in teacher definitions. The society views and judges teachers based on the morality, and the teachers do the same with themselves and each other. The morality becomes something taken for granted and it largely contributes to teacher identity formation. Teachers assume that they need to have certain qualities to be good teachers, among which morality appears dominant. Accordingly, they train themselves in certain ways and shape their perceptions along these lines. However, this does not suggest that the identity formation process takes place naturally and easily. Rather, it is made a conscious process, in which the common overshadows the personal and the personal is mixed with the common. The degree of mixture between the common and the personal makes teachers different from one another, despite their shared values. Chi might be less controlled by the common while Lien seemed to confine herself to it. Trang, Linh and Vy appeared to be more articulate about the personal while Thu seemed to be more concerned with social norms and regulations. However, their perceptions of the representation of the personal were not the same. If Linh was more concerned with her will, Vy asserted her personality in relation to her job. This observation suggested that individual choice or volition played an influential part in the negotiation between the personal and the professional.

These teachers' perceptions of teacher morality and ethics showed the human side of the concepts. They included a good sense of responsibility, love and kindness to students, enthusiasm for the profession and awareness of moral responsibility to young generations. This is the meaning and value of the Vietnamese educational practices, which the West often misreads as 'authoritarian' and 'imposing' (Phan Le Ha, 2004). I discuss this point in detail in subsequent sections. It is the close association of morality and ethics with teachers' images that gives them an identity. Both the society and these teachers fastened their identities and thus gave them an insider status. Also, these values and their negotiation of identities make them Vietnamese teachers, not teachers from Australia or Britain, for example.

## How Identity Formation Processes Take Place: The Moral Guide and/or the Teacher of English

When defining themselves as teachers, these Western-trained Vietnamese teachers of English located themselves under two identity umbrellas: a teacher of English and a Vietnamese teacher. As the former, they wanted to be facilitators and get students involved in communicative activities to improve their English. But as the latter, they also saw themselves as taking responsibility for their students' moral development. So the moral guide walks side by side with the 'facilitator' teacher of English in them, in which the former constitutes an imperative role and the latter means little interference. How these teachers accommodated the situation and dealt with the tensions revealed their identity negotiation process, in which identity fastening and unfastening seemed to dominate.

Since this section focuses on the teacher as moral guide and/or the teacher of English, it has much in common with the previous one, where the dichotomy of the personal and/or the professional was discussed. The most noticeable commonality is the role of demonstrating morality in teaching in Vietnam, and how teachers take up this role.

When these teachers expressed their opinions about a teacher's role, the role of 'moral guide' appeared equal to the role of possessor of knowledge or facilitator, and in certain cases, the former even played a more important part. Being a teacher includes being a moral educator. Therefore, although they were teachers of English, these teachers did not forget their role as moral guide. However, this does not suggest that they performed these two roles separately or they divided themselves into two different parts to fulfil their duties as both teachers of English and Vietnamese teachers. Instead, their constant identity fastening, unfastening and refastening allowed them to harmoniously and efficiently play these dual roles, without doing a disservice to their students and their perceptions of being teachers.

## Perceptions of 'moral guide' role

I now look at these teachers' perceptions of 'moral guide'. As Reed (2001) argues, identity fastening occurs as individuals submit to available categories. I show that these teachers defined themselves by both adopting the 'moral guide' role – the identity available to them in Vietnam – and constructing it.

Presenting themselves as both Vietnamese teachers and teachers of English, these Western-trained teachers of English seemed to emphasise the former role. Teachers in Vietnam often find it necessary and important to educate students morally, no matter what subject they teach. They care for personal development as well as knowledge achievement, and the former is closely associated with morality education. Teachers are moral educators or moral guides. For these teachers, being teachers of English did not stop or prevent them from performing their 'moral guide' role, the role that made them Vietnamese teachers.

The teachers expressed various ways of performing the 'moral guide' role. Linh saw teachers' 'moral guide' role as showing students what 'proper behaviour' was.

When my students don't behave properly, I'll tell them what proper behaviour is. … Ah, I remember one class they often had private talk. I was quite easy when they had group work, 'no problem', but when someone in the class spoke, others should listen. Yeah, these students, they didn't listen, and in such a situation, I normally interfere. I told them gently that when someone spoke, you should listen to him or her and you should show that you knew how to listen. I used English to tell them that 'if you want to be a good speaker, be a good listener first.' Normally I only educate my students when they don't behave properly. If not, I won't say anything because they're all grown-ups. I mean I don't give them moral lessons but I do tell them how to behave when an incident occurs as I've just mentioned. … When they behave badly I'm willing to tell them that they're wrong and they should do this or that. For example, they should know how to listen to other people because listening is a way of support.

Vy and Thu perceived their 'moral guide' role as introducing students to literary works or reading passages that carried moral lessons, and from those lessons, students would be directed to 'good behaviour'.

# 114 Teaching English as an International Language

We always select what we teach. We tend to select works that have moral or ethical lessons to teach students. In my subject, after each lesson, I often draw some values or my students and I all draw good things from every work we study. Sometimes we also choose works full of negative images but the purpose of it is to highlight works with positive moral lessons. I mean we introduce both 'bad' and 'good' characters to our students but through the introduction of 'bad' characters, we direct our students to 'good' behaviour in life. I think it's good to do so. (Vy)

Conveying a somewhat like an ethics message to students often occurs in teaching languages because, for example, when we teach them reading or teach them a story, there is always a moral lesson embedded in the reading or in the story, and students draw their own lessons and I give them some feedback. … I myself like such readings because I can absorb them as I'm reading, then I present them to my students who often like them too because they think they learn a lot from them … One of the advantages of learning languages is that it's more humanity-oriented. (Thu)

Vy gave one example of the selected works, *Hamlet*, in which her students would have to discuss whether or not Hamlet should take revenge.

Chi explicitly defined herself as a moral educator, who consciously directed students towards good behaviour and proper personality development.

Since I started teaching at university, I've always been aware of my role as somewhat like a moral educator. I often spend my break time to talk with students, listen to them and try to understand their problems and why they behave in such a way … I also tell them stories about how to become a good person. I don't know whether they think of me as a young teacher who likes to teach morality, but I believe that those who listen to me will become better. I tell them such stories to realise them that besides learning English well, they also need to know many other things, like how to behave properly in different social situations. I often teach them such things through the teaching of English. In other words, through my teaching, I also concentrate on moral education and teach them how to become a person with good morality and personality. I think all teachers can do such things … There are so many opportunities to do so through teaching.

Lien clearly defined a teacher as someone who should both 'teach' and 'educate' students (as she used Vietnamese to express this idea, 'day' and 'do', I have tried to convey it in English although it is not completely equivalent to the original meaning). Lien reported that she developed her teacher self in light of this definition. She emphasised the necessity and importance of teaching morality to teachers-to-be, since morality was the very quality that could make them good teachers later.

Besides teaching, I want to be close to my students ... I know that university students are grown-ups but many of them still need advice from someone older on how to behave or what to do. And I want to become one of those older people who can give them advice ... I always think that a teacher should both teach and educate students, especially those who would later become teachers. They need to be directed. When they're students, they need to follow standards and moral norms. This will make them good teachers in the future ...

Trang talked about teacher morality and in her perception, the 'moral guide' role could also involve setting a good example for students.

For me teacher morality is very important, morality towards my university, students and myself ... I want to become a good example for my students. I play many roles with them.

It is clear that although these teachers all talked about morality and the 'moral guide' role, their perceptions were not exactly the same. Each of them performed their roles in their own ways but all were based on shared concepts of morality. They took on the available identity the society and others constructed for them, the 'moral guide', but they also enriched the notion by submitting their own interpretations and enactments to it. Put differently, they contributed to constructing the 'moral guide' role along the lines of the morality concept, which I discussed in earlier sections. Here the 'moral guide' role expressed by these teachers confirmed the humanist side of morality. Morality was taught through examples, works, experiences and incidents that embodied moral lessons. Teaching morality, as these teachers' perceptions suggested, served two main purposes, fulfilling their role as teachers and making their students morally good individuals. They did not teach morality by imposing on students or forcing them to learn it through 'dry' norms. Neither did they feel forced to do it. Instead, they did it as it was a felt responsibility coming from a teacher's morality and conscience.

Their perceptions of the 'moral guide' role suggest a shared identity among Vietnamese teachers. It also confirms their belonging to the Vietnamese community of teachers. These teachers taught English, a foreign language accompanied by a foreign culture, but they seemed to develop their teacher selves along the lines of the Vietnamese pedagogical culture. They fastened their identities to find a way to belong, as argued by Reed.

## Negotiating two identities: The moral guide and/or the teacher of English

As these teachers taught English, they unfastened their identities to feel they belonged to the community of teachers of English and at the same time fulfilled their 'moral guide' role. This combination allowed them to identify themselves with both groups of teachers and simultaneously constructed their own identity, the identity of Vietnamese teachers of English. I will explore how their enactment of 'moral guide' was incorporated with being a teacher of English, which they described more or less as 'facilitator'.

All these teachers reported that they performed their 'moral guide' role through the teaching of English. That means they did not treat their university students as small school pupils, who needed explicit moral lessons. Instead, they maintained an active 'moral guide' role while performing the 'facilitator' role by shifting and incorporating their multiple identities harmoniously. By doing so, they presented themselves as Vietnamese teachers, who could teach both English and morality well. At the same time, they did not alienate themselves from those teachers of English worldwide, who claimed to know how to teach English most effectively by acting the so-called 'facilitator' role.

### The teacher of English

These teachers viewed the 'facilitator' role in their own way, and their perceptions were not the same as what CLT theories often mean. They did not think that they were imposing on their students or applying the teacher-centred method in an inflexible way to teach English. Following are examples of how they taught their students.

As a teacher of general English, Linh taught first- and second-year students, and thus the focus on grammar was strong. The criticism the West often has of ELT is that Asian teachers heavily depend on a grammar-translation method, giving students almost no chance to speak. But looking at how she taught, it is clear that on the one hand, Linh did introduce grammar rules and structures to her students with thorough explanations and repeated homework, on the other hand she developed activities based on her students' grammatical knowledge to help them master both their linguistic and communicative competences. With first-year students who undertake a subject called 'English grammar', and whose language proficiencies range from elementary to upper-interme-diate or even advanced, teachers normally have to spend the whole lesson revising, explaining or teaching some grammatical structures to make sure that all students can benefit from the teaching. So did Linh. For second-year students, who do not have a grammar subject, Linh felt she had more flexibility to design her own syllabus and more freedom to create activities for her students. To prove herself as a teacher who is 'very flexible' in her teaching methods, Linh gave examples of how she made her grammar lessons more diverse and communicative.

> [When teaching grammar] I create many activities to get students involved. And these 'communicative-oriented' activities are designed in relation to a specific grammar structure. After these activities, students will have to sum up what has been studied, and based on these they will ask more questions to further their understanding. Other students can help answer, or I can help them if necessary. In general, the way I teach is very flexible. (Linh, journal entry)

So even though Linh focused on grammar when teaching, the way she taught was not 'boring' (her own words) nor did it lack a communicative orientation as the West may assume. Importantly, she offered what her students needed, and was very confident that she always performed at the highest level.

Linh expressed her perception of teaching and what she thought was important when teaching languages. She stated that 'I encourage my students to do things by themselves and ask questions instead of "pouring knowledge into their minds".' To make this stronger, she asserted 'I never impose my ideas on my students, I never force them to be for or against anything or never force those who're for to be against or vice versa.' For her, she did not impose her ideas for the sake of having 'a meaningful argument' in her classes. Linh confidently saw herself as a 'very flexible' teacher who 'created many activities for [students] to speak and let them speak more'. How Linh helped her students in class is an accurate reflec-tion of what she expressed as being her pedagogical role; encouraging students to ask questions helps them to become engaged in 'reflective thinking and critical thinking'.

As a literature lecturer, in the individual interview Vy clearly asserted that she liked to be her students' friend, 'a facilitator, a companion, but not a controller'. She stated that English literature was not just English. However, she also expressed the idea that students did need a good command of English to study the subject well. Obviously, her subject requires much practice of writing and writing cannot be perfect without good grammar knowledge. Vy emphasised the importance of equipping students with grammatical knowledge prior to and through her literature teaching, although teaching grammar was not her focus.

Seeing literature as having much to do with personal attachment, Vy always reminded her students that not all she said was correct, 'I want them to express what they think and feel rather than me standing in the lecturing area imposing them.' This is a sign of encouraging students to explore and develop their own voice, particularly in literature, a world of the soul, the heart and inner thinking. Vy saw her 'students' satisfaction' as being 'very important'. She reported giving priority to her students' eagerness to explore knowledge, and this challenges the West's perception of the Other teacher who likes to impose ideas on students. Vy had strong confidence and high self-esteem as a teacher when she stated: 'I'm very confident with my way of teaching, and my students really like it.'

> [When teaching literature] I divide the class into several groups and each group reads one chapter, then each group presents the chapter to the class. By doing so, all students understand the whole book. (Vy, individual interview)

Vy reported that she often encouraged her students to tell her what they thought.

> Why should I be angry with you [if you don't agree with my opinions]? Not everything teachers tell you is correct, particularly in the literature subject, which requires you to have your own ideas depending on your own feelings and appreciation. You've got your own appreciation. (Vy, individual interview)

As a teacher of morphology, a theory-oriented subject and a compulsory subject included in the final examination, Thu was aware of how she should teach it best to make sure that students could meet the examination's requirements. She described her way of teaching as 'traditional', but also stressed that this traditional method was the very way her subject needed, given the limited time she had to teach it.

Traditional methods are the very ones morphology teaching needs. Different activities need different methods. For example, because morphology is a difficult subject, I need to lecture a lot and give students time to take notes, and so it's traditional. Moreover, I have a very limited time to teach such a difficult subject, only 30 sessions (each lasts 45 minutes), so I don't have much time for discussion or giving feedback on students' exercises. If I had more time, I would divide students into small groups and each group would study a particular part of the subject, then they would discuss with each other, and I would give them some feedback. It would be interesting to do that way, and it is assumed CLT, if I had more time. (Thu, individual interview)

Feeling that she had more freedom in designing her own syllabus, since her subject, which was about cultures, was not the core one, Trang seemed to give her students more chances to explore the subject. She also revealed that the nature of the subject enabled her to diversify class activities.

[When teaching a cross-cultural subject] I often don't follow any particular textbook. Instead, I introduce students to a number of books needed in the course. In the first lesson, I normally give them an intro-duction of the subject, and this introduction follows different themes and has some questions. I want students to realise that they will have the chance to explore those themes and answer those questions in the subject. I also want to generate students' interest in the subject by making them more curious about the subject through those themes and questions, since they may ask themselves 'do I know this or that?' For example, I ask them 'what is the favourite sports of American people?', and students may have different answers, like 'football', 'baseball', and so on. And then I may or may not give them the answer. I draw their attention by telling them that they will have the chance to know the answer while they are learning the subject. I mean I really have to motivate them. I then divide the class into groups and each group is responsible for one topic. And each week as I teach a partic-ular topic, one group presents the topic to the class, then all students will discuss, and ask questions. And then I play the videotape covering the topic to the whole class, ask students questions, let them discuss and draw some lessons in comparison with Vietnam. (Trang, individual interview)

It seemed that these teachers knew how to teach their subjects best. Moreover, they appeared to leave necessary space for their students to co-

construct knowledge and develop interest in what they were learning. They also seemed to be aware of how they taught, whether they gave students enough discussion time or whether students participated actively enough in class activities, as seen in Thu and Vy's examples. They seemed to be familiar with CLT norms, though they did not explicitly refer to it, except Thu. However, they asserted their optimal ways to teach their own subjects, which did not necessarily reflect the CLT approach, but still benefited their students.

### The teacher of English and the Vietnamese teacher

As Ellis (1996: 215) suggests, in ESL contexts, teachers 'act more as a facilitator'. But this does not mean EFL teachers do not see themselves as facilitators. What I would like to argue here is that how these Vietnamese teachers performed 'teacher as facilitator' is not necessarily the same as the way their Western counterparts do. When asserting themselves as 'facilitator', they located themselves under two identity umbrellas: a teacher of English and a Vietnamese teacher. In other words, they did 'facilitator' in harmony with their cultural expectations. As a good teacher of English, they wanted to encourage their students to have free and stimulating discussion or to take part in as many language activities as possible for the sake of learning English. But as a good Vietnamese teacher, they also needed to perform their duty as 'behaviour educators' or 'moral guides'. Put differently, they instigated cultural performance, such as politeness, which is not the same as what the West expects.

As discussed earlier, these teachers performed their 'moral guide' role in various ways. Linh used English to direct students towards good behaviour, such as 'if you want to be a good speaker, be a good listener first.' She said she told her students how to behave when she observed that they did something wrong. She did it as if she was teaching them an expression in English which would make them think, but not as an explicit moral lesson. She achieved both aims, teaching English and norms of behaviour.

Vy and Thu performed their teacher roles differently from Linh. Vy proactively selected works with moral or ethical lessons to teach students. Thu let her students raise moral issues from the readings she introduced to them. Then they both gave feedback to students and helped students become aware of moral lessons and what they should follow. In doing so, they were able to teach English and educate students morally.

Chi, even though she explicitly defined herself as a moral educator, did not introduce obvious moral lessons to her students. Instead, she found her own way to incorporate teaching morality with English lessons. She took any possible opportunities in her English teaching to draw students' attention towards moral messages. She made her students realise that English was just one thing, and besides it they also needed so many other things, among which norms of behaviour or morality appeared significant. In other words, knowledge should be accompanied by good personality, and good personality requires good moral education.

As both an 'expert knower of the language' and a 'moral guide' (Kramsch & Sullivan, 1996: 206), these Vietnamese teachers seemed to have succeeded in providing their students with the knowledge they wanted, without alienating them from their familiar home culture. In other words, they had taken into consideration both the culture of the target language and the culture of the students.

These Western-trained Vietnamese teachers of English unfastened their identities by making their English lessons a means of conveying moral messages. Instead of making themselves dependent on the so-called 'facilitator' role assumed by CLT theories, they made English serve their purposes. Still, they perceived themselves as good teachers of English and good Vietnamese teachers. They fastened their identities by confirming their 'moral guide' role. They refastened their identities as they invented their own ways of incorporating both English and morality lessons in one.

## Conclusion

This chapter has examined processes of identity formation manifested in the two dichotomies, namely the professional and/or the personal, and the moral guide and/or the teacher of English. These apparently contradictory roles and selves have been explored to understand how these Western-trained Vietnamese teachers of English saw themselves as teachers and as individuals in relation to their society and professional contexts in Vietnam and in the future.

Though they expressed tensions presented in these apparently contradictory roles and selves, these teachers all suggested ways to accommodate these tensions. By fastening, unfastening, and refastening their individual identities, and co-constructing a shared teacher identity, they claimed a professional identity and a national identity, which gave them a sense of belonging and continuity in the development of their teacher selves.

Morality plays an important and significant role in these teachers' negotiation of identities. Morality becomes an identity filter, through which they grouped themselves and others. Their negotiations often came down to their perceptions of morality and how to demonstrate morality, so as to measure one identity up against the other. Although they showed certain resistance to new values as teachers of English, a foreign language, they demonstrated an awareness of such values, which in collaboration with their existing values gave them an identity – Vietnamese teachers of English.

The examination of these two dichotomies, particularly the moral guide and/or the teacher of English, acts as a bridge to Chapter 5, since it partly opens up a new direction for looking at teacher identity formation. In contributing to the disproval of commonly held Western views about Asian teachers of English, it links to the politics of Self and Other, which are explored in the next chapter.

# Identity Formation: The Teacher and the Politics of ELT

## Introduction

The notions closely associated with images of teachers of English illustrated in the literature (Holliday, 2005; Pennycook, 1994, 1998; Phillipson, 1992) are re-examined in this chapter in light of the data obtained from these Western-trained Vietnamese teachers of English. Issues arising from dichotomies suggested by the way they expressed their experiences and perceptions, such as native and/or non-native teachers of English, Western-trained and/or non-Western-trained teachers of English, and teacher of English in Vietnam in relation to language, culture and identity are explored. Furthermore, how these helped reveal resistance to such dichotomies are also be investigated.

Self and Other as discussed here have moved very far from their original images of the coloniser and the colonised. In this book, apart from representing the dichotomy of native and/or non-native teachers of English, these participating teachers also referred to Western-trained and/or non-Western-trained Vietnamese teachers of English, and teachers of English and/or teachers of Russian. Through their discussion, it was evident how their teacher identity was constructed, shifted, negotiated and reshaped within these dichotomies.

## Teacher of English in Vietnam in Relation to the Politics of Language, Culture and Identity

In this section, I explore how these teachers defined themselves as teachers of English in relation to the politics of language, culture and identity. Particularly, in the context of English as a global language and Russian having lost its dominant status in Vietnam, I am interested in how languages and politics have influenced teacher identity.

English has given these teachers of English a certain status in Vietnam and has simultaneously made teachers of Russian 'jobless'. English intrinsically is not to blame but what accompanied it carries issues of ethics. All of the teacher participants began either teaching or learning English in the 90s when English had been establishing its dominance in Vietnam. They all eye-witnessed the decline of Russian and people's eagerness to learn English. Let me take an example from Linh's story to demonstrate this.

> I started learning English in 1989 when I was in grade 10 ... At that time we didn't have the right to choose what language to learn but we had to kind of play lottery to try our luck. They had plenty of secret ballots in a box and in each ballot they wrote the name of a foreign language. We had to pick a ballot to see what language we would learn. You know I was so nervous when I had to do it that I didn't see clearly what was written in my ballot and I told the person in charge there that it was Russian. Then she read the ballot again and told me 'Silly. It isn't Russian. It's English.' You know I was so excited that I jumped and shouted and cheered. Yeah, that's how I started learning English. (Linh, individual interview)

Learning English meant opportunity while learning Russian was subject to risk. This made those who learned English feel advantaged while those who learned Russian became disappointed. Since almost all students wanted to learn English, a 'lottery' game acting as a gate-keeper was set up to make some students learn Russian.

**The important and dominant role of English**

These teachers all stressed the importance and dominance of English, and then discussed whether learning English was an inevitable and natural choice and whether Vietnamese people chose to learn it actively or felt obliged to learn it.

> Compared with Russian and French, English has a higher status. The learning of English has been blooming since the government introduced the reform policy in 1986. Particularly, after the collapse of the former Soviet Union, Russian became less and less attractive, giving way to English to blossom. However, the learning of English varies according to educational levels. At school level, more and more students learn English, but at tertiary level it has become saturated. Learning English at universities now is more like learning a means to

serve other purposes than taking English as a major. More and more students of other majors learn English but the number of English major students is decreasing ... The role of English? Why does it have such a dominant status? It's because English-speaking countries have become more and more economically and politically powerful, thus making English a global language. Therefore, Vietnamese people now have the need to go overseas for study, business or cultural exchange. And we need to use English more often. If French and Russian used to be dominant, then English has now replaced them. Knowing English gives one a better chance to get a job. (Thu)

I don't know whether my observation means generalisation or not, but I think learning English is like a social habit. It's not something we do willingly and neither are we forced to learn it. It's like a social habit and we're either forced or feel necessary to learn it. Let's take example of children whose parents want them to learn English when they're only three or four years old. Yes, they think it's necessary to know a foreign language and English is now the very language their children should learn. Or people in general think they need to learn English because others learn it. (Chi)

I think it's because of socio-cultural changes in Vietnam that makes people want to learn English. During the Vietnam–America war, people in the South of Vietnam had to learn English to communicate or work for Americans, because then the US poured a lot of money in American–Vietnamese associations or the like. After the war, there were still people learning English. But since Russia had won influence throughout Vietnam, people rushed to learn Russian. And then when the former Soviet Union collapsed, they turned to English. Why? Because capitalist countries invest a lot in Vietnam and people see knowing English as an economic advantage. English closely attaches to opportunities. So I think learning English is a result of social reality. I still remember some years ago when Francophone countries invested in Vietnam and offered scholarships for students to study in France, a lot of students chose to learn French as their major. I personally think people choose a foreign language to learn because of underlying benefits rather than their real interest. Vietnam is still a developing country and we tend to choose the language that brings more benefits to us. (Trang)

It seems to me that learning English is not something vital in Vietnam despite people's realisation of its dominant status and accompanying benefits.

## Learning and teaching English change one's identity

Thu, Chi, Lien and Trang suggested that learning and teaching English contributed to changing their performance and thus their identities.

Teachers in my Faculty used to be commented as somewhat open in the way we dress. They often assume that those who learn foreign languages tend to be open and foreignised. But it's not exactly like that. But from my observation, I find that whenever Faculties of foreign languages have meetings, we don't either sit quietly and formally or criticise one another as other faculties do. Instead, we laugh a lot and make jokes and tell jokes. Why is that? Maybe because we have absorbed some Western culture and tended not to pick out for hostile criticisms among one another. I think definitely there's some kind of influence. (Chi)

Even our teaching methodologies are more open and casual. (Trang)

English lessons are always more relaxing than other lessons. I don't know whether by saying this I'm in favour of teachers of English, but I think that these teachers know how to make their lessons less boring. Of course there are still boring English lessons but less than those in other subjects. In English lessons, students don't have to suffer for hours from listening to lectures. From what I've heard from you all, I know that not only teachers of English in your universities are like that. Same as teachers of English in my university. Their ways of teaching and their performance seem more special. (Lien)

Lien saw all teachers in her English faculty as having a good sense of humour. This made their classes more relaxed and enjoyable. She even saw her learning and teaching of English change her personality. It helped change her from a serious and quiet person to a cheerful and humorous one. She said she was influenced by her classmates, teachers and colleagues. She felt she could see this influence and change more clearly.

Thu commented that Vietnamese people were often afraid of rumours. They also tended to criticise others. But since she came to Australia, she realised differences between the two practices. In Australia, people looked at two sides of everything and they often respected others' private life so as not to criticise people's ways of living.

What these teachers had said showed their belief that English and ELT had brought about more positives than negatives. They affirmed that

English and ELT not only helped change their performance such as teaching methodologies but these also converted English language teachers' values and personalities. This suggested that the influence was deeper and more serious than it appeared on the surface. This on the one hand disproved Liu's (1998) assertion discussed in Chapter 3 that learning English did not mean losing one's identity. Once these teachers realised that they had been changed, they at the same time realised a hybridity in their values. On the other hand, this confirmed the argument about the relationship between language, culture and identity. How these teachers saw English change their values and practices consolidates Fairclough's (1989) perception of language as social practice. The more we use a language the more familiar it becomes, and the more familiar it becomes the more likely it turns into a social habit.

## Learning and teaching English: Negative influences

Although 'learning a language broadens our minds', as Thu stated, and learning and teaching English brought about positive changes, as these teachers suggested, they were also concerned with negative influences resulting from their attachment to English.

I think learning a foreign language is to learn others' culture. And when learning culture, two people have two different viewpoints. For example, if one adopts the foreign culture, he/she will view the one who refuses to adopt it very differently. Neither of them are bad, but one will accuse the other as bad and vice versa the other one will blame one as being foreignised. But no culture is bad or good. For example, if you think both Vietnamese and English values are good and it's necessary to adopt some English values too, but if I am very conservative and blame you as being de-rooted, then? I think these problems do exist. I don't know whether they're good or bad but we do face them when we learn a foreign language. (Chi)

But [the way teachers of English teach and perform, as praised by Lien earlier] could lead to bad habits as well, not necessarily bad habits but definitely there will be teachers who are too open and cross the allowed border. Thus, this is a shortcoming. (Chi)

Well, I acknowledge that there are certain bad habits that are formed by the learning and teaching of English, such as code-mixing and telling dirty jokes. Students also seem to respect teachers less. Don't you think so? (Trung)

I told them a story of a teacher who after being trained in an English-speaking country wore shorts to class and often sat on the table to teach students. Below are their responses.

Like I've just said, learning a language means learning its culture. But in many cases, the introduction of foreign cultures isn't accepted in the society. And I think this is the ugly side of learning a foreign language. (Chi)

Our educational environment can't accept that way of dressing, so students feel shocked at how that Western-trained teacher changes his way of dressing. That teacher might teach very well and students still respect his knowledge, but his way of dressing reduces students' respect. If he goes out with shorts, it's fine. But it's definitely unacceptable to wear it at university. (Lien)

From administrators' perspective, teachers of English are criticised for their casual and undisciplined teaching. We can start earlier and also can finish a lesson sooner than scheduled. We can also plan lessons in our own ways, very different from standard samples. We even organise classes more freely. For all of these, we're assumed to have less sense of discipline and order than teachers of other subjects. Particularly for those who hold traditional views of teachers, they can't accept the teachers of English's performance. Thus, they tend to complain to us rather than try to understand the nature of language teaching. Those English teachers who're trained overseas are even more open in everything. They sometimes sit on tables or do things to show that they've been trained abroad. Some teachers also copy Western teachers' performance from workshops, and then practise it in their teaching. (Trang)

That teacher is too much. As a male teacher myself, I can't accept his way of dressing. You know, respect from others really matters, particularly for our teaching job. (Trung)

## English, ELT and the role of Russian in Vietnam

Almost all of these Western-trained Vietnamese teachers of English had some connection with Russian, either as learners or teachers of it. Four of them had taught Russian before they became teachers of English. For Binh, An, Van and Minh, who used to teach Russian, they felt a significant change in their teacher selves.

I was more relaxed before. I didn't have to negotiate my values with those embedded in Russian. Teaching Russian was like teaching our mother tongue. (An)

I wasn't rich but had a comfortable life when I was a teacher of Russian. I wasn't under pressure of making money. We just didn't have the kind of impact that English has now on teachers. Now I find myself very busy earning and there are always things to do, lots and lots of private classes to teach and it's hard not to feel tempted. (Binh)

It's more challenging now in a way, but the pace of life is also very fast. I miss the days when my students and I sang 'My Russia' and danced 'Kalinka'. It was a good life. But I'm not complaining about the current situation. English has given me a lot too, but a different kind of life, which is not bad, either. (Van)

I hate to say that I can't speak Russian well now. I feel like betraying my own identity. Who do I speak Russian to? Even my former colleagues now prefer speaking English. We, Russian lovers, do gather from time to time to make 'Russian salad' and drink 'vodka', but to talk about sending our children to America or Australia for further studies. The peaceful golden Moscow in autumn has seemed to stay only in our memories. (Minh)

And for those teachers of English who had never taught Russian before, their views are as follows.

I don't know about other universities but at my university teachers of Russian fiercely confront teachers of English. There is a teacher who used to publicly declare that she would never ever learn English because she hated it. She said she would rather learn something else than learn English. But the reality in the Faculty of Russian is that there are more teachers than students. Thus, the abovementioned teacher who used to make the declaration and terribly hate English then had to learn English. What if one day we faced the same reality? We aren't feeling assured, are we? (Trang)

You know, we sometimes can't stand the low teaching quality that former teachers of Russian perform in English classes now. They only learned English quickly for about two years or so, and now they are teaching like us. (Trung)

I can tell you a lot about how former teachers of Russian teach English in Vietnam. No doubt the quality is so low. They all need retraining. (Vinh)

But I don't think former teachers of Russian are allowed to teach students majoring in English. They only teach English to students from other majors. But this is a serious problem because those students will never learn good English. (Thanh)

We can't deny that those former teachers of Russian catch up with us very fast. You can find lots of English language centres run by them and we actually work for them. We, teachers of English, only know how to earn little money, but they know how to earn big money. (Thao)

Through the words of these teachers, I discovered that a number of teachers of Russian and teachers of English did not seem to like and appreciate each other much. The rise of English meant the fall of Russian. Likewise, the more wanted English had become, the more neglected Russian was. Consequently, teachers of Russian had lost their status and attached benefits. They fell from the sky to the ground and at the same time were seeing teachers of English changing their lives overnight. This had confirmed what I said earlier about how uncomfortable life was for teachers of English before the late 1980s. Obviously, English has contributed to unhealthy treatment of certain groups in the Vietnamese society. English and ELT have lent a hand to creating distance and even confrontation between teachers of different languages. Some of these teachers felt empathetic to teachers of Russian and they were also worried about their future, though only vaguely. But some of them did raise their concerns regarding the teaching of English by many former teachers of Russian. It seemed that the status of teachers of English was very much driven by political and economic pictures. They suddenly felt unsupported. Teaching and learning a language is no longer neutral or politics-free. Rather, it is controlled by forces having power. This confirms Phillipson's (1992) and Pennycook's (1994, 1998) point that English and ELT are not neutral and power-free. Teachers of English may have power today but they might lose it one day, as happened to teachers of Russian.

When these teachers indirectly and directly mentioned the declining role of Russian and teachers of Russian in Vietnam, they implicitly suggested the victory of English and the comfortable status of its teachers. They realised that English and the politics of languages had created the difference and differentiated teachers of English and Russian. But they did not realise that they had become part of the politics game, when some of them described teachers of other majors as less open, less democratic and more conservative than them – teachers of English, who had been influenced by English and its values. Here they were, teachers of the global language, and here were the 'them', the teachers of the unwanted Russian. This status made the difference and created two different identities under the same umbrella: Vietnamese teachers.

## Vietnamese Teacher and/or Teacher of English: How Are These Roles and Selves Mediated, Shaped and Reshaped?

The tensions between themselves as Vietnamese teachers and themselves as teachers of English were apparent in the voices of these Western-trained teachers. As the former, these teachers were expected to perform and behave in certain ways, which are socially and culturally appropriate. But as the latter, they were also required to 'do' teacher in ways embedded in the ELT norms. These ways meet one another at some points but contradict in many other points. Moreover, as teachers of English – an international language – they both benefited and were affected by the language and its underlying values. As they were trained in the English-speaking West, they were more exposed to English and the norms of ELT. At this point, the politics of ELT is called into question. Whether or not they became more aware of the tensions between their existing teacher values and the values presented to them during their stay in the West is explored. The shift of contexts from Vietnam to the West also contributed to their awareness.

### The curriculum: English as a global language

In this section, I discuss the politics of Self and Other and the politics of 'English as a global language', presented as a subject in the TESOL Master's course introduced to some of these teachers. It is not something general, something theoretical or ideological discussed in books, but it is something real that four teachers experienced in their classroom in Australia. It is incorporated in the curriculum, pedagogies and classroom interactions. It is clearly presented with powerful and concrete instances given by these teachers. Such a sensitive issue as this could only be broached in a group discussion, where the participants supported each other and held on together to assert their professional values and their Vietnamese identity. Not all of them were equally articulate about the issue, but however resistant or reluctant, they all showed their attitudes, clearly expressing when and how they were affected.

As teachers of English in Vietnam, these teachers had a certain position in the society and somehow were proud of mastering English, a global language. However, when they faced the issue of English as a global language presented in their Master's course, they realised that they were no longer masters of it. Instead, they were assumed to be its 'servants'. As such, the tensions between themselves as teachers of English and themselves as Vietnamese became visible. The Vietnamese part in them seemed to win over the other part, the part that made them feel inferior rather than proud of what they taught.

When talking about their TESOL programme, Thu, Chi, Lien and Trang in a group interview pointed directly to one subject called 'English as a global language'. Trang saw the subject as problematic. Thu shared her views, admitting that Vietnamese people generally were so tolerant that Thu and her peers themselves did not want to criticise the unethical side of the subject. Although they were somewhat aware of unethical performance in their course (as they reported), they found excuses to tolerate it. For example, Lien gave her opinion 'if we think our course has some problems of ethics, then it sounds insulting to Australian lecturers.' Nevertheless, no matter how hard these teachers tried to resist their true feelings, they finally, in the interview, reported on the issue of 'English as a global language' and how the subject was presented. Thu, Chi, Lien and Trang all stated that the subject really made them feel uncomfortable and 'hurt' because it boasted of the power and global status of English.

### Unethical representations of 'Other' in teaching examples

These teachers commented on the Australian lecturer and how she addressed the subject.

The way she lectures is very untactful. She always gives negative examples of developing countries. So we don't feel easy at all in such lectures. (Trang)

She always gives very negative examples of how English is taught in Vietnam. (Chi)

She only came to a workshop in Hanoi for a few days [in the late 1980s or early 1990s], but she has seen everything in Vietnam in a negative way, and her examples of Vietnam are negative, too. ... And she generalises everything there in such a negative way. ... She never gives any positive examples of other countries. (Thu)

She also uses the word 'barbaric' or the like in her lectures. (Chi)

In terms of pedagogy, the Australian lecturer was obviously excluded from the category of what might be considered a good teacher by these Vietnamese teachers. Also, she clearly defined herself as belonging to developed countries as opposed to these Vietnamese teachers (her Master's students) who came from 'developing countries' or 'barbaric' ones, as they reported the lecturer having said. By emphasising negative examples of how English was taught in Vietnam, she made these Vietnamese teachers feel as if their own practices were looked down upon. This helped unite them together as one solid group of Vietnamese teachers, who were non-native teachers of English and all confronted the lecturer, a representative of the other tongue – English. They encouraged each other 'to be prepared' to listen to the lecturer's examples.

We often tease each other that we should 'get ready' to face her examples about Vietnam. She assumes that the teaching of English in Vietnam has nothing good, all memorisation, not exactly her words but something like that. (Lien)

When she talks about Vietnam, she talks as if what she saw there would never change. (Thu)

And she always affirms that Vietnam or ELT in Vietnam is like this or like that. (Lien)

Because she always stereotypes how English is taught in other countries, we students feel very hurt and this makes us think that teaching is only good in Australia or America. (Trang)

These teachers seemed to work together to contest the stereotype. On the one hand, as insiders, they knew much better about how English was taught in Vietnam than the lecturer. Moreover, what they said suggested that the teaching of English had changed, and thus the teacher identity had also changed compared to the time the lecturer went to Vietnam. On the other, they teamed up to argue that ELT in Vietnam might not be best but it was not as negative as the lecturer described. It needed to take into account social and cultural factors. They denied the lecturer's assumptions, and by doing it they grouped themselves under a unitary identity. They fastened their identities to find a way to resist the imposition of a negative identity.

### Unethical representations of 'Other' as teachers

When Thu, Chi, Lien and Trang described how other international students in their classes felt when the issue of English as a global language was presented to them, they revealed unethical issues embedded in the subject.

> She [that Australian lecturer] wants to 'advise' us that English is a global language and as we come here to study, we have to learn it, no matter what; and compared to English, other languages are only sub-languages. And the way she lectures is very insulting as one overseas student comments. He says that we come here to learn how to teach English, but not to serve English. Other overseas students feel insulted too. Teaching this subject is like boasting of English-speaking countries' power, implying that other countries are not good, and we would lose our identities one day. So, such a subject shouldn't be taught in TESOL courses. ... This subject obviously reflects discrimination. (Trang)

Suddenly, these teachers were defined as 'servants of English'. Rather than being seen as teachers of English, they were seen as agents who served the benefit of English-speaking countries and English itself as a global language. Moreover, they felt that their mother tongues were suddenly assumed to be sub-languages, acting as subordinate forces besides the bullying growth and flowering of English. However, they did not accept this idea. Instead, they disapproved of the introduction of the uncritical focus on 'English as a global language'. As they came to Australia to study different teaching methodologies, they were aware of their roles as teachers of English, but not as 'servants of English' as part of their courses might assume. So, instead of appropriating what had been presented to them, these teachers questioned the given knowledge. They confirmed their status as equal and thus disapproved the fixity of representation.

## The united identity to contest Western pedagogy

### Identify fastening and unfastening

I can see multiple identities within these teachers. Their Vietnamese identity came to the fore while their identity as teacher of English stayed in the background when they together fought against stereotypes about Vietnam. But the latter became stronger when they faced negative examples about ELT in Vietnam. Their identity as non-native teachers of English became predominant when their classmates shared their feelings. Their identity as teachers of English who enjoyed an equal status to teachers from any other country appeared strong when they denied the fixity of representation. The shift in identity seemed to be the same with these four teachers but they also showed different degrees of being affected by the issue. Trang appeared to be most concerned and articulate about it while Chi did not often express her views. Rather, she listened and nodded her head. If at first Lien tried to deny the unethical side of the subject, she could not do it anymore after Trang had pinpointed the problem. Although Thu was not the first one who thought of the subject, she then became actively engaged and critical about it.

The nature of group interviews and open discussions allowed these teachers to unveil such a sensitive matter. They felt supported and they could rely on each other to contest the values attached to English. As teachers of English, they might not be sensitive enough to realise such things or they might think of them but might not be brave enough to accept the unethical aspects of their course. But when they talked together, they found themselves stronger and more unified as one group who belonged to a unitary identity. This identity could be a hybrid one, a mixture of their multiple identities, but most importantly it gave them power to assert themselves and criticise their course. The teachers constantly fastened and unfastened their identities to create this power, which ran throughout the fluidity of their hybrid identities.

### Co-constructing a professional identity and a national identity

The tensions between themselves as teachers of English and Vietnamese teachers were seen when the teacher participants assumed themselves to be good Vietnamese teachers who did not teach in such an untactful way as their Australian lecturer did. At least they considered both what they taught and how they performed it. Although they were non-native teachers of English, they considered themselves better than a native one who failed to make them love English. They did not appropriate what was given to them because inside them there was another voice wanting to be heard. The voice of the Vietnamese teacher identity did not allow them to adopt such unethical values of English. It also prevented them from seeing Vietnamese as a subordinate language. Hence, although the tensions were not transparent enough to be seen, their shift of identities helped reveal them.

## Native and/or Non-native Teacher of English: How Are These Roles and Selves Mediated, Shaped and Reshaped?

The dichotomy between native (NS) and non-native (NNS) teachers of English was both explicit and implied in the perceptions of these Western-trained Vietnamese teachers of English. When it was explicit, the tensions between these two selves were clear, but when it was implied, there seemed to be no tensions or the tensions were transformed into a discussion of the productive nature of differences.

It is often assumed in the literature that there is a clear-cut distinction between non-native and native teachers of English (Brutt-Griffler & Samimy, 1999; Phillipson, 1992), but what these Vietnamese teachers of English reported did not support this view. Rather, they seldom defined themselves based on the dichotomy. They addressed it when I asked them to write about it in their reflective writing and to talk about it in one group interview. I noticed only one time when several of them indirectly described themselves in relation to native English-speaking teachers.

Whether colonial and postcolonial paradigms of non-native speaker and native speaker affected the way these teachers defined themselves, it was found in this study that they constructed their own ways of identifying their teacher selves. They did not actively employ the dichotomy to view themselves in relation to the so-called superiority and inferiority between the former and the latter, as the literature has pointed out (Brutt-Griffler & Samimy 1999; Pennycook, 1994, 1998). Instead, they viewed the dichotomy in their own ways, which were different from conventional views (Phillipson, 1992). The dichotomy was not necessarily seen as 'negative' or 'colonial' or 'deficit'. It was mainly used as 'different' and 'complementary'. From how their identity formation took place, it was also clear that the dichotomy itself did not work sufficiently to understand the complication of identity formation, particularly when these teachers shifted their identities.

What did emerge was that these Western-trained Vietnamese teachers of English clearly defined themselves (and others) in terms of their competence and their pedagogical content knowledge (PCK) rather than in relation to their condition as native speakers or non-native speakers. Shulman (1987: 8) defines pedagogical content knowledge as a 'special amalgam of pedagogy and content'.

### Seeing the dichotomy not as 'negative' but as 'different'

Before the group interviews, when I asked them to write about the dark and bright sides of being NNS and NS, these teachers appeared to believe that both NNS and NS had weak and strong points. Accordingly, it was impossible to say which was better. They did not see the other (NS) as the primary object against which they defined themselves. This supports Phillipson's (1992) argument that teachers are made rather than born. Also, this disproves the assumption that NS are ideal models for NNS in language teaching and learning, which Carrier (2003) implies (though I assume that the author does not intentionally argue for the implication). These teachers defined themselves as non-native teachers of English and different from the native ones. But they did not at all see themselves as inferior to the native. They presented the dichotomy between the two to reveal differences rather than tensions or contradictions. By defining the other, they identified themselves, or their images were constructed through their descriptions of others. This confirms that identity is constructed through difference, as discussed earlier in this book.

Linh wrote:

> Vietnamese teachers of English have the following *advantages*:
>
> Being bilingual in both English and Vietnamese helps them communicate better with students, and thus helps them understand better underlying messages, requirements, explanations and so on. This is certainly better when English fails to prove its efficient role. L1 is especially important at beginners' level and when advanced students come across complicated notions. L2 often fails to satisfy them, while using L1 saves more time and makes things clearer.
>
> Knowing students' L1 facilitates student-teacher contact, to a certain extent, because students can be sure that they can let teachers know their problem, by explaining to teachers in L1.
>
> Moreover, as non-native speakers, teachers also share the same culture with students, the general culture, and thus they can adjust materials/activities to make them more culturally appropriate. Also, if teachers teach L2's culture, they still know which parts needing more focus. Furthermore, they understand their students' learning styles better, for example, some students feel shy to ask questions or take part in speaking activities. Thanks to this, they can think of activities to gradually promote effective learning habits, such as group-work or presentation.
>
> One more advantage of sharing the same mother tongue with students is that it helps teachers understand better difficulties faced by students when learning L2, since teachers themselves have experienced those. They thus have empathy and understanding for students. One example of difficulties in learning L2 is pronunciation, and teachers tend to know what kind of mistakes students often have, such as l-n, s-sh. They thus have solutions for teaching pronunciation. An example in teaching writing is that teachers know when students write by thinking in English and when they write by translating from Vietnamese.

There are more advantages, of course; otherwise non-native teachers of English might be fed up with their job. Isn't it true?

Vietnamese teachers of English have the following *disadvantages*:
They're not able to speak English as fluently as native speakers and of course they can't master the language as the native speakers. This thus causes difficulties in teaching, for example, intonation, rhythm, listening and even pronunciation. In shorts, being a non-native teacher of English causes certain disadvantages in teaching for some teachers. I don't say all teachers because in Vietnam many teachers are extremely good at English and teaching methodologies.

Another disadvantage is background and culture. Materials used for teaching in Vietnam are mainly written by native speakers. These materials require teachers to have understandings of L1's culture and societies. For example, not all teachers can explain 'first class mail', or they can't explain how 'validating tickets' works if they don't know about the train and tram system in Australia, etc. These things seem to be taken for granted with native teachers of English, because these are part of their life. However, with our teachers, particularly those who don't have many contacts with real-life and authentic materials, media and culture of L2, it's a big difficulty for them.

There may be more disadvantages but I think that's enough for now.

Kien wrote:

Non-native teachers of English often understand better the difficulties faced by their students because they share L1 with their students. Moreover, they tend to know grammar of the target language better than native speakers. They can explain in L1 if their students don't understand properly in L2. However, their language proficiency is not as good as native teachers' of English.

Native teachers of English have some advantages. Because they teach their mother-tongue, they don't have language difficulties. However, they don't often analyse their grammar as well [as non-native teachers]. They have the advantage with pronunciation. They can also know what is appropriate to say, since they're more familiar with their mother-tongue styles. They also understand their cultures, and they can explain many concepts only existing in English.

Vy wrote:

The *bright side* of a native teacher:
– good at four macro-skills; have a deep knowledge and understanding of culture and history of his country, so that he will not have any trouble in explaining the language he is teaching; has plenty of experiences and illustration to make his lectures more vivid and interesting; takes less time for preparing vocabulary, pronunciation, grammar.

The *dark side* of a native teacher:
– cannot catch up the difficulties that non-native students get involved in their expression, writing or speaking; sometimes there's no understanding between teacher and students due to different cultures, different styles of living; don't know where and when they need to stop in their lecture to give more explanation to their students.

The dark and bright sides of non-native teachers of English are opposite to what I've mentioned above.

I observed that Linh, Kien and Vy all wrote about the issue in a similar manner, in which none saw the dichotomy as a negative criterion to judge who was better. Instead, they pointed out the advantages and disadvantages each possessed, to conclude that being a non-native teacher of English was not necessarily less advantageous. The other also had disadvantages. The overall balance seemed to fall into the question of 'who owns English' and 'who knows how to teach English better', in which, as Kien, Linh and Vy suggested, the NS tended to take over the former, while the NNS seemed to be masters of the latter. This point was extended further when they discussed the matter in a group interview. So, the dichotomy in this case proved its positiveness rather than negativeness as shown in the literature; or it has changed into different forms to fit in different cases produced by the complexity of identity formation.

## 'Who I am' as teacher in parallel with the politics of difference

In the group interviews later, Kien, Linh and Vy brought into the discussion the notion of 'who I am' as teacher in parallel with the politics of difference. They were different from the native teacher of English because English was not their mother tongue, but not because they were non-native teachers of English. They differentiated the language they taught from their profession and professional practices. Speaking English as L1 or L2 was not a matter to make them at all inferior in terms of teaching methodologies. It was the quality and values teachers from both sides owned and practised that mattered, and superiority in methods did not depend on who they were, native or non native. In fact, these teachers defined themselves more through their pedagogical content knowledge than through their English knowledge alone.

As teachers of English, Kien, Linh and Vy admitted that they sometimes lacked confidence about their English. But their lack of confidence, again, resided in the question of 'who owns English'. English was not their mother tongue.

> I sometimes don't have enough confidence about some things but they're only related to language alone. I lack confidence not because I'm a teacher, but because I'm a non-native speaker of English. For example, I can't be sure of intonation or stress in English. But I never compare my teaching methodologies with those of native English teachers. (Linh)

> I'm not confident about my intonation and my fluency, but my writing is not at all worse than theirs. (Vy)

Despite these disadvantages, these teachers affirmed that they were not afraid of teaching speaking and listening to students. They also agreed with each other that native English speakers had better speaking and listening in English, but it did not guarantee that they had a better method to teach these skills. Moreover, they indicated that native English speaking teachers could not train students in TOEFL or IELTS better than Vietnamese teachers because they had never experienced taking these tests.

These teachers, in the discussion, apparently defined themselves as non-native speakers of English, but at the same time they were competent teachers of the language. So as speakers, they were non-native, but as teachers, they were equal to native teachers of English, since they all taught English. They marked the difference as between 'speakers' rather than 'teachers' of English. They also differentiated the language they taught from their profession and professional practices. They defined themselves in relation to their pedagogical content knowledge.

### Being able to speak English at native level versus being an English person

Later in the group interviews, although Linh, Vy and Kien were quite consistent with what they wrote in their reflective writing, instant peer-interactions and questions raised in the group interviews teased out feelings and thinking behind their written words.

These teachers seemed to have a high self-esteem and highly valued their images as non-native teachers of English. Particularly, Linh was highly aware of her status. She saw herself equal to a very good university lecturer in Australia. Not all native speakers of English were considered to reach her standard. What she wanted was to possess extremely good academic English, and not all lecturers were a good enough model. Linh's tensions were not only between her Vietnamese self and English, but also between general English and academic English.

> If I ever wished, then as a teacher I only wish that my English were as good as that of an English-speaking academic, but definitely not any native speakers, not anyone in the street. (Linh)

Kien said he only wished his English were as good as a native English speaker's, but he never wished to become a native speaker. Linh once more confirmed Kien's point and added that she never wished to become an English person, either.

Vy only wished her English were perfect but she never wanted to become an English person. Linh again affirmed herself.

> I'm myself and I always want to maintain everything I have in me. I only want my English to be as good as that of, if I have to compare, then a very good university lecturer here [in Australia].

When these teachers had to assert themselves as they did in the interviews, it seemed to be a process of reaffirming their right to self-esteem. They clearly wanted their English to be at a native level, but they did not desire any other features typically possessed by native English speaking teachers. They did not want to change their status and they were confident of their status as Vietnamese and as non-native teachers of English. Being 'an English person' or 'a native speaker' did not necessarily mean 'better' in English and teaching English, and Linh, Kien and Vy seemed to treat 'being an English person' as something irreconcilable with their selves. I found a strong sense of national identity among them when they discussed this matter.

## Work quality as the most significant criterion of teachers' performance

Although these Western-trained Vietnamese teachers of English tried to avoid the dichotomy, they still used it, but they used it to assert that it was not the right criterion to judge teachers. For them, quality of work was the most important and thus they did not look at a teacher based on where he/ she came from. Instead of using the dichotomy to judge teachers, they offered a different parameter to compare teachers' teaching ability.

> I don't base on the dichotomy to judge teachers. What I'm more concerned about is teachers' personalities and their ways of teaching. I don't generalise. I don't pay attention where they come from and who they are, but I care how they perform and how they teach. That's all. (Linh)

Kien, Minh, Trung and others did not think that native or non-native teachers were better. For them, whether they liked a native teacher of English, it depended on specific contexts.

Again, the dichotomy of Self and Other did not work here. These teachers did not identify themselves in line with this dichotomy. Specifically, they saw themselves as having equal status with native teachers of English. The dichotomy was not the first and most important matter for them to think of when they identified themselves. For them, all teachers needed to make students appreciate their lessons, no matter who they were. This was the shared thing that both native and non-native teachers of English needed to have so as to be liked by students.

These teachers also reported that they had the same attitude towards their lecturers in Australia, Britain and the US. They did not treat them differently because they were Anglo, Asian or Latino. They all said that work efficiency and quality was more important than who the teacher was, native or non-native. So, the value these teachers tended to use to view their lecturers rejected the postcolonial dichotomy of Self and Other, in which the Self is often seen as superior and more civilised than the Other. This discussion disrupted it and opened up a different way to look at teacher identity formation, a way that takes into account teacher voices comprehensively rather than treating it in such a closed and fixed dichotomy.

### Experiences in the English-speaking West disrupting the belief that native teachers are better teachers

For Thu and Chi, who reported that they had had pre-assumptions about the superiority of native teachers of English, their views changed after being physically exposed to the Australian TESOL classroom. Their experiences in Australia helped disrupt their belief that native teachers are better teachers, and simultaneously made their assertion of their identities as Vietnamese teachers of English stronger.

They had believed native English speaking lecturers possessed somewhat better, more interesting, more advanced and more communicative-oriented teaching approaches than their counterparts in non-English-speaking countries. This had an impact on their teacher identity formation. They thus reported that they had had a sense of an inferiority complex when comparing themselves with NES lecturers, although professionally speaking they were all university lecturers. However, when they observed that not all native English speaking lecturers performed well, while other lecturers originally coming from China and India were very good, they realised teaching well did not depend on where one came from or what language one spoke as L1.

Specifically, Chi used to think that Western teachers were all very good before she commenced her course in Australia, but from what she had experienced in her lectures, she concluded that 'human beings are the same everywhere, have good and bad qualities' (individual interview).

What Thu and Chi saw in their course led to their conclusion that there were good and bad teachers everywhere; that native teachers did not necessarily mean better teachers; and what mattered was not 'who you are' but 'how you teach'. This helped them realise that native teachers of English were not guaranteed to be better teachers.

## Western-trained and/or non-Western-trained Teacher of English: How Are These Roles and Selves Mediated, Shaped and Reshaped?

This section partly explores the politics of Self and Other, in which I discuss these teachers' processes of identity formation. The notion of Self and Other is used very differently from its original meaning, in which Self refers to Western-trained teachers of English, while Other represents non-Western-trained ones. Self also represents Western teachers, while Other stands for Vietnamese ones. My intention is not to create dichotomies. Rather, I aim to employ these notions to draw a more comprehensive picture of identity construction, which contains fluidity, fragmentation, appropriation, resistance, contradiction, conflict and a sense of national identity and belonging.

### Teachers being trained in the English-speaking West and/or teachers in Vietnam

Although what these teachers reported disrupted the postcolonial dichotomy of native and non-native teachers of English as discussed earlier, there seemed to be a clear-cut distinction made between Western-trained and non-Western-trained teachers of English, particularly suggested in one group interview. Thu, Chi, Lien and Trang implied that those teachers who were trained in the West were worthier, and thereby better than those trained in Vietnam only. They also implied that non-Western-trained teachers at home would never change the way they taught. This suggested fixity in ELT in Vietnam, and at the same time strengthened the assumption that the adoption of teaching practices in Vietnam practised by Western-trained teachers would bring about changes and enhancement in language teaching. Moreover, teachers at home were seen as conservative forces who held back the movements of teaching as well as turned a blind eye to changes. Consequently, these Western-trained teachers defined themselves as somewhat different from and worthier than their colleagues at home. However, when aligning themselves with Vietnamese teachers, they seemed to merge with them and consider themselves part of the community.

### Non-cooperation from non-Western-trained colleagues

When Thu, Chi, Lien and Trang discussed how they would apply methods they had learned in their Master's course in their teaching in Vietnam, they predicted a number of constraints, among which non-cooperation from their colleagues appeared dominant. They argued that they could not improve and change teaching practices if other teachers did not support them. In their eyes, other teachers were depicted as those who envied Western-trained ones so much that they would probably not support changes.

> We're now trained in Australia, how come they would cooperate with us? (Lien)

> It's difficult to make changes because the way they look at us would be the same, full of envy. (Chi)

> It's difficult because how can those who are not trained overseas like us support changes? (Thu)

The dichotomy 'Us' and 'Them' was clear-cut in these statements. Teachers at home were pictured as those who would not cooperate, were full of envy and separated from Western-trained ones. This also suggested that before going to Australia, these teachers might have also been like those teachers at home. By being exposed to the West, they changed their views and distanced themselves from their colleagues in Vietnam. They had absorbed something new and were no longer the same as they were before. Their colleagues at home might also change, but these teachers did not see it and assumed that only they could change thanks to their exposure to new practices and values.

Vy also observed that older teachers trained in Vietnam had a fixed viewpoint about language teaching, even though many of them received further training through workshops operated by the British Council or other organisations from English-speaking countries.

> They're not open but very sceptical. For them, applying new teaching methods or not doesn't matter. They're very sceptical and they still follow their own way, the traditional method. Although they've attended workshops held by the British Council or Australians or Americans, they don't change their way. I mean they're very sceptical. One of them, an old male teacher in my faculty, voiced to me 'Well, you're young and you can act or play with your students. But I'm old now and imagine an old man with grey hair like me jumps and makes jokes in class, it's unacceptable.' I think he has valid reasons. (Vy, individual interview)

The politics of identity and difference was clear in Vy's example. By defining others, Vy defined herself and likewise excluded herself from 'Them', who were sceptical and traditional. She also saw their tensions and why they did not welcome changes. Change meant implementing new practices and they could not afford the time and effort to do it, given their familiarity with the existing conventions and their age. It did not mean they denied the advantages of new teaching approaches, but the notion of 'acceptable and unacceptable behaviour' caused tensions and discouraged them from trying those approaches. Still, face and images of teachers in terms of behaviour appeared extremely important in whether or not to change. By seeing such tensions, Vy was convinced that those teachers had their reasons not to do certain things, but not because they were not trained in the West. Clearly, she was not one of them, and she could not share their feelings, since she did not belong to that 'old' and 'non-Western-trained' group. To assert herself more strongly, she stated that when she grew older, she would develop her own way of adjustment taking into account proper behaviour as well, but this did not mean she would be conservative about changes. So, to some extent, Vy aligned herself with those Vietnamese teachers in terms of behaviour, but presented herself more as Western-trained and one who was eager and open to change. This compromise did not contain tensions; in other words, tensions led to compromises.

### Social judgements about Western/foreign values

These teachers also suggested that the society also had its judgements about Western-trained and non-Western-trained teachers, in which the former were highly regarded.

> The society has a different look towards Western-trained teachers. They're regarded more highly than teachers at home. (Chi)

> One reason why I wanted to go overseas for my MA TESOL is that it is something that our society appreciates. (Minh)

> Some teachers in my department did their postgraduate studies in Australia, New Zealand and the US, and they seem to be quite well treated by the admin people in my university. (Binh)

However, being trained in the West was subject to prejudices, too.

> We want to bring about changes because we think changes are good and necessary, but they may think that we like to show off. (Lien)

> They pay attention to every word we say and every activity we do in class, because we are trained in the West. It's just so hard. I feel so stressed that I want to go somewhere now. (An)

> And any idea I suggest, they think I try to lecture them. I have to be careful with how I dress when I am in class. They may just think I am going away from the code of dress in a Vietnamese classroom. (Huong)

'They' here referred to both the society and teachers at home. The above expressions revealed a social prejudice against those who adopted foreign values and wanted to implement these in Vietnam. Such teachers faced resistance and non-cooperation because they created a clash of values that forced traditional practices to be examined and contested. Teachers at home are the ones who are affected if new teaching techniques are introduced because they will have to adjust. Moreover, changes in teaching methodologies will affect social and cultural values embedded in local teaching practices.

Why the society has prejudices against those who are trained in the West is partly because of the idea that anything hybrid or foreignised tends to have a negative effect on Vietnam. It is due to its long history of contacts with and fighting against the West and its assumption that anything unhealthy or ill-cultured is a result of Western influence, as is highlighted by Phan Ngoc (1998) and Tran Ngoc Them (1999) in their discussions of the importance of national identity in identity formation for Vietnamese. Western teaching methods are thus not exceptions.

### Training in the West bringing about broad-mindedness

These Western-trained teachers seemed to think that after being trained in the West, unlike teachers at home, they became more broad-minded and tended not to take things personally. This suggests a positive change in their performance, and simultaneously implies that other teachers are narrow-minded, closed-minded and easily affected. Trang gave one example.

> I've observed that in my Faculty in Vietnam, after each semester, all teachers have to write a self-evaluation to help them evaluate whether the way they teach is efficient or whether they need to change anything. Those who have been trained overseas find this a normal, impersonal and necessary practice. They want to get feedback from their students too. But those who haven't been trained overseas find this irritating because they explain that self-evaluation is nothing but a way to let students freely express their views. They're afraid that their students will say something negative about their teaching, so they think they will lose their face. So, you now can see clearly that the difference in these two perspectives ... Additionally, they don't like class observation at all because they always assume that class observation is mainly for fiercely criticising and thus devaluing each other. So I think it's not easy to change such perceptions in one or two days.

Trang admitted that she used to be like the teachers at home before she came to Australia for training. Chi challenged Trang, stating that class observation was indeed sometimes aimed at fiercely criticising each other. She sourly revealed that teaching well even sometimes attracted unfriendly attitudes from colleagues. However, these teachers all said that they wanted to implement changes but not at the cost of causing mismatch between their ways and those of teachers at home. They admitted that they did not want to bear too much responsibility, either.

It seems to me that at the surface these teachers identified themselves more with Western teachers, who they assumed not to have 'bad' but very 'human' qualities as teachers in Vietnam. Being exposed to a new set of practices, they tended to appropriate new values and build up a new identity, which was labelled 'Western-trained'. They formed their own circle of Western-trained teachers, by whom they felt they were better understood. At the same time, they seemed to exclude themselves from their previous circle. One might think that they betrayed their own values, but it was more like they tended to view Western values uncritically and superficially. Instead of judging the pedagogy in Vietnam, they judged the Vietnamese teachers' psychological and impulsive feelings, which they saw as rather personal. They noted that this emphasis on the personal was rooted in their society's ways of making judgements.

The reason why Vietnamese teachers feel uneasy asking students to give feedback on their teaching is partly because of a powerful notion of 'face' given to and taken from teachers according to how well they perform. Losing face to students is a humiliating experience. Meanwhile, Western-trained teachers may feel it much easier to do so, since they are labelled as being trained in the West. That means they are assumed to be more open and democratic with students. This also makes students tolerate them more easily because students may benefit from their teachers' Western-oriented styles. Furthermore, the aim of having class observation in Vietnamese universities is very different from that in the West. If in Australia for example, teachers have more autonomy in their classrooms and they can decide whether they allow class observation, in Vietnam, teachers normally have no say if the authority wants their lessons to be observed. So, they feel they are under pressure and tend to see class observation as an instance of criticising each other more than self-improving their teaching. However, these Western-trained teachers tended to see the idea of getting students' feedback and class observation as related to open-mindedness, thanks to being trained in the West.

These Western-trained teachers sought support from one another in such a discussion to strengthen their appropriation and absorption of Western values. They once more confirmed what they had spelt out in the individual interviews with me. My feeling is that they consciously aligned themselves with Western teachers without considering their role in the English-speaking West sufficiently. Over there they were teacher-learners but not teachers. Their observation was based on their experience as learners and their engagement with Western ideologies and theories written in books and provided in their lectures. They could not see critically the politics that Western teachers may have and what values attached to Western pedagogies. Thus, they were more inclined to appropriate what they saw on the surface. Hence, by the time they made their appropriation, they tended to have a somewhat idealised view of Western pedagogies.

Being exposed to the West resulted in these teachers' ways of thinking and ways of doing changing. This related to their ideology and value changes. The story now becomes more complicated, since teacher training programmes have dual effects, changing both teachers' teaching methods and teachers' values and ideology. The construction of identity takes place in this process of changing. Superficially, it is very tempting to judge that these teachers easily became Westernised in many ways. But a closer look at the issue demonstrates that they had been undergoing complicated processes of negotiation. Although they seemed to be eloquent about changes for improvement, they also knew their limitations. In terms of 'ideology', they might like to be identified with Western teachers. But regarding reality, they showed some hesitation in drawing a clear-cut border between Western-trained and teachers trained at home. They were both but they were not either of them in full because they had been trained in two different modes of pedagogies, which present clashing values and practices. This required instant negotiations to mediate between the two to find a place where they belonged.

## Vietnamese teachers versus Western teachers

Tensions between themselves as Western-trained and/or non-Western-trained teachers of English were also shown indirectly between themselves as Vietnamese teachers versus Western teachers. If these teachers seemed to suggest a clear-cut distinction between Western-trained and non-Western-trained teachers of English, they tended to deny the dichotomy of Vietnamese teachers and Western ones. Simultaneously, their viewpoints contributed to disrupting the assumption that the West and anything related to it was better. In doing so, they constructed a professional identity as well as a strong Vietnamese national identity.

### Denying stereotypes about Asian teachers

In one group interview I had a feeling that the teachers somehow subconsciously created a dichotomy between Vietnamese and Western teachers. It was embedded in their comparisons and judgements about the two. To clarify my feeling, I told Kien, Linh and Vy common stereotypes Westerners often had about Asian students and teachers to explore their perceptions, such as that Asian teachers were mainly knowledge transmitters, authoritarian and imposing, and Asian students were passive. Linh interrupted me and denied those stereotypes. She said:

> It's not like that. I think any generalisation or stereotype is not always true. We need to place them in contexts to justify their reliability. We can't just believe in them naïvely.

Vy asked me whether those stereotypes were specifically about Vietnamese teachers and students. I told her that they were about Asian students in general and they were very powerful. Then, I decided to challenge them to obtain my aim. I told them that what they had said in the interview seemed to indicate that they indirectly supported the stereotypes and that they might not be aware of it. I gave one example: Linh had said that when she was in Vietnam she created many activities in her teaching and did not know what to name them. When she came to study in Australia, she could theorise what she had done at home. I told her that what she told me applied to anyone and anywhere. I asked her whether she thought that teachers in Australia could all name exactly what teaching activities they used every day at university. Linh disagreed with me, saying:

> What I meant is general to everybody, no matter what nationalities they have, British, Westerner or American. If one doesn't learn how to teach and one self-learns teaching, then one can only teach impulsively. One can't clarify or theorise what one is doing. One isn't conscious of what values attached to one's ways of teaching, either. For example, one may observe that having group-works encourages students to speak, but one doesn't know the underlying 'values' of this activity. That is we respect individual learners and treat them as 'potential learners' who can 'generate knowledge'. These are the underneath values that one can't think of. So I think everybody is the same if they don't study. There is no difference between Asian and Westerner. I think we're not at all inferior to Westerners.

Kien referred to pragmatic reasons and the lack of resources and facilities to explain why teachers and students in Vietnam could not fully develop their skills.

Our discussion then led to comparing Vietnamese with Western teachers in terms of ability. Linh strongly expressed her views.

We can't talk about ability because it's very difficult to judge it and because of the fact that people can't show their ability due to a lack of opportunities/chances or some reasons, for example. It's not because they're unable.

Vy confirmed Linh's opinion and admitted that in her university in Vietnam, both teachers' and students' potential was affected by the lack of facilities and resources. Linh further explained that students and teachers in Vietnam could reach higher if they were better equipped.

Apparently, what these teachers had said helped disrupt the commonly held view that Western teachers were better. They appeared confident. They did not place themselves any lower than Western teachers. Also, they seemed to be familiar with stereotypes the West often had towards Asian teachers. They did not get shocked or surprised. Instead, they denied the stereotypes to assert their status. Regarding teacher ability or potential, there was no difference between Vietnamese and Western teachers. The difference fell into how teachers' potential was fostered by facilities and resources.

### Constructing a professional identity and a national identity

By denying Western stereotypes about Asian teachers and students, these teachers implicitly constructed a professional identity and a national identity. Their construction was first based on the difference between 'Us' and 'Them', for example in Linh's expressions '*we* need to place [generalisations or stereotypes] in contexts … We can't just believe in *them* [Westerners] naïvely', or '*we*'re not at all inferior to *Westerners*.' Then, they constructed their professional and national identities by shifting their generic observations about teachers in general to specifying the situation in Vietnam. They shifted the third person singular pronoun '*one*' to the first person plural pronoun '*we*' to assume a group solidarity. This can be seen in Linh's case, 'if *one* doesn't learn how to teach … *one* can only teach impulsively. *One* can't clarify … *One* isn't conscious of what values attached to *one's* ways of teaching … I think *we*'re not at all inferior to Westerners.' This is also evident in Linh and Kien's views when they specifically used the word '*Vietnam*' as opposite to Australia – a representative of the West – and the word '*our*' to assert a shared identity: '*our* teachers in *Vietnam* … in *our* institutions … ' (Linh), and 'in *Vietnam*, we … whereas in Australia … ' (Kien).

By constructing a professional identity and a national identity, these teachers indirectly highlighted the difference between themselves as

Vietnamese teachers and the Other as Western teachers. However, the difference did not suggest 'deficit' or 'superior' as versus 'inferior' between the two.

## Conclusion: How Does the Identity Formation Take Place?

### Identity fastening and unfastening

*Identity unfastening* is obvious since these Western-trained teachers moved from the Vietnamese cultural context into several English-speaking West contexts, where the membership norms and rules are different. Their insider status was challenged as well as extended and somehow changed. On the one hand, their moving from Vietnam to the Western world challenged their membership status. They defined themselves as teachers of English in Vietnam, who enjoyed a respectable status as teachers who taught English in the society. They then went to the English-speaking West for their Master's degree, finding themselves losing the status and being marginalised by ELT norms. They suddenly 'became' teachers from underdeveloped and developing countries who possessed backward teaching methods. They were assumed to be 'servants' of English instead of its 'masters'. They were described as the Other, who did not belong to that top circle of teachers of English. As their mother tongue was seen as sub-language compared to English, their status was accordingly subordinate to that of the Self. They were excluded, and thus their insider status was challenged and denied. They were made to see themselves as Vietnamese teachers who found it uneasy to fit in the norms of ELT. They were teachers of English, yet, they were still the Other.

On the other hand, their moving from Vietnam to the English-speaking West enabled their membership status to extend and renew. They had opportunities to experience differences, interact with teachers of English from many countries and question their own teaching methods. Their views had been widened and they became more willing to change, or at least willing to negotiate different practices. They were given the chance to identify different roles and selves embedded in their teacher selves. If in Vietnam they were more concerned with how to mediate between the personal and the professional, and the facilitator and the moral guide, in the English-speaking West they became aware of how they were seen in the ELT norms. They were exposed to dichotomies of Self and Other. They were labelled 'Western-trained' and tended to take a different view of non-Western-trained teachers in Vietnam. Moreover, their exposure to new values and practices enabled them to disrupt the commonly held view that 'the West is better'. If some of them used to think that Western lecturers were better, they then realised there were good and bad teachers everywhere. Also, their self-presentation and exposure helped deny the literature of ELT about the native and non-native teachers of English. They did not see the dichotomy as a deficit, or as tensions or contradictions. Instead, they saw it as differences so as to recognise and appreciate diversity in language teaching.

*Identity fastening* happened as these teachers experienced different sets of pedagogic performance, which governed their acts to claim insider status for themselves and others. Before going to the English-speaking West, they were members of Vietnamese teachers of English in general. While overseas and being exposed to new values and practices, they found themselves different from both the West and Vietnamese. They suddenly became non-members of either. But to be included in the circle of teachers of English, they needed to mediate the differences. They had to accommodate so as to fit in the given circumstances. They needed to build a way to belong. Therefore, their identity fastening was somehow a conscious and aware act. Through their mediation of tensions discussed above, they were tempted to align themselves with Western teachers in terms of 'being open-minded', but they were inclined to align themselves with Vietnamese teachers in terms of teachers' roles. They grouped with teachers of English from other non-English-speaking countries to form a unitary identity to fight against hegemonic ELT norms. But when their turn came, they pictured their colleagues in Vietnam with similar images, such as those teachers who always opposed changes and stuck to out-of-date teaching methods. As they claimed insider status for themselves, they did the same thing with others. Others were created through their visions, and as their visions changed, others' images would accordingly change.

Since identities are always subject to being unfastened, as individuals are in constant contacts with new cultural values and norms as they move from one place to another and are positioned in various contexts, identity fastening and unfastening always take place side by side. In other words, they walk hand in hand and correlate. But one is also obtained at the cost of the other. As Reed (2001: 329) asserts, they 'usually occur simultaneously and in multidimensional ways'. For example, these teachers fastened their identities to assert their belonging to the circle of teachers who were trained in the English-speaking West, but at the same time still asserted their belonging to the world of teachers in Vietnam who could not tolerate their colleagues' inappropriate self-presentation, such as wearing shorts to classes. They at the same time unfastened their identities to both welcome changes and defend their values, and to both acknowledge their contacts with the West and assert their Vietnamese roles. They shifted from one group to others and found themselves belonging to different but overlapping identities. Their movement between spaces allowed their identity fastening and unfastening to happen, and as these processes occurred, they were subject to constant reshaping and reforming. They are part of the ongoing process of identity formation and identity negotiation. However, the arguments about identity fastening and unfastening do not suggest that these processes are fixed. Rather, they are progressive processes.

### Identity and difference

Self is constructed through other; or identity is constituted 'through the eye of the needle of the other' (Hall, 1991: 21, cited in Dolby, 2000: 901). Thus, for example, when these teachers drew a line between Western-trained and non-Western-trained teachers of English, they constructed their identities as they pictured the other. Their identities were shaped through their perceptions of others. By making others, they made selves.

When these teachers depicted non-Western-trained teachers of English with certain values, they simultaneously drew their own picture. By describing the others as those who were nosy and often took things personally, they implied that they were not so and did not do so. By stating that the others were not open for changes, they implied that they were more open and willing to change things. They were different from when they used to be, and because of their contacts with new practices and values, they were enlightened, whereas their colleagues at home were not. But interestingly, they all denied their similarity to the Vietnamese teacher who were trained overseas and later wore shorts to class in Vietnam. They were different from him because they knew to select appropriate things. By accusing him of being improper and adopting Western practices arbitrarily, they claimed their properness and awareness, and thus asserted a certain identity for themselves. They, at least, did not give away their Vietnamese part and did take cultural and social sensitivities into consideration.

### Identity as relational

As Dolby and Cornbleth (2001: 293) observe, 'identity itself is a relation – or set of relations and interrelations', and hence, 'we see or define ourselves in relation to various individuals and groups, specific life situations and particular contexts.' In this view, these Western-trained teachers of English saw and defined themselves in relation to teachers in Vietnam, teachers trained overseas, native teachers of English, teacher-learner and teacher of other languages and so on; in specific life situations, such as when they were doing their Master's in the West; and in particular contexts, for instance, during the interviews or while they were writing their journal entries.

The interviews and journal entries allowed these teachers and me to identify and understand their different roles and selves. By talking to me and with each other, they explored themselves and shaped their identities. As Vy admitted, the interviews were the very first time she had the opportunity to express her teacher self. She had never seen herself that clearly. The interviews were instances of identity formation. They shaped their identities as they went on in the interviews. These teachers defined themselves by relating to others. They confirmed, disconfirmed, shaped and reshaped certain identities by negotiating with their own selves, with me and with one another. With different relations, they presented different selves and roles. When they had to write journal entries, they presented themselves differently from when they were discussing with me in the interviews. For example, when Kien, Linh and Vy were asked to write about the dark and bright sides of being a non-native and native teacher of English, they seemed to construct their identities based on the assumed dichotomy embedded in the question. But when they discussed this matter in the group interviews, they did not define themselves in relation to the dichotomy. In specific life situations, such as while they were in Australia, their tensions between the Western-trained and Vietnamese parts became obvious and tended to dominate their identity formation. All of these relations, situations and contexts were intertwined and together influenced their identities.

In relation to their lecturers, they were both peers and students. As the former, they also enjoyed the difference of being Vietnamese. As the latter, they were different from Australian students and those coming from other countries. In relation to Vietnamese teachers, they were Vietnamese but Western-trained. Unlike Russian teachers, they were teachers of English, a global language. With different relations, their different identities became visible and stronger.

With me, Vy appeared quite confident, but with Linh and Kien, she seemed reserved and far less assertive. Her identity became 'dim' and hidden, whereas Linh's identity was strong and visible. While Thu did not enthusiastically participate in the group discussion, Trang appeared very active and often took up a critical stance. She was often the one who teased out issues first, and then others started to extend them. Her identity formation seemed smooth and clear, while it was not easy to comment on Thu's identity formation. If Chi and Lien were more enthusiastic in the individual interviews, they became quieter in the group interview. They presented a different image from what I had observed the first time I met with them. So, different situations obviously influenced identity formation.

## Identity as hybrid

As discussed above, identity unfastening allowed these teachers to add something new to their existing values. Seeing themselves no longer the same as they used to be and different from Western teachers, these teachers defined themselves as Western-trained, a group incorporating both but having their own code for their identity formation, the code that could not be shared by outsiders. But the code itself varied from one teacher to another. This process of identity formation applied differently to every one of them and adjusted itself according to his or her own circumstances.

These teachers' existing values were subject to transformation, examination, confirmation and disconfirmation. Consequently, something hybrid was created, but it did not make them totally new individuals. Instead, I suggest this process of identity formation works similarly to reconstitution, in which hybrid identities are constantly created and recreated, both consciously and unconsciously, in close association with a sense of continuity and connectedness. For example, when I interviewed Vy for the first time, I found her very eager to implement new teaching methods in her teaching in Vietnam. She tended to adopt what had been presented to her in her course. She seemed to stay away from 'traditional' teachers. But when she was in the group interviews with Linh and Kien, she became cautious and less eager, seeing herself questioned by her peers. The Vietnamese part seemed to support her and gave her a way to belong. Although the formation of hybrid identities operates as an on-going process, here, at least, it goes along the lines of existing values, which helps maintain continuity in identity formation. As can be seen, hybrid identity is never static, always dynamic, changing, despite the possibility of a thread of continuity.

## How the sense of belonging and continuity operates within the notion of identity as multiple, constructed, hybrid and dynamic

Although I agree with the arguments that identity is understood 'as a phenomenon that is actively produced and reproduced, instead of as a stable entity that exists before the social world' (Dolby, 2000: 900), and that identity is constructed, multiple, hybrid and dynamic (Farrell, 2000; Hall, 1997a, b), I would like to examine how the sense of belonging and continuity, discussed by Vietnamese and Western authors, operates within these arguments.

Since identity fastening and unfastening take place simultaneously and in multidimensional ways, the sense of belonging and continuity is maintained. Also, that the formation of hybrid identities operates as an ongoing process helps sustain existing values as well as causing them to transform and renew. This results in continuity being guaranteed. Identity is not a stable entity, but rather it is constructed, produced and reproduced. For example, since the interviews acted as a vehicle of identity formation, these teachers' identities were constructed on the spot. When I asked them to write about the dark and bright sides of being a non-native teacher of English compared to a native one, I placed them in a certain position to define themselves. This act was a conscious act, whereas their act of constructing teachers of English in Vietnam appeared subconscious but active.

These teachers had multiple identities, which were subject to reconstructing and reshaping, since the identity formation was continuously active and could cause any identities to hybridise. Their multiple identities did not appear together, but they took turns to come to the fore when necessary. Some of them might be hidden, and there were always some to be created during the hybridity process. As such, their multiple identities held on together to maintain the sense of belonging and continuity.

## The relationship between language, culture and identity

I would like to specifically employ Hall's (1997a) presentation of the relationship between language, culture and identity to explore how English and ELT contributed to these teachers' identity formation.

*First*, culture is about 'shared meanings' (p. 1) and meanings are produced and circulated through language. The 'shared meanings' the teachers had was their perception of to what extent ELT allowed them to act certain ways and what performance they, teachers of English, could fulfil. These meanings were represented in a shared language called the language of English teachers, including the way they dressed, how they taught and how they saw themselves. These Western-trained Vietnamese teachers of English had their own *culture*, a small culture surrounded and overlapped by multiple layers of bigger cultures. Within their cultural surroundings, they constructed their own identity, which was different from teachers of other subjects. The difference rested in their ability to make their lessons interesting, their sense of humour and their own discipline and order. Their *culture* constituted its own set of practices, while their language visualised, conveyed, sensed, illustrated and constantly constructed these practices. More explicitly, their perceptions of themselves as teachers of English were reflected through their presentation, appearance and performance with each other and with teachers belonging to other cultures. However, like other Vietnamese teachers in the society who are influenced by social and cultural contexts, these Western-trained teachers shared values of respect and the concept of acceptable versus unacceptable behaviours so as to set limit for their performance. Although they built their own identity, it was mediated in order not to be rejected. It was their awareness and consciousness to form a hybridity, which was negotiated and renegotiated through their profession, their professional values and local contexts.

*Second*, meanings are constructed through language and socially constructed. The teachers' shared meanings were both constructed through their own perceptions and what the society thought of them. As they reported, the society and teachers of other subjects often assumed teachers of English were liberated and foreignised. Thus, they tended to take on this assumption and appeared the way others assumed them to be. The language they used then signified their *culture* and affected it as well. The more positively they saw themselves, the more often they acted their felt, shared ways, and thus this strengthened and extended their shared meanings. At the same time, since the society is changing and moving, the more they negotiated with local contexts and their professional values, the more they adjusted and negotiated with their *culture*, keeping it under constant construction. At this point, again it was their consciousness that maintained their attachment to the Vietnamese teacher circle.

*Finally*, Hall argues that 'meaning is what gives us a sense of our own identity' (p. 3), since we construct meaning as we go on. I could see multiple identities within these teachers' overall identity as teachers of English. Their appropriation of being liberated, open and casual and having their own disciplines and order associated more with English, but their resistance to Western behaviour made them closer to a Vietnamese teacher. Moreover, although they shared certain meanings and belonged to a certain culture, it does not mean that they were the same. Within their cultural loop, they were different selves. They had different degrees of appropriation and resistance to being influenced by English and ELT. For example, if Thu was very concerned about changes, suggesting that those changes might become bad habits if one was not aware, then Lien saw her changes as something positive.

From the discussion with these teachers, it was clear to me that they subconsciously aligned themselves with Western teachers in many ways. To begin with, by contrasting Vietnamese people as often picking to pieces others' shortcomings to the indifferent attitudes of Westerners, they indirectly suggested that their exposure to the West made them better. Accordingly, by aligning themselves with the West, they became better. They clearly showed that their learning English and going to the English-speaking West gave them the chance to change positively at least in terms of evaluating other people. Next, they positioned themselves as opposite to Vietnamese teachers who held traditional viewpoints in teaching. They implicitly assumed that many Vietnamese teachers followed traditional teaching methods, which were seen by them as inflexible, strict and stiff as opposed to their liberated, open, interesting and humorous teaching and performing manner. However, they differed themselves from those teachers who adopted unselectively Western values and practised them in their teaching in Vietnam. Also seeing themselves as being somewhat Westernised, they drew a line not to be crossed and created a screen to filter Western values. They really stood in-between Westernised teachers such as the teacher who wore shorts for teaching and teachers in Vietnam. This is a conscious act of constructing identity containing constant negotiation and renegotiation.

To conclude, these teachers' identity formation processes were shaped by tensions, contradiction, fragmentation, fluidity, consistency, accommodation, negotiation and mediation. The Self and the Other were intertwined and correlated. They did not deny one another. These Western-trained teachers often crossed the border to become the Other and got back to be the Self. Their movement between time and space created hybridity, but it maintained the sense of belonging and continuity. Also, their mediation and negotiation of tensions played an essential part in the process. Importantly, not all of them experienced the same tensions. They did not accommodate the tensions similarly, either. This made them different from each other but still belonging to one group, the Western-trained Vietnamese teachers of English.

# Chapter 6
# An EIL Teacher's Identity Formation: Kien

This chapter explores how identity formation takes place at the individual level. Although the processes of identity formation of all these Western-trained Vietnamese teachers of English underwent tensions, contradiction, fragmentation, consistency, fluidity, accommodation, negotiation and mediation, it is not guaranteed that they all experienced the processes in the same way. Hence, it is important to look thoroughly at one teacher's experience to get an insight into the processes.

I decided to explore Kien's case for this purpose for the following reasons. *First*, he appeared to take part in the data collection process enthusiastically, both with interviews and written forms. Therefore, I had rich data about him. *Second*, I observed that in his negotiation of identity he seemed to have more contradictions and fragmentation than the other teachers, though he did not show any obvious tensions. *Third*, he often seemed to make spontaneous judgements in the beginning, and then reasoned his judgements as he went on, either after being challenged by his peers or after realising some pragmatic reasons. Put differently, he had his own way to negotiate his identity, which presented more fragmentation than appeared to be the case for the others. *Finally*, despite obvious fragmentation and contradiction, the way Kien's identity was negotiated and shaped demonstrated connectedness and a sense of belonging, which followed a flow of continuity. This is not to say that others did not experience this. However, in Kien's case, the process to express this was complex and thus seemed to deserve close attention.

Kien's processes of identity formation are told like a story, and I have three stories to tell. Each story places an emphasis on different contexts. Story One looks at Kien's processes of identity formation in a particular one-to-one social context, which is the individual interview with me as the researcher, and in which I focus on the interview as a vehicle for identity formation. Story Two explores these processes in a cultural context with culturally based content. Story Two has two parts. In Part One, the cultural context is Kien's classroom in Vietnam, and the cultural content is a culturally value-laden topic used in Kien's teaching. In Part Two, the cultural context is pubs and bars in Australia, and the cultural content is Vietnamese teacher morality. Story Three investigates these processes in a second kind of social context, in which I focus on the role of multichannel interactions in the process of identity formation, in this case when Kien discussed teachers' roles with his peers in a group interview. These contexts are strong elements in producing identity. This way of story-telling then suggests that identities are shaped by the social and cultural contexts that we experience, and these identities are equally shaped by the contexts within which we express them. At the same time these accounts indicate how identity is shaped dynamically.

## Story One: How Did Kien's Processes of Identity Formation Take Place in the Individual Interview with Me?

This section exemplifies how Kien's processes of identity formation took place in a social context, and in this case in the individual interview with me as the researcher. I acknowledge that I had known Kien as a friend before he participated in this study. Thus, this interview was somewhat like a conversation between two friends who came from very similar intellectual and professional backgrounds. His trust in me as a friend enabled him to talk openly and informally, without me having to ask frequently. This contributed to the construction of his identity, in which the interview in effect acted as a site of identity formation, and the researcher became a catalyst in this process. How his identities were shaped as the interview was going on and how I as researcher was actually instrumental in some of this shaping are presented in the form of a story.

The story tells Kien's experience of studying teaching in Australia after several years of being a teacher in Vietnam. It focuses on his comparisons of teaching and learning styles and the relationship between students and teachers in Australian universities with those in his Vietnamese context. Kien highly appreciated what he had learned from his course in Australia. He saw almost everything in his Master's course as better than what he had undergone in Vietnam. He seemed attracted to the Australian style. However, as the story was being told, his appropriation of, resistance to and reconstitution of new values and practices were also manifested in accordance with his own desires and reasoning. These processes were taking place within a mixture of realities, such as pragmatic factors, Kien's movement in space and time between Vietnam and Australia and his apparently contradictory roles and selves.

## Learning and teaching styles

Kien started his comparison with learning and teaching styles. While comparing these things, Kien was actually defining his position. His experiences in Vietnam were expressed from both a teacher and a student's points of view, whereas his observation in Australia resulted from his being a student there. As a teacher, he saw his students' way of learning as negative and dependent. His point was strengthened when he juxtaposed Vietnamese students with Australian students. He also defined himself as a student in Australia, and he thus saw the value of self-study. He criticised Vietnamese educational practices while appreciating values of Australian independent learning. He appropriated this value and saw it as a good thing he had learned from his studying experience in Australia. This was a site of hybridity, where Kien found himself equipped with a new and better value as he saw it.

Although Kien seemed to appropriate the Australian way of learning and teaching, his appropriation tended to take place within resistance.

It is common sense that students in Australia have more self-study; meanwhile our students (both when I was a student and when I am a teacher) find it difficult to take notes in lectures if a lecturer doesn't read his/her lecture slowly for them to write it down. Our students often wait for lecturers to ask them to take notes. If a lecturer doesn't let students take notes, they don't like him/her because our students often think that having something written down means learning something. And they often fail to take any notes or just have some poorly expressed notes. So when exams come, students normally feel nervous because they have nothing to read, and if a lecturer asks them to read the textbook, they complain that the book is difficult and long to read. Generally speaking, students in Australia have less lecture time but they read more by themselves.

Although Kien was obviously not in favour of the learning habit possessed by students at his university back home, he at the same time gave reasons to excuse the habit, 'because our students often think that having something written down means learning something.' This explanation actually links to his description of how he taught.

Whenever I teach a theory subject, I always give examples and analyse these examples to make sure students understand the nature of any question. With the subject I teach for example, the important thing is that students have to know pronunciation and be able to do it. According to the way we teach in Vietnam, I often read some important lecture notes, so that my students can take notes.

Kien's concern about the aims of education, what counts as knowledge and how one shows one has got it presented more contrasts than consistency. This also demonstrated his resistance while reasoning his appropriation. Regarding pedagogical practices in Vietnam, he criticised the 'passive' and 'dependent' learning habit of students, implying that they possessed little sense of independent learning. But when he moved to describe how he taught, he defended his way of teaching, seeing it as important and necessary. He legitimised his method while still acknowledging the positiveness of training students to be more independent. He apparently wanted to adopt the positiveness of the 'new' way but simultaneously viewed his 'old' way as good and effective. As a student in Australia, Kien had learned how to be independent with his study, but as a teacher in Vietnam, he also knew how to teach appropriately. His negotiation was 'travelling' between himself as a student and himself as a teacher. Also, it was travelling between his 'here' reality in Australia and his 'there' reality in Vietnam. The space and time made his negotiation more complicated and full of contradictions.
Kien continued to compare teaching styles.

> And the teaching style is also different. If in Vietnam, teachers often impose you with their ideas and if you don't follow them you lose your marks, here everything is more open. I can develop my argument in my own way provided that I can support it well.

Although Kien emphasised the 'difference' between the two teaching and learning styles, what echoed here seemed to reflect his attitudes of appropriation. He showed that he had mastered the 'right' way to pursue knowledge, the way that allowed his individuality to flower.
When talking about teaching styles, he actually provided a cultural model of Vietnamese teachers who were socially and politically expected to transfer ideas to students. Teachers are 'knowledge experts' and 'role models'. For the sake of students and the society, students should be guided to a particular set of moral behaviour or normative attitudes. This has been seen as positive, since teachers – also as gardeners – ideally wanted to 'grow healthy trees' both inwardly and outwardly. This also

reveals the importance of the experienced and the old in the society, but at the same time implicitly addresses a concern and belief that the young can only become socially good citizens if they are properly educated and fully guided. This also discourages the development of individualism and personal identities. Therefore, when Kien was a student in Vietnam, he did not have enough freedom to voice his own ideas. He did not realise it until he came and studied in Australia. When he had experienced both, he could compare them. He could clearly see disadvantages of having ideas imposed on him. Thus, when placing the Vietnamese approach next to the Australian one, it is always very tempting to fall in love with the latter because of its openness, freedom and the applause of individualism. Kien was not an exception. As his identity was unchained, his voice and personal creativity could brilliantly blossom.

### The relationships between teacher and student

When Kien talked about the relationship between student and teacher in the two societies, Vietnam and Australia, his dilemma became clearer. His identities were unfastened, fastened and refastened simultaneously and in a multidimensional way.

He contrasted the 'distant' relationship in Vietnam with the equal and free relationship in Australia. On the one hand, he implicitly showed a preference for the latter. But on the other hand, as a Vietnamese teacher, he found himself caught in social norms that determined how teachers should behave with students. Additionally, Kien revealed the fact that because teachers in Vietnam had to work under financial pressure, it was understandable that they could not spend extra time with students. It was not because they did not want to help. It was a matter of maintaining their lives. This implied that teachers in Australia worked in far better conditions than those in Vietnam. Kien actually did not criticise Vietnamese teachers for not offering students more time, what he wanted to say was the hardship of being a teacher and the dispute between dedication to teaching and life management. It was obviously difficult to both devote oneself to teaching and work overtime elsewhere to earn one's living. As an insider, Kien understood the situation deeply. However, he still saw the Australian way as desirable, and he implicitly wished teachers in Vietnam could be offered excellent working conditions and sufficient salaries as are their Australian counterparts.

The relationship between teachers and students in Vietnam is different from that in Australia. Due to Confucianism influences, there is always a distance between students and teachers, except in special cases. Teachers always want to have a distance with students. And so students find it hard to ask teachers about their study. Moreover, in Vietnam our teachers don't spend a lot of time with students because they have to work overtime to earn their livings since their salaries are very low. And if they have to be at uni four to five days a week without being paid higher, they can't manage their lives with such low salaries. Meanwhile, Australian teachers normally stay at uni during weekdays and therefore they can spend more time with students. ... So in Vietnam, normally teachers only spend their lecture time with students and I think this is very limited. And if students want to ask a teacher any extra questions, they often ask during breaks. In contrast, in Australia if students want to ask anything, they just need to make an appointment with a teacher in advance, and then they can talk freely with the teacher.

Kien seemed to realise he might have been too critical at first when comparing the two sets of relationships, as he gradually rationalised his criticisms. His views were shaped and reshaped as he was negotiating and reasoning with his own arguments. As he talked more, unprompted, his views were constantly reconstructed.

Kien first referred to Confucianism, a commonly held ideology, to explain the difference between the two. It sounded common sense, since anyone would feel tempted to associate a particular set of practices with a certain ideology. But then when Kien actually gave reasons why Vietnamese teachers could not spend more time with students, he directed his arguments to pragmatic reality. No matter how Confucianism influenced teachers' practices, what they were facing was the reality. Teachers everywhere would act the same way if they had the same reality. As an insider, Kien understood that and he clearly defined himself as a teacher who wanted to devote more to students but at the same time needed to live. Given this context, even the most fascinating things generated from the Australian ways would do no good to his situation in Vietnam.

In a sense, Kien liked the idea that students could talk freely with teachers. But at the same time he saw the 'distance' as necessary. However, the degree of 'distance' had been reduced and remeasured from its starting point. As a student in Vietnam, Kien felt the distance and when he became a teacher, he still felt it, but he rather took it for granted without actually thinking of how it might affect his relationships with students. Not until he experienced a new set of teacher–student contact, did he automatically sense the comfort of a student enjoying an informal and equal status with teachers in Australia. He apparently wanted to offer his students a similar comfort and enjoyment while he was talking to me. But he could never separate himself from the reality as a teacher in Vietnam, so he again negotiated with his own desire: would he actually bring back something good or just do something unwanted; and if it was good, how would he eventually practise it. Would he do it individually with his classes or would he introduce it to other teachers? He finally came to a conclusion: 'when you are in Rome, do what the Romans do.' That means he had not yet found a way to do what he wanted without alienating himself from the norm.

When asked whether he still showed respect to his Australian teachers the way he did with his Vietnamese ones, Kien again said, 'do what the Romans do.'

> I think 'go to Rome and do what the Romans do.' Of course it depends on individuals, but I think here (in Australia) we don't have to show too much respect. And 'respect' is not just the way you greet your teachers, it is also the way you talk to them, your attitude, etc. It means that you're a student and they're your teachers. I always want other people to respect me and behave properly to me. Of course I don't like my students to call me with my first name as students do here, and therefore I find it impossible to call my teachers in Vietnam with their first names.

Despite Kien's preference for the open and informal teacher–student relationship in Australia, he clearly rejected its appropriacy for Vietnam. He gave the very specific example of calling a teacher by first name. This represents informality and friendliness in Australia but signifies disrespect and impoliteness in Vietnam. As a student, he preferred the Australian way but as a teacher, he felt more comfortable and respected with the Vietnamese way. He did not need to relate this sense of respect to any ideology, but he related it to his own principle, 'I don't like my students to call me with my first name as students do [in Australia].'

Kien's preference for the Australian way and his simultaneous rejection of it suggested his awareness of the negotiation process. He tended to visualise the two worlds of 'here' and 'there' at one time and positioned himself as well as his desire. He simultaneously fastened and unfastened his identities. He observed that in Australia students could be equal and rather overfriendly with teachers, but in Vietnam this needed to occur in moderation. He definitely could be friendly with his students and he expected his students to be friendly with him, but moderately and acceptably friendly. He clearly stated, 'you're a student and they're your teachers', which means students were students, teachers were teachers and they should not be treated as if they were from the same flock. He implied two _'cultural models'_ here: a student and a teacher in the Vietnamese society. As a teacher, one has certain rights and responsibilities. As a student, one has to follow certain rules of respect. Kien also implied the distance and status between teachers and students, or in other words, between the two hierarchies. So as a teacher although Kien wanted to 'borrow' the Australian relationships between teachers and students (he clearly felt part of such practices as a student), he could not deny his status as a teacher in Vietnam. He was also very explicit about how students should behave to him. He could not be the same as them. He was their teacher and thus he should be treated the way a teacher deserved.

His comparisons and explanations about differences in the teacher–student relationships in the two settings presented his ability to control and adjust. He tended to choose a safe and effective way to perform. So the process of negotiation took place in rather complicated ways here. Kien showed his activeness to select the suitable, reject the unsuitable and trans-form them to best serve his context in Vietnam. Put differently, his appro-priation and fastening, unfastening and refastening of identities were under his control, taking place in both 'here' and 'there' with him as both a student studying in Australia and a Vietnamese teacher in most cases.

While talking and making comparisons about learning and teaching styles and the relationship between teacher and student in Vietnam and Australia, Kien was also speculating about how to apply the Australian way to his teaching in Vietnam. He then faced the barriers that caused him to be more realistic.

If teachers want to implement this style, they must be knowledge-able, not everyone can do that, even here [Australia] ... If we want to introduce this style to Vietnam, I think all teachers must follow the Australian teaching methodology. But I think this methodology can't be applied to our universities. I mean ... [thinking] ... because it is impossible that all teachers would do it simultaneously, and if only a small number of teachers [Western-trained ones] do it, students would feel bored and assume that those teachers don't know how to teach. Let's say while other teachers read their lectures for students to passively write down, we [Western-trained ones] in contrast, ask them to read a lot, of course students would complain us. They prefer the other way.

As Kien explained why it was impossible to apply the Australian way to his university in Vietnam, he also showed his resistance. Even though he tried to appropriate this way of teaching, his resistance appeared stronger. He did consider the local circumstances and acknowledged the mismatch of expectations as well as the impracticality and inappropriacy of the Australian way. His explanations revealed his preference for the Australian way but also presented his unwillingness to pursue it.

The most important point is that Kien often tended to criticise ideologies and values embodied in pedagogies before he pointed out that the practices he critiqued were due to the lack of facilities and resources in Vietnam. That meant after negotiating with his reasoning, he always found pragmatic reality the main problem for his teachers and students.

I found Kien always in the process of negotiation with either his own desire or reasoning. His negotiation showed contradictions within his own reasoning. For example, if he began by criticising students for their lack of independent learning, he ended by focusing his criticisms on curriculum and the reality in Vietnam.

> I think one of the reasons why our students can't follow the Australian style is that in Vietnam students have to take so many subjects at one time. They are actually overloaded. In Australia, students have to go to class three or four times a week but our students go to uni all week from 9 a.m. to 5 p.m. Reading references are available here [Australia] so students can find a lot of books themselves, whereas our students still complain even when they have to read only one textbook. The problem is that our students don't have time for reading because they have to learn too much at school. For example, besides specialised subjects, they have to take irrelevant subjects like maths, geography, etc. When I was a student I didn't have to study those 'crazy' subjects.

It was not because Vietnamese students did not want to read more. It was because they had to study many more subjects than their Australian counterparts. They could not afford time and effort to read more. So instead of blaming students for their dependence, Kien was actually empathetic with them. As a teacher in Vietnam, he understood his students and appreciated their effort. This conflicted with his initial criticisms. It could be explained why this happened. At first, he compared everything in Vietnam with what he had experienced in Australia and viewed the latter as the standard, so he tended to appropriate the Australian things while criticising the Vietnamese ones. But then, as he went on to compare and criticise, he realised his students were not to blame. They even had to study harder under more pressure of examinations and curriculum. He also realised teachers in Vietnam had the same story. So his views became softened and part of his criticisms turned into empathy. He obviously became less overwhelmed and less overexcited by the Australian way.

It is clear that although Kien applauded the Australian pedagogies, he was also aware of how pleasant yet how unwanted they were to ELT in Vietnam. His conscious awareness was a result of his negotiations with his values, desires and reasoning.

### The social context: The effect of the researcher on identity formation

The interview in which Kien displayed his fastening and unfastening of aspects of his identities as teacher and learner was dominated by Kien's enthusiastic and emotive accounts of his experiences. My initial question had been 'you've already studied and taught in Vietnam and studied teaching in Australia. Can you tell me about your feelings and experiences on coming back to a student's life?'

The social context of the interview thus invited, implicitly, comparisons between teaching and learning experiences and in different locations. Moreover, because Kien knew I shared his culture and status as a student in Australia, he freely and without further prompting or hesitation, expressed his range of experiences. Little turn-taking was expected in this social situation and few inhibitions or sense of a need for formal explanations seemed to operate in the interview. In this way I feel that the social context of the interview on the one hand elicited the contradictions, unfastening, fastening, appropriation, resistance and negotiation of identity formation and on the other hand gave Kien the freedom to explore his ideas and emotions through reasoning and to express his own uninterrupted accounts of these different moments in his life as teacher and learner.

### Story Two: How Did Kien's Processes of Identity Formation Relate to a Specific Cultural Context and Content?

This story tells how Kien's processes of identity formation related to a specific cultural context and content. In other words, it explores how cultural contexts and contents shape identity formation while taking into account processes of identity fastening, unfastening and refastening.

This story has two parts. Part One presents one example of how Kien's identities were negotiated in the cultural context of Vietnam, where he taught English to his students. Part Two demonstrates how his identities were shaped in the cultural context of Australia, where he, as a Vietnamese teacher, was exposed to Western values. Specifically, how he negotiated his teacher morality in relation to the act of going to pubs and bars in Australia is discussed.

## Part One

In Story One, it is clear that Kien was very much attracted to the Australian way of teaching, although he always negotiated this attraction with his own reasoning, values, pragmatic factors and multiple roles and selves. When he described how he taught English to his students in the cultural context of Vietnam, Kien showed a strong commitment to his Vietnamese teacher role, which overshadowed other identities seen in him in other contexts.

He stated in the individual interview that certain topics should not be open for enthusiastic discussion in the classroom. I hence asked him how he dealt with topics relating to 'romance/love', for example.

> Yeah, it's rather sensitive and quite personal when talking about love because our students often don't feel open to talk about it. It's because in Vietnam people often takes things personally and cares about others' life, so if one says something, others will assume that one's lifestyle is like this or that. I'm myself like that too. If a student in my class talks enthusiastically about love, of course other students will think 'she/he is too open, too easy or too hot, so adventurous, etc.'. And I may also think the same way about the student. If in Australia, people easily say what they think about love and others don't judge their personalities, in Vietnam it's different. They care what you say and then relate it to your personality. I think because love is something normal, something open in Australia, so people don't care. But in Vietnam, it's still not that open.

Kien's identity fastening, unfastening and refastening was evident in the conflict between himself as a teacher of English and himself as a Vietnamese teacher. The conflict was manifested in his awareness of incorporating culture with language in both content and appearance. In other words, he took account of contexts and mediated the global with the local. Interestingly, he located himself quite clearly in the negotiation between the local and the target language's cultural appropriateness. On the one hand, he knew for sure that participating in a discussion about 'love' in an English lesson may have nothing to do with one's own personality or lifestyles. On the other, he still fell into the trap of judging others if they did discuss 'love' with enthusiasm or approached the topic from a different point of view, the view that was not approved by the majority. Still, he felt the majority was the winner and in the right, although the minority was not necessarily wrong nor did it lack moral input. The problem often lay in the way the society thinks and expects its citizens to behave, and Kien was caught up in this. In a group interview later, Kien reinforced this notion that he was heavily affected by what he believed society expects of teachers. When discussing with other Western-trained Vietnamese teachers of English in the group interview the pressures society placed on teachers, Kien was adamant that teachers should not fall in love with students, at least openly. It should be noted here that there is no law or regulation in Vietnam that forbids teachers to fall in love with students at tertiary level. It was Kien who claimed that teachers should not fall in love with students to avoid social judgements or rumours that placed pressure on teachers' personal lives.

Kien's expression about the way he dealt with the topic 'love' in his class called into question the 'lifestyles' which have a great influence on the Vietnamese classroom. Truly, what happens in the classroom reflects what happens in the society, or the former is a zoomed-out picture of the latter. So the Vietnamese teacher in Kien was more attached to the society than the English part. English was just the language in which he and his students talked about the notion of 'love' accepted in the Vietnamese society. Even though English was considered the language of 'more open' societies, discussion in English in the Vietnamese classroom could not neglect Vietnamese social norms. The language could not be used as a mask to get away with personal judgements and social prejudices. This was the conflict of identity that Kien faced. He had to bargain between English – the language he taught – and Vietnamese – the society he lived in. So he performed two duties, those of a teacher of English and a Vietnamese teacher. As the former, he enabled his students to have open discussion so they could practise English. But as the latter, he was both expected and chose to set a limit on 'openness' because he himself could not separate his way of thinking from judging students in an English class. His identity was negotiated and then defined as developing along the lines of a 'core' Vietnameseness, to which he belonged.

It appears that Kien's focus on a single cultural context and value-laden content affected the balance in the contradictory identities he expressed. His emphasis on his Vietnamese teacher identity seems a result of his focus on a particularly culturally value-laden topic – that of 'love' – as a theme for teaching in a Vietnamese classroom. Thus once again, the content of discussion within the interview context and the broader contexts of the two educational cultures affected the ways he talked about his identity.

## Part Two

Studying in Australia, Kien was exposed to Western values and practices, many of which were totally different from what he had experienced in Vietnam. Was he fascinated by these new things? Was he trying to stop himself from being Westernised? Was he negotiating with himself on what to follow and what to stay away from? In one conversation with me when I wanted to clarify some of his points relating to the issue of teacher morality, Kien talked about nightclubs and pubs in Australia and what those places had to do with teacher morality.

Kien showed his curiosity about pubs and bars, since he had only vague ideas what they were like. Yet, at the same time he made up his mind not to have those experiences.

> Sometimes I also wanted to go to a nightclub to see what it is like, but then I decided not to do so. We are teachers. If students in Vietnam know that I go to such places, they would treat me differently. If other Vietnamese teachers who study in Australia go to a nightclub, I wouldn't judge them as bad, but I myself can't do it.

Why? Because he was a teacher and a Vietnamese, and a Vietnamese teacher should not go to those places, which were rumoured in Vietnam to be places of unhealthy and ill-cultured behaviours and activities. Although he realised that nightclubs and pubs in Australia may be different, he still did not find the courage and daringness to explore that experience. He explained to me that as a teacher, he felt uneasy to be in such places. He was afraid of being caught and judged by others as a bad teacher. In his thinking, it seemed that everybody knew he was a teacher, particularly he thought his students were watching over his shoulder. Kien did care what other people thought, particularly when what they thought might have bad effects on his teaching profession and values. His own desire or curiosity was controlled by his professional values. In other words, his profession set rules and limits for his personal acts. He took on what others thought about him. His identity was partly formed by the society's expectation, and this even won over his personal desire. So, even though he was in Australia, away from home and social norms, he still chose to perform his Vietnamese 'teacher' self.

Moreover, the 'here' and 'there' reality and the Vietnamese teacher part in him held him back. He could not escape from the real world. He obviously restricted his freedom, reasoning himself into not doing certain things, as a Vietnamese teacher. Thereby, although he was in Australia, he still felt he was watched and judged by unseen faraway but powerful norms. The Vietnamese part in him made him stay with reality instead of flying with fantasy, which possibly led to unwanted results, as he admitted.

Kien also used 'We' when he reminded me that 'we are teachers'. He seemed to include me in his circle and seek my solidarity with his decision. He also implied that I would act in the same way if I were him. Although he tried to appropriate some Western individual freedom, he still found it very foreign to him. On the one hand, he wanted to have more freedom, but on the other, when it came to his turn to 'enjoy' the freedom, he resisted it and chose to stick to his own values. He felt safer to do so.

The above example demonstrates that Kien's strong sense of being a Vietnamese teacher affected the way he negotiated his multiple identities. The fact that he was in Australia made his Vietnamese identity more important and solid to him. He seemed to feel more Vietnamese, as he was in Australia. The content 'teacher morality' too added more weight to his negotiation of identities. As a teacher he talked about teacher morality, and this clearly strengthened his awareness of being a teacher. Once again, contexts and content affected the ways Kien talked about his identity.

## Story Three: How Did Kien's Processes of Identity Formation Take Place in Group Iinterview?

This story tells how Kien's identities were shaped by interacting with his peers in a group interview. Kien participated in the group interview with two other teachers, Linh and Vy. Three of them had known each other rather well, and Linh was a quite close friend of Kien, while Kien and Vy were acquaintances. Thus, in a sense the interview was like a discussion or a conversation among friends.

It should be noted that although I had also known Kien as a friend before he participated in this study, the relationship between him and me was different from that between him and Linh. While I knew him more as an acquaintance, Linh and Kien were friends in both the professional and social environments. Hence, the way Kien presented himself to me in the individual interview was very different from the way he did so in the group interview with his friends, although both occasions involved interactions. This very difference plays an essential role in how Kien's identities were presented and negotiated.

This story focuses on how Kien perceived his role as a moral guide. In order to reveal how his identities were shaped in this context, I first talk about how he perceived his enactment of this role when he talked to me in the individual interview, then how he negotiated this role with his peers is discussed.

In the individual interview with me, Kien both implicitly and explicitly acknowledged that he played a role of a 'moral guide' with his students. As discussed earlier in this book, when a teacher is a 'moral guide', he/she needs to be proper in every way, including the way he/she plays the role. When Kien was talking with me, what I noticed was his consciousness of playing the role. For example, Kien reported that he often shared with students his thinking and what was important to him. In discussing teachers' responsibilities with students in Vietnam, he said:

> as a language teacher, it is necessary to share with students our conceptions of a particular issue, let them know what is right and what is wrong, or share with them how responsible we need to be with each group of people.

He also described how he reacted when he was not happy with his students' behaviour. For example, to show his anger or dissatisfaction with his students when they did not listen to his lectures properly, he either kept silent and stopped his lessons or reminded them of the importance of the subject. His students then would know how to perform more properly. He said that students were all grown-up, it was not necessary to be mad at them or to teach them how to behave explicitly. He normally reminded them of what they should do to benefit themselves and to respect his lectures in order to obtain something out of each lesson.

I interpreted his behaviour as proper acts as socially and professionally expected from an ideal teacher in Vietnam. However, in the group interview, when Kien, Linh and Vy discussed teacher values in Vietnam, I saw a different Kien.

Having listened to Linh's and Vy's perceptions of teacher values, Kien reported that he tended to absorb teacher values embedded in social norms and made them his own values. He admitted that he tried to perform teacher in light of these norms, as he saw their necessity and positiveness.

> I think values attached to teaching come from many sides, but mostly from social norms. For example in Vietnam, a teacher needs to set good examples for students in many ways. We have to follow the

norms because if we don't, or misbehave, we will become eccentric and people will say we're not teachers. Teachers are expected to be good at both knowledge and morality, then we have to follow these norms. Of course there are other things influencing teachers' values, but I think social norms play the main role.

In my opinion, these social norms are generally good and reasonable, because they are not made up by one person but drawn from generation to generation.

At this point, Kien still talked ideologically, which was no different from the way he talked to me in the first interview. Kien still appeared to act on these norms and at the same time tried to make these norms part of his teacher values. He showed his willingness to be tied to the social norms, and thus to develop himself in accordance with these norms.

Linh and Vy continued to extend their points as well as Kien's points, and Kien concluded that:

It's good to follow these socially constructed norms. But the problem is to what extent we can follow them. It doesn't mean that we can perfectly follow all the norms. If so we were gods, not human. For example, although it is expected that teachers mustn't scold students harshly but I still do it [laughing]. But I do it just for students' sake. I want to make them study. If I am irresponsible, then I won't care, but I'm not.

Linh and Vy did not agree with Kien's example. Linh challenged Kien, saying 'what kind of teacher are you, you always scold students.' Kien replied to Linh the way he did to someone who knew him so well, 'so what? I scold them because I want them to be better.' Linh and Vy said there were other and proper ways to do it, and scolding was not at all acceptable. The way Linh challenged Kien and replied to him suggested that Kien was notorious for being harsh with students.

Only at that moment did I realise that Kien himself 'offered' to reveal his 'hidden' identities. He could not just talk ideologically any more. He was being watched and judged by Linh, so he could not afford to present himself the way he did to me. He did not wait for Linh to unveil this aspect of his teacher identities. It appeared that she had known his scolding of students so well that he had to say it first, and he admitted it both boldly and humorously. It looked as if he shifted his identities suddenly but this shift appeared to be very smooth and natural by his taking a proactive role in doing it. Also, it was clear that he tended to take on the identity others constructed for him, that of 'scolding students'. He saw it as part of his teacher identity.

Again, the social context of the group interview, the topic discussed, the interactions among Kien, Linh and Vy and their relationships affected the ways Kien negotiated his identities. Although he talked about teacher values ideologically, the way he performed teacher was not at all ideal, as he and his peers saw it. I was not able to know this aspect of his identities in our one-to-one interview, but this multichannel interaction enabled me to see it. This indicates that identities are equally shaped by the contexts within which we express them.

## Discussion and Conclusions

The above three stories present Kien's processes of identity formation in various social and cultural contexts. The ways he expressed and negotiated his identities were vastly influenced by those contexts, and in each context Kien's identities were expressed and negotiated differently. For example, when he was in the individual interview with me, he appeared more as a confident professional who enthusiastically talked about his range of experiences of teaching in Vietnam and studying in Australia. When he revealed how he handled topics related to 'love' in a Vietnamese classroom, his identity as a Vietnamese teacher became dominant and came to the fore, while other identities stayed silent. However, when he was discussing teacher values with his peers, he seemed to show his awareness of being challenged and judged by them. He thus tended to identify himself in accordance with what others usually thought of him, how they represented him (Pennycook, 1998; Said, 1978), in this case, as 'scolding students harshly'. All of these examples indicate how identity is shaped dynamically through work practices in a particular social context (Farrell, 2000). They also suggest that identities are shaped by the social and cultural contexts that we experience, and these identities are equally shaped by the contexts within which we express them (Gee, 1999; Hall, 1997a, b; Phan Ngoc, 1998).

Despite the differences in the ways Kien dealt with the contradictions, fastening, unfastening and refastening of his identities, his sense of himself as an appropriately moral teacher in Vietnamese terms is a consistent feature of his accounts of himself and forms an important part of what he presented as his core identity. His awareness of his felt identities and identities constructed for him by others and his control of his relation to the various contexts contributed to the fluidity in his negotiation.

His identities were shaped, negotiated and reconstructed by identification of himself in relation to others and their representations of him (Woodward, 1997), by his fastening and unfastening (Reed, 2001) and by his claiming a Vietnamese national identity which guaranteed his belonging despite his exposure to Western modes of thinking and pedagogical practices (Phan Ngoc, 1998; Tran Ngoc Them, 1999, 2001a, c). His choice to retain his Vietnamese teacher values contributed to constructing this national identity and strengthening it (Phan Ngoc, 1998). That Kien's statements were often full of conflicts with his own reasoning suggested fragmentation in his identity. This is the main difference between Kien's and the other teachers' ways of self identification. While the other teachers appeared to be quite consistent and coherent in their expressions of their identities, Kien seemed to experience obvious fragmentation and contradictions in presenting himself.

However, the way he reasoned his statements and how he performed teacher (as he reported) indicated consistency and fluidity. Some of his performances were against the social norms of teachers in Vietnam, such as scolding students harshly, but the responsible teacher in him appeared to function consistently. Additionally, this very identity among the multiple identities manifested in his accounts demonstrated connectedness and continuity, which made Kien's identities coherent. He scolded students because he wanted them to learn for their own sake. This act seemed to contrast with his claim to be a morally good teacher, since it was not considered 'proper' by the society and the teaching profession. However, all of these seemingly fragmented and contradictory identities were well connected by a thread, which was called responsibility and teacher's conscience noticed in Kien. Despite fragmentation and contradiction, Kien's identity developed along the lines of a coherent growth (Phan Ngoc, 1998; Tran Ngoc Them, 1999, 2001a, c).

To conclude, Kien's identity formation processes were fluid, fragmented, appropriating, resisting, contradictory and conflictive, but nevertheless involved a sense of belonging, connectedness, continuity and a strong sense of a Vietnamese national identity.

*Chapter 7*

# Teacher Identity and the Teaching of English as an International Language

## Introduction

At the moment, sitting in front of the computer, thinking of what to write to close this chapter, I feel really confused. I am writing in English, not Vietnamese. Yes, I have been writing in English for so long because it is the very means of communication that makes me understood by the outside world. But at the same time, it is not my mother tongue, so it makes it harder for me to naturally think in it. And I think around.

Thinking of my flight home with Malaysia Airlines and a two-day stop-over in Kuala Lumpur, I feel eager. There, I will see some of my friends again after more than two years. How can we communicate with each other? English, thanks to it we can be friends. How wonderful it is to know English! We, people from different parts of the world, totally strangers, have now become closer because we all have a shared language, English. Yes, English has its own bad images, but it also has many good images that make every one of us feel good at least one time when we can talk to a person coming from a different country.

Thinking about the film *Chicken Run*, I burst out laughing when I remember the cock from America, who suddenly found himself surrounded by strange hens, asking those hens, 'Is that English what you're speaking?' Definitely, English is deliberately advertised as a world language. Thinking about the story told by a friend that the English text-book she used to teach her students was filled with racial discrimination, in which people found pictures of a slave being an African, a housekeeper being an Asian and a happy retired person being an Anglo, I feel somewhat uncomfortable. Thinking about the inappropriacy and problems of ethics of English and ELT, I realise that I am now fully aware of how I should develop a course on TESOL/ELT for postgraduate students in

178

Vietnam and how I should write English exam papers for my undergraduate students there too. I also think hard on how to empower my own students in Australia and in those countries where I will teach.

I want to see TESOL courses give students opportunities to be engaged in postcolonial theories. These theories, as discussed throughout the book, can be used as a vehicle for critical literacy, in particular for TESOL teachers. One way of doing this is having explicit discussions about the teacher's role in TESOL classes, where students come from many different cultural backgrounds. They need to be given the chance to express their perceptions of themselves as teachers through class activities, such as group discussions and teacher–student discussions. Students should not be left to reflect on the application of theory to their roles in their own contexts by themselves. Rather, explicit debate about these roles needs to be encouraged, and this needs to be included in teaching units.

In order for this suggestion to better serve TESOL students, it is important that TESOL curricula should be pervaded with critical literacy. Theories that have given the Self a comfortable position need to be presented to students for challenging and questioning. Likewise, students also need to be introduced to theories that have defined them as a particular group of people, for example 'Asian students' or 'non-native teachers of English'. They need to have opportunities to discuss these matters critically in class and in written tasks. Local and international students then would understand and appreciate each other better.

I continue my thinking. Thinking of the publications I have had and the papers I have given at international conferences, I know that at least I have presented myself well in English and in ways that are meaningful to me and my values. At this moment, I do not think of English as an imperial language or the language of power, instead, I think of it as a friendly language that makes the huge world a small village. I think of English as the language of common understanding among scholars, the language that we can appropriate to reflect our bilingual/multilingual minds and multiple practices. Thinking of the claim that non-Western academics are admitted to the sacred halls of international publishing only if they learn to play by Western rules, I actually think otherwise. Writing in different languages and thinking in a bilingual/multilingual mind is one way of enriching the world. This very characteristic owned by the vast majority of World TESOL professionals should be seen as their strength and power instead of as deficit and disadvantage. This could be incorporated in TESOL courses. Specifically, to better serve English users, it is important that TESOL discourse both acknowledges the multiplicity of ways of viewing the world and incorporates these ways in its whole repertoire. The TESOL curriculum thus needs to look at different practices and values through the lenses of more than one perspective. This benefits both TESOL providers and its users. While TESOL providers can enrich and broaden their understanding of multiple theoretical bodies of knowledge, TESOL users can better represent themselves and hence can participate more actively in TESOL activities at all levels.

Thinking of the obvious tensions in the ways my colleagues, students and I had to negotiate while experiencing apparently contradictory roles and selves expected and resisted in TESOL courses, I recommend explicit on-going orientations about changing senses of self be introduced in TESOL courses. This practice needs to be done before, during and after a course of study. These orientations should act as an arena for TESOL students to express and exchange their perceptions of their identities. For example, before commencing their course, TESOL students can be divided into groups, and each group maintains on-going contacts among its members, through means such as focus-group discussions. In such discussions, they will talk about how they identify themselves as teachers and learners of English, and how their views change as they go on with their course. Those focus groups will have a channel, by which they can give feedback to teaching staff. They may also choose to have a mentor or liaison person who can act as a bridge to staff on their requests to deal with issues that affect their identities negatively.

Thinking of what Vy said to me in one interview that she had never had any chance to reflect on her own teacher self that explicitly and that she thanked me for asking her to talk and write about her being a teacher of English, I have realised how important it is for TESOL students to 'communicate' their identities. I hence suggest that by encouraging TESOL students to write about identity, we can help raise their awareness of their own identities and this would help them negotiate their identities in a way that serves their development. Moreover, it would further inform lecturers in their growing understanding of the users of English whom they teach.

Thinking of the unpleasant experience Thu, Chi, Lien and Trang had with the unit on 'English as a global language' in their MA course and thinking of why these teachers refused to behave in the same way as 'the Australian students' would do in classes (Phan Le Ha, 2007), I see the need to make the TESOL classroom a site of mutual understanding. As addressed in this book, the TESOL classroom serves as a site of identity formation and we can control its context to some extent; what we need to do more is to make it a site of respectful and open interchange of ideas. Together with explicitly introducing postcolonial theories to students, this could be achieved by encouraging students to form multinational groups. These groups would then reflect on identity-related issues in the class in a respectful and open manner.

And I think more. Acting as the language of international communication (McKay, 2002; Rajagopalan, 2004), English has enabled me to extend the multiplicity of my positioning in the world and the multiplicity of conceptual tools to research into this complicated issue of identity formation. Importantly, the cultural politics of English as an international language has enabled me to bring two completely different bodies of knowledge, the Vietnamese and the Western, together in this book. One complements and harmonises with the other to best understand the complicated and sophisticated processes of identity formation of Western-trained Vietnamese teachers of English. The international status of English helps me introduce Vietnamese philosophies as equally valid conceptual theories for research and knowledge development to many others, to whom Western scholarships seem to be the only valid tools of inquiries.

Given what has been addressed and discussed in the previous chapters, I now argue for the understanding of these Western-trained EIL Vietnamese teachers' identity in relation to 'core' identities and locality, together with viewing it in light of multiplicity and mobility. I also affirm that identity and difference walk hand in hand, and both are multifacetedly constructed and reconstructed. Identity depends on and responds to contexts, and hence is context-driven. Teacher-as-moral guide, a socially, culturally and professionally constructed notion of what it means to be a teacher in Vietnam, appears to be the most important factor holding together these teachers' multiple identities. In parallel with my arguments about identity, this chapter challenges postcolonial theories of Self and Other in how their ways of shaping identity according to dichotomies may fail to unpack processes of accommodation, negotiations, renegotiations, fastening, unfastening and refastening of these teachers' identity formation.

## The Construction of the Vietnamese Identity – the Core Identity – alongside Multiple Identities

The Western-trained EIL Vietnamese teachers experienced changes in their identities as a result of their exposure to a new context with different cultural and pedagogical practices, but they seemed to negotiate their identities on the basis of 'dominant' identities. These consisted of Vietnamese national/cultural identity, Vietnamese teacher and Vietnamese student. These are the very identities that provided them with strong foundations and commitments, on which they asserted all their identities.

These teachers negotiated their Vietnamese identities alongside their multiple identities. They identified themselves with different groups, such as Australian lecturers, Vietnamese students, Vietnamese teachers of English, Vietnamese teachers and Western-trained teachers, and acknowledged changes in their identities. However, they insisted on holding on to their 'existing' and persisting Vietnamese values. They suggested the notion of 'existing' values, which I interpret as a sense of connectedness in their fluid negotiation of values, instead of as a single stable entity.

Although these teachers' identities were constructed in different sets of relations and interrelations, what appeared dominant was their strong sense of belonging. For example, Kien's identities were shaped, negotiated and reconstructed by identification of himself in relation to others and their representations of him (Woodward, 1997), by his fastening and unfastening (Reed, 2001) and by his claiming a Vietnamese national identity which guaranteed his belonging despite his exposure to Western modes of thinking and pedagogical practices (Phan Ngoc, 1998; Tran Ngoc Them, 1999, 2001a, c). His choice to retain his Vietnamese teacher values contributed to constructing this national identity and strengthening it (Phan Ngoc, 1998). Another example is Linh's argument of the 'out there' Vietnamese cultural values. Vietnamese cultural values were something 'out there', available and inside her, something immutable that she would never lose, no matter how she grew or developed. By using the word 'lose' and the expression 'there's no way we can lose our cultural values', Linh assumed that Vietnamese people possessed the same values, the Vietnamese values. A Vietnamese identity became visible and it was named 'cultural values'. Also, Linh's descriptions and expressions of herself and her teaching values showed that she was open to some practices but conservative on others, and what influenced her decision was her Vietnamese identity, which she strongly stated she would never lose. This gave her a sense of belonging and continuity in her teacher self formation.

Through their identity formation, the Vietnamese teachers constructed a national/cultural identity, which strongly supports Phan Ngoc's (1998), Tran Ngoc Them's (1999, 2001a, c) and Tran Quoc Vuong's (2000) arguments of national/cultural identity as one united element and a core sense of 'wholeness', which each Vietnamese should maintain and develop. Also, this helps challenge the argument that identity does not involve a sense of a core value (Hall & du Gay, 1996).

Although the teachers' fluid negotiations of their multiple identities also suggest the notion of hybridity in their identity formation, hybridity was obtained on the basis of some core Vietnamese identities and the sense of 'Vietnamseness'. Thus, hybrid identities are understood as reconstituted identities which enjoy dynamic change and fluid movements rather than fragmentation. Hybrid identities are not necessarily different identities.

They are, rather, new identities constructed within negotiation and aware-ness of change and the sense of resistance which incorporates both appro-priation and reconstitution, as discussed in Chapters 2 and 3. The teachers held on to the sense of 'Vietnameseness' to negotiate changes in their hybrid identities and maintain the sense of belonging.

The teachers constantly constructed their identities as they went through different stages of their exposure to the English-speaking West. Their identities continued to be shaped and reshaped, as they negotiated their existing values with other new values. They tended to present them-selves through their multiple identities, which seemed to hold on together on the basis of a shared professional and national identity. This suggested a sense of continuity in their identity formation processes, despite the obvious tensions, contradictions and fragmentation they experienced in the movement in space and time between Vietnam and the English-speaking West. Above all, their sense of Vietnameseness seemed to influ-ence all their processes of identity formation, and in each process, they constructed and reconstructed the Vietnamese identity.

The way the teachers constructed their multiple identities with constant references to their Vietnamese identity confirms and supports the role of place-based identities in identity formation (Lin, 2002). This also consoli-dates the complex and multifaceted interrelationship and interdepen-dence between mobility and identity. Truly, despite the teachers' mobility, locality or place of origins, in this case Vietnam, plays a significant role in their transnational identity formation. This affirms that place-based iden-tity is one of the many fundamental forces operating behind the scene of mobility, and it is mobility that offers the ground for place-based identity to assert itself.

Let me now come back to Holliday's (2005) suggestion of adopting 'cul-tural continuity as a solution to native-speakerism' (p. 157) embedded in every aspect of TESOL. I would like to argue that while this positioning offers useful grounds for understanding the struggles to teach English as an international language by certain groups of World TESOL profes-sionals, it seems to ignore other TESOL professionals whose professional identities are significantly influenced by their national and cultural identi-ties. These TESOL professionals may well construct their identities along-side some core identities which are necessarily culture-driven or locality-driven, as the Western-trained EIL Vietnamese teachers referred to throughout this book did. What is more important to them is the sense of belonging, connectedness and continuity attached to their strongly felt Vietnameseness, rather than a vague 'global' umbrella seen through the lenses of cultural continuity.

## Morality in Teacher Identity Formation

The notion of morality played an important part in the teachers' professional identity formation. Morality became an identity filter, through which they grouped themselves and others. Their negotiations often came down to their perceptions of morality and how to demonstrate morality, so as to measure one identity up against the other. Although they showed certain resistance to new values as teachers of English, a foreign language, they demonstrated an awareness of such values, which in collaboration with their existing values gave them an identity – Vietnamese teachers of English. They negotiated their identities along the lines of morality and moral values embedded in their cultural and professional practices. They presented a strong sense of self as teacher in relation to morality and the cultural model of the moral guide role. This integral part of their identities was consciously maintained and fostered. This part also played the role of a core identity, based on which their multiple identities held together.

As discussed earlier, their teacher identities were clearly subjected to pressures and tensions for change in the new context, and these pressures and tensions were negotiated on the basis of their 'dominant' identities, and along the lines of their persisting identities, which all made their Vietnameseness hold firm. The notion of morality appeared to play a significant role in these teachers' identity formation. Morality-related identities were the very identities that the teachers relied on to negotiate the pressures and tensions caused by their exposure to the new context. They were also elements that maintained the fluidity, continuity and the sense of connectedness in the processes of identity formation. In the same way, they guaranteed the sense of simultaneity of space and time – Vietnam and the English-speaking West, here and there, now and then, past, present and future. They made the processes of transnationality, hybridity and mobility, which were discussed in Chapter 2, fluid and continual, taking into account the specificity of both locality and time (Crang *et al.*, 2003; Lin, 2002; Werbner, 2001).

These teachers saw themselves as moral guides and morality demonstrators. Even if much else around them was more dynamically shaped, their perceptions of this role remained more or less non-negotiable. Despite their being teachers of English and their studying in Australia, Britain and the US, these morality-related identities remained quite stable and were not open for negotiation as compared to many other identities perceived by the teachers. Morality and ethics were seen by the teachers as criteria to differentiate Western and Vietnamese values.

Why these teachers' morality-related identities were consciously maintained and fostered is partly supported by how absolute this moral sentiment in Vietnamese society has always been, and how it has been developed since the early socialisation of the Vietnamese people, as discussed in Chapter 1.

These Western-trained Vietnamese teachers of English always saw themselves as moral guides, no matter where they were. This moral sentiment has been consolidated and encouraged by Vietnamese society's respect and love for teachers and the teaching profession. The rules and regulations of the demonstration of morality by teachers also support teachers' awareness of their responsibility for providing moral education to students. Vietnamese (educational) philosophies have been the cradle that nurtures and flourishes moral values in teaching in Vietnam.

These teachers' perceptions of teacher morality and ethics showed the human side of the concepts. Morality and ethics may be thought of as strict rules, regulations and inflexible sets of behaviour, and teachers may be forced to follow them. But in their expressions, these concepts appeared to be attached to the heart, to come from the heart and to be different from 'dry' norms. It is the close association of morality and ethics with teachers' images that gives them an identity. That was why the teachers emphasised these icons in their discussion of teacher identity. Society 'pictures' them as teachers by expecting them to practise teachers' values, and they make themselves teachers by conforming to these values and making them their own property – teachers' property. Both society and the teachers themselves fastened their identities and thus gave them an insider status. Also, these values and their negotiation of identities make them Vietnamese teachers, who both teach knowledge and demonstrate morality.

These Western-trained Vietnamese teachers of English had always been well aware of the necessity and responsibility to address morality in their teaching. This supports Johnston's (2003) arguments for the role of morality and values in ELT, which, as the author shows, has been neglected and left out of the TESOL field. Particularly, for English to become an international language which serves its users effectively and morally, that teachers as moral agents are vital to the negotiations, mediations, appropriation, resistance and reconstitutions of values and identities. Moreover, these teachers' perceptions of the role of a teacher show that in the context of mobility, transnationality and the dominance of the Western academy, the role of teachers as moral guides becomes the most powerful element in the processes of teacher identity formation that bind Vietnamseness and give these Vietnamese teachers a sense of belonging, continuity and connectedness. This role operates as the moral foundation on which new elements are interpreted, negotiated, resisted and reconstituted.

## Identity Fastening, Unfastening and Refastening

Identity fastening, unfastening and refastening (Reed, 2001) occurred quite consistently in these teachers' identity formation processes. Importantly, their identity refastening was more like the reconstitution of identity, which suggested the construction of hybrid identities in many theorists' terms (for example, Bhabha, 1994; Hallward, 2001; Hiddleston, 2004; Pennycook, 2001; Werbner, 2001). Their identity fastening, unfastening and refastening suggest a notion of hybridity that is critical and useful for recognition and appreciation of difference and cultural creativity, not a notion that denies the right to be different (Werbner, 2001). This notion of critical hybridity involves a new awareness of and new take on the dynamics of group formation and social inequality (Nederveen Pieterse, 2001). It also embraces the sense of agency, ambivalence and third spaces (Bhabha, 1994), in which third spaces should not be understood as bounded, fixed spaces. Rather, these third spaces are subjected to constant dynamic formation and re-formation, and fluid movements within these spaces are closely linked to 'first spaces' with an awareness of 'second spaces' to form third spaces of dynamic change, continuity and connectedness (Duong Thieu Tong, 2002; Phan Ngoc, 1998; Tran Ngoc Them, 1999, 2001a, c).

As discussed earlier, the notion of morality is the essential element in determining these fluid and continual identity formation processes. That was why despite apparently contradictory roles, selves and tensions in negotiating these roles and selves, these teachers fastened, unfastened and refastened their identities in relation to morality-related images of the teacher perceived by Vietnamese culture. Being seen and treated with respect, these teachers tended to both behave as expected and act to consolidate their images. 'A teacher should be like this or that' seemed to be a motto for them and they fastened, unfastened and refastened their identities accordingly to be included in the teacher circle, as well as to be seen as teachers by others. Identity fastening, unfastening and refastening seemed to take place along the lines of certain 'core' identities assumed to be possessed by teachers.

To a large extent, these teachers showed their obvious compromise to become good teachers, as pictured and expected by society and their own wishes. Nevertheless, their compromises embodied tensions. Even though they had to or offered to give priorities to the professional in most cases, it did not guarantee that they were happy with their decisions. Whether the personal or the professional should dominate made them negotiate constantly. Such negotiations both enabled and suppressed tensions. So, together with compromises, tensions became an inevitable factor in the negotiation process between the personal and the professional. This was confirmed when Linh, Vy and Kien expressed in one group interview how teachers' personal lives in Vietnam were heavily interfered with by norms, ethics and social prejudices. For example, Linh suggested that teachers' personal lives should not be too closely watched. In other words, they should be more liberated. Society and others should not just look at teachers' lives to judge them and put pressure on them. However, these teachers still insisted on preserving and promoting teacher morality, conscience and social conventions, but argued that teachers' lives should not be confined to these criteria only. In the light of these perceptions, they fastened, unfastened and refastened their identities to reshape their teacher identities and make this an ongoing process.

When Thu, Chi, Lien and Trang discussed the unethical sides of 'English as a global language', I can see their multiple identities. Their Vietnamese identity came to the fore, while their identity as teacher of English stayed in the background when they together fought against stereotypes about Vietnam. But the latter became stronger when they faced negative examples of ELT in Vietnam. Their identity as non-native teachers of English became predominant when their classmates shared their feelings. Their identity as teachers of English who enjoyed an equal status to teachers from any other country appeared strong when they denied the fixity of representation. When they talked together, it seemed that they found themselves stronger and more unified as one group who shared a unitary identity. This identity could be a hybrid one, a mixture of their multiple identities, but most importantly it gave them power to assert themselves and evaluate their Master's course critically. These teachers constantly fastened and unfastened their identities to create this power, which ran throughout the fluidity of their hybrid identities. This supports Bhabha's (1994) arguments of hybridity, ambivalence and liminal space, which equip these teachers with the agency and power to resist the unethical practices of English as a global language and to recreate and strengthen their cultural/national identities.

These teachers' hybrid identities did not merely mean 'new' identities. Instead, these identities were negotiated and reconstructed in a way that took into account both the 'being' and the 'becoming' of identity, in which the 'being' seemed to dominate. This, again, supports the Vietnamese authors' arguments about identity, wherein they believe in the dominant 'being' of identity as compared with its 'becoming'. The teachers' identity fastening, unfastening and refastening processes reflected this notion of hybridity, 'being' and 'becoming'. These processes take place 'simultaneously and in multidimensional ways' (Reed, 2001: 329), and they are always progressive processes.

Another important argument in relation to processes of identity fastening, unfastening and refastening is that these teachers showed a high degree of control, adjustment and negotiations in these processes. For example, Kien's comparisons and explanations about differences in the teacher–student relationship between Vietnamese and Australian universities presented his ability to control and adjust. Kien showed his aptness to select the suitable, reject the unsuitable and transform them to best serve his context in Vietnam. His appropriation and fastening, unfastening and refastening of identities were under his control, taking place both 'here' and 'there' and 'now' and 'then' with him as both a student studying in Australia and a Vietnamese teacher in most cases. One more example was the shifts of identities manifested in four teachers' (Thu, Chi, Lien and Trang) identity formation. Simultaneously, they aligned themselves with Western lecturers in terms of 'not taking things personally', defined themselves as Vietnamese teachers who demonstrated morality and strongly opposed those Western-trained Vietnamese teachers of English who brought home unacceptable Western values and practices, such as the one who wore shorts to class.

That these teachers presented a high degree of control, adjustment and negotiations in their fastening, unfastening and refastening of identities supports the tendency in postcolonial theories that seeks to investigate the question of agency, active resistance and reconstitution from the so-called Other, such as the work of Canagarajah (1999), Chakrabarty (2000) and Djebar (as presented by Hiddleston, 2004).

## Identity and Difference

These Western-trained Vietnamese teachers constructed their identities in relation to difference from others (Wodak *et al.*, 1999; Woodward, 1997). The notions of 'us' and 'them' were often brought into their negotiation. The notions of 'us' and 'them' are not necessarily created by the way I asked questions, nor are they a product of deliberate positioning. Rather, they are in part functions of the tasks these teachers were undertaking in Vietnam and the English-speaking West. Within fluid processes of fastening, unfastening and refastening, and within constant moments of contradiction, fragmentation and negotiation, there was a strong tendency to construct their identities in relation to similarities and differences perceived through cultural lenses. Very importantly, although they constructed their identities in binary terms in relation to Western lecturers and other Western-trained teachers, they always negotiated and reconstructed these identities on the basis of the very 'core' Vietnamese morality-related identities. This guaranteed their sense of belonging, their difference as Vietnamese teachers and their attachment to the commitment to demonstrate morality.

Although the construction of identity in relation to difference has been criticised as another form of essentialism (Windschuttle, 1999), the ways these teachers constructed and reconstructed their identities both utilised the necessity of essentialising and used essentialisation as a means of affirming their agency and power to resist, reserve and reconstitute. This is further supported by the discussion in the following section on challenging postcolonial notions of Self and Other. It should be noted that for these teachers to essentialise and avoid being essentialised, teacher morality and morality-related identities appeared to be the decisive elements.

## Challenging Postcolonial Notions of Self and Other

Interestingly, although these teachers essentialised their identities and others' identities to a certain extent, they actively resisted being essentialised. On the one hand, they both consciously and subconsciously identified themselves in relation to others, such as Australian lecturers, the West, non-Western-trained teachers of English and teachers of Russian. But on the other hand, they constructed their identities by moving fluidly and dynamically alongside those others' identities. They insisted on the right to be different and actively constructed the differences, but at the same time appeared to be open to negotiations. In other words, their boundaries were not fixed, and both 'organic' and 'intentional' hybrid identities (Bakhtin, 1981, cited in Werbner, 2001) were present in their identity formation. This suggests that postcolonial notions of Self and Other (such as those discussed by Pennycook, 1998; Phillipson, 1992; Said, 1978) do not work efficiently enough for these teachers' identity formation to be understood. Clear-cut dichotomies of Self and Other in fact simplify the question of identity and thus fail to acknowledge the fluid processes of identity formation.

Postcolonial notions of Self and Other, I argue, need to treat identity formation in light of other critical notions, such as the West, transnationality, mobility and hybridity. These notions, as discussed in many recent postcolonial writings (Chakrabarty, 2000; Crang *et al.*, 2003; Hallward, 2001; Hickling-Hudson *et al.*, 2004; Hiddleston, 2004; Ingham & Warren, 2003; Lal, 2002; Lin, 2002), have closed the gaps in identity formation caused by the dichotomy of Self and Other. They have also encouraged new ways of looking at identity formation, ways that have not necessarily come from the West and Western assumptions of the divided world of East and West, North and South and colonising Self and colonised Other.

Because postcolonial scholarship pays tremendous attention to the West and the Western academy without committing itself to engaging with universals and non-Western theories as well as taking into account cultural and historical difference (Chakrabarty, 2000; Ingham & Warren, 2003), the colonised Other is consequently a product of the imagination of the colonising Self. The Self's imagination backed by the assumed superiority of the West (the Self) is so powerful that images of the Other have been seen as 'truths'. What has been discussed in this book so far, together with the support of recent critical postcolonial theories (such as Charkrabarty, 2000; Hickling-Hudson *et al.*, 2004; Ingham & Warren, 2003), has indicated that postcolonial notions of Self and Other in many ways have in fact served the dominance of the West and masked the Other's power to resist and represent themselves in their own voices. Also, these notions often fail to acknowledge the Other's active resistance and reconstitution of their hybrid identities which incorporate agency, creativity, fluidity, negotiations, accommodations, continuity, dynamic change and connectedness.

Postcolonial theories have been criticised for their focus on modernity, which sees colonial modernity as a fact of history rather than an ideology of colonialism (Ingham & Warren, 2003). As a result, everything related to the Other is seen as 'static', 'traditional', 'fixed', 'backward', 'underdeveloped' and 'irrational' (Pennycook, 1998), as compared to the 'changing', 'modern', 'developed', 'progressive' and 'rational' qualities of the West. This has been partly reflected in the expressions of these Western-trained teachers, particularly when they at times saw the teaching methodologies used by other teachers in Vietnam as 'out-of-date', 'traditional' and 'worse' than those of the West. They thus showed their eagerness to change and appropriate some Western teaching practices. However, their appropriation did not take place as easily and without negotiations as a number of scholars suggest. Likewise, the politics of English as a global language and ELT as a dominant profession in language teaching partly affected these teachers' identities, but not necessarily in the way that some of the postcolonial literature suggested. For example, Phillipson (1992) remarks that teachers trained in English-speaking countries tend to adopt everything from the West and consequently can be harmful to their home countries upon returning to their teaching. The teachers in my study, however, on the one hand appeared to be tempted to appropriate certain Western values and practices, but on the other resisted them. Moreover, they strongly resisted values and practices which were considered 'disrespectful' or 'harmful' to the tradition of teaching in Vietnam, such as wearing shorts to class. Their appropriation took place alongside resistance. They negotiated one identity over others and took into account pragmatic factors so as to find a place where they belonged. This act of identity formation needs to receive more attention from postcolonial scholarship.

What has been addressed so far in this book may offer more, perhaps new ways of treating postcolonial notions of Self and Other. Western-trained Vietnamese teachers appeared to view various dichotomies, such as native and/or non-native teachers of English, and Western-trained and/or non-Western-trained teachers of English, in a different way from postcolonial theorists. Rather than treating the dichotomies as 'colonial' and 'negative', they viewed them as 'different' and 'complementary' factors contributing to the construction of multiple and dynamic identities. They did not feel that they had been pushed away and that Self and Other had been seen as totally mutually exclusive. Both were reflected in their identity formation. They used these dichotomies as resources for their fluid movements among multiple identities, with and without an awareness of contradictions.

The way Self and Other are constructed in postcolonial theory is an unbalanced process rather than a mutually negotiated two-way interaction (Chakrabarty, 2000; Ingham & Warren, 2003). The Other are created by the Self and made to view themselves in the Self's way. Postcolonial notions of Self and Other have actually silenced the Other's voices, and this results in the Self treating the Other as 'empty vessels' in their own construction of identity, at least as teachers of English. However, some of the Western-trained teachers' awareness of their own identity and how it is affected by the Centre's images of the 'Other' is the key to whether there is some control over their identity formation. For example, in their TESOL courses, each teacher has gained awareness of their positioning in different ways (for example, one set of ways for those who were introduced to thinking about postcolonial issues and another for those who were not or were only asked to look at it from the Centre's perspectives).

## 'Daughter-in-Law of a Hundred Families' in the Teaching of EIL

The identity formation of these Western-trained Vietnamese teachers of English was affected by multilayered relations and different contexts, and with every relation and in each context these teachers had to negotiate, sometimes compromise, and then assert themselves in a way that would protect them best from social judgements, stereotypes and fixed representations in the teaching of English as an international language. They played the role of 'the daughter-in-law of a hundred families', the daughter that had to try hard to 'please' all parties, yet relate to her sense of her own identities.

It is assumed in Vietnamese society that being a daughter-in-law is tough, since a girl has to try hard to please her in-law family, which often involves her husband's extended family members and relatives. She will have to distribute her attention everywhere so as not to be judged as being bad. She has to 'please' many parties. Also, her ethics and morality are seen as crucial as to whether she will be in favour or not. Walking into her husband's family, her ethics and morality are observed through her behaviours toward her in-law family members and to what extent she can suppress her dissatisfaction and expectations to please them. She is expected to love, respect and satisfy her in-law family and at the same time sacrifice her personal life to an extent that can secure her favoured position in her husband's family. So when being a teacher is compared with being a daughter-in-law, it suggests that being a teacher is already hard, but being a daughter-in-law of a hundred families is a hundred times more difficult. How can a teacher satisfy all expectations from multiple parties? This expression indicates how difficult it is to play the teacher role in society, where whatever a teacher does is being judged by the whole society.

Being a teacher of English in Vietnam, teaching English in an increasingly mobile, transnational and global world, these Western-trained EIL Vietnamese teachers had to consider all these factors so as to perform best, particularly in terms of ethics and morality. Taking into account global English and the literature of critical notions of English as an international language discussed in Chapter 3, teachers of English have to perform morality in an even more conscious and aware manner, which responds to both social, cultural, professional expectations of teachers and the potentially negative impacts of the global on local/national pedagogical values and practices. These Western-trained teachers of English in Vietnam take all of these responsibilities and play all of these roles, yet commit to constructing their identities, which are their own and embrace the sense of connectedness and continual development of dynamic change.

## The Work is Complete, but the Identity 'Journey' is On-going

On completion of this book, my understandings have changed and grown, so has my identity. I have learned how to appreciate others' ways of doing, their values and practices. I have learned to live in harmony with diversity and multiplicity. If I used to think that there was only one way to interpret the world, the Vietnamese way, then I have now enriched my ways of communicating with the world. By bringing two seemingly completely different bodies of knowledge together in this book project, the Vietnamese and Western, I can see the East and West complementing and harmonising with each other. Without one the other does not do the job. By making them work together, what is presented in this book does not deny the multiplicity of identities. Likewise, through my use of multiple tools, not just Western and Vietnamese perspectives on language, culture and identity, without forcing them into a coherent model, this book project reflects the multiplicity of experiences of identities.

I have realised that identity is multiple and dynamic, and that people interpret values and practices differently based on their ways of knowing and their positioning in the world (Dolby, 2000; Farrell, 2000; Gee, 1999; Hall, 1997a, b). I have come to understand that identity is not one stable entity, but it is not just about changing and fragmentation, either. Identity still gives people a sense of belonging (Phan Ngoc, 1998; Tran Ngoc Them, 1999, 2001a, c; Tran Quoc Vuong, 2000). It incorporates continuity, fluidity and connectedness, which all create dynamic change within a wholeness. Identity is about both the 'being' and the 'becoming'.

This book project has affirmed the seemingly non-negotiable role of morality in Vietnamese teacher identity formation. This has made me more confident in pursuing my self development as a transnational mobile Vietnamese lecturer in the fields of education, TESOL and applied linguistics. This has also consolidated my perceptions of teachers in Vietnamese society. Morality has, indeed, been proved in this project to be the very element that holds firm the Vietnamese teachers' multiple, even contradicting identities.

Doing this project has given me strength and confidence in voicing my positioning in the scholarly world. The literature on the West, mobility, transnationality and hybridity has strongly supported my will and intention to introduce to the academic world my understandings of Vietnamese scholars' work, which has, not in any sense less equal to the work by Western scholars, shaped my views and influenced my interpretations of teacher identity formation in the context of transnationality and mobility.

If I used to look at English from one angle, I have now looked at it from multiple angles. With each angle, I see different 'mes'. Writing this book has also offered me more ways of identifying myself in relation to my identity as a Vietnamese teacher of English. My multiple identities have been dynamically shaped, changed and reconstituted, but developed along the lines of my existing and persisting identities. I have changed, but I am not a different Ha. I, instead, have multiple 'Has' inside Ha. And this identity 'journey' is always on-going.

Finally I would like to leave you with the borrowed voices of the teachers participating in this project, as they identify themselves as teachers, teachers of English, Vietnamese teachers and Vietnamese teachers of English trained in the English-speaking West. Their voices from the jungle of multiple identities close this book and simultaneously present an open-ended story about teacher identity formation in the teaching of English as an international language.

*Teachers of the English word,*
*we are tossed about,*
*defined by others,*
*insecure*
*yet whole.*
*We are special,*
*knowledge experts, moral guides*
*and yet the public's tails.*
*We have access to the world,*
*we belong,*
*yet seem foreignised,*
*unselectively*
*Westernised.*
*We are not allowed to be human,*
*to fall in love*
*(with students),*
*yet we need to live, to change.*
*We are nobody in this world of Others*
*yet not the shadow of native English teachers*
*we light the way for our own.*
*We are the daughter-in-law of a hundred families*
*And proudly ourselves,*
*growing.*

# References

Auerbach, E.R. (1995) The politics of the ESL classroom: Issues of power in pedagogical choices. In J.W. Tollefson (ed.) *Power and Inequality in Language Education*
(pp. 9–33). Cambridge: Cambridge University Press.

Bakhtin, M.M. (1981) Discourse in the novel. In M. Holquist (ed.) *The Dialogic Imagination: Four Essays by M.M. Bakhtin* (pp. 259–434). Austin, TX: University of
Texas Press.

Ballard, B. and Clanchy, J. (1991) Assessment by misconception: Cultural influences and intellectual traditions. In L. Hamp-Lyons (ed.) *Assessing Second
Language Writing in Academic Contexts* (pp. 19–34). Norwood, NJ: Ablex Pub.

Ballard, B. and Clanchy, J. (1997) *Teaching International Students: A Brief Guide for
Lecturers and Supervisors*. Deakin, ACT: IDP Education Australia.

Baurain, B. (2004a) Editorial. *Teacher's Edition* 15, 2.

Baurain, B. (2004b) Teaching as a moral enterprise. *Teacher's Edition* 15, 35.

Bax, S. (2003) The end of CLT: A context approach to language teaching. *ELT
Journal* 57 (3), 278–287.

Beaverstock, J.V. (2002) Transnational elites in global cities: British expatriates in
Singapore's financial district. *GEOFORUM* 33, 525–538.

Bhabha, H. (1990) *Nation and Narration*. London: Routledge.

Bhabha, H. (1994) *The Location of Culture*. London: Routledge.

Block, D. (2005) Convergence and resistance in the construction of personal and
professional identities: Four French modern language teachers in London. In
S.A. Canagarajah (ed.) *Reclaiming the Local in Language Policy and Practice*.
Mahwah, NJ: Lawrence Erlbaum.

Breach, D. (2004) What makes a good teacher? *Teacher's Edition* 16, 30–37.

Breach, D. (2005) What makes a good teacher (Part II)? *Teacher's Edition* 17, 28–35.

Brodkey, L. (1994) Writing on the bias. *College English* 56 (5), 527–547.

Brodkey, L. (1996) I site. *Open Letter* 6 (2), 17–30.

Brown, R. (2000) Cultural continuity and ELT teacher training. *ELT Journal* 54 (3),
227–233.

Bruton, A. (2004) Keeping the NNS customer happy, perhaps? A response to
Sandra McKay. *ELT Journal* 58 (2), 183–186.

Brutt-Griffler, J. (1998) Conceptual questions in English as a world language:
Taking up an issue. *World Englishes* 17 (3), 381–392.

Brutt-Griffler, J. (2002) *World English: A Study of Its Development*. Clevedon: Multilingual Matters.

Brutt-Griffler, J. and Samimy, K.K. (1999) Revisiting the colonial in the
postcolonial: Critical praxis for nonnative-English-speaking teachers in a
TESOL program. *TESOL Quarterly* 33 (3), 413–431.

Canagarajah, S.A. (1999) *Resisting Linguistic Imperialism in English Teaching*. Oxford: Oxford University Press.

Carrier, K.A. (2003) NNS teacher trainees in Western-based TESOL programs. *ELT Journal* 57 (3), 242–250.

Chakrabarty, D. (2000) *Provincializing Europe: Postcolonial Thought and Historical Difference*. Princeton, NJ: Princeton University Press.

Chen, C.J. (2003) 'Are we there yet?': 'History' as a postcolonial dilemma [review of Chakrabarty (2000)]. *JUVERT: A Journal of Postcolonial Studies* 7 (2). On WWW at http://social.chass.ncsu.edu/jouvert/v7i2/cjchen.htm. Accessed 7 February 2005.

Chew, P. (2005) Remaking Singapore: Language, culture and identity in a globalised world. Paper presented at the third Asia TEFL International Conference, Beijing, China, 3–6 November.

Chowdhury, R. (2003) International TESOL teacher training and EFL contexts: The cultural disillusionment factor. *Australian Journal of Education* 47 (3), 283–302.

Constitution of Vietnam. On WWW at http://www.vietnamembassy-usa.org/learn_about_vietnam/politics/constitution/chapter_three/. Accessed 14 July 2005.

Cook, V. (1999) Going beyond the native speaker in language teaching. *TESOL Quarterly* 33 (2), 185–209.

Crang, P., Dwyer, C. and Jackson, P. (2003) Transnationalism and the spaces of commodity culture. *Progress in Human Geography* 27 (4), 438–456.

Crystal, D. (1997) *English as a Global Language*. Cambridge: Cambridge University Press.

Davis, D.R. and Moore, W.H. (1997) Ethnicity matters: Transnational ethnic alliances and foreign policy behaviour. *International Studies Quarterly* 41, 171–184.

De Cillia, R. Reisigl, M. and Wodak, R. (1999) The discursive construction of national identities. *Discourse and Society* 10 (2), 149–173.

Do Anh (1993) Tieng me de va muc tieu phat trien van hoa cho nguoi hoc [Mother tongue and its role in developing cultural awareness in learners]. In *Viet Nam: nhung van de ngon ngu va van hoa* [*Vietnam: Issues in Language and Culture*] pp. 77–80. Hanoi: Linguistic Society of Vietnam and Hanoi College for Foreign Languages.

Do Huy Thinh (1999) Foreign language education policy in Vietnam: The emergence of English and its impact on higher education. In J. Shaw, D. Lubelska and M. Noullet (eds) *Proceedings of the Fourth International Conference on Language and Development*. On WWW at http://www.languages.ait.ac.th/hanoi_proceedings/proceedings.htm. Accessed 1 July 2004.

Dolby, N. (2000) Changing selves: Multicultural education and the challenge of new identities. *Teachers College Record* 102 (5), 898–912.

Dolby, N. and Cornbleth, C. (2001) Introduction: Social identities in transnational times. *Discourse: Studies in the Cultural Politics of Education* 22 (3), 293–296.

Du Gay, P., Hall, S., Jones, L., Mackay, H. and Negus, K. (1997) *Doing Cultural Studies: The Story of the Sony Walkman*. London: Sage Publications in association with The Open University.

Duong Ky Duc (2000) Tan man xung quanh mot chu thay [Discussing the meanings of 'teacher']. *Ngon Ngu Va Doi Song* [*Journal of Language and Life*] 11 (61), 1–2.

Duong Thieu Tong (2002) *Suy Nghi Ve Van Hoa Giao Duc Vietnam* [*About the Culture of Vietnamese Education*]. Ho Chi Minh City: Tre Publications.

Edge, J. (1996) Cross-cultural paradoxes in a profession of values. *TESOL Quarterly* 30 (1), 9–28.

Edge, J. (2003) Imperial troopers and servants of the Lord: A vision of TESOL for the 21st century. *TESOL Quarterly* 37 (4), 701–709.

Education Law of Vietnam.On WWW at http://www.edu.net.vn/VanBan_Luat/LuatGD_1998/law_in_english.htm. Accessed 14 July 2005.

Ellis, G. (1996) How culturally appropriate is the communicative approach? *ELT Journal* 50 (3), 213–218.

Fairclough, N. (1989) *Language and Power*. London: Longman.

Farrell, L. (1994) Making the grade: A study of the writing in English of non-English speaking background students in the final year of schooling. Unpublished PhD thesis, Monash University, Australia.

Farrell, L. (1997a) Doing well ... doing badly: An analysis of the role of conflicting cultural values in judgments of relative 'academic achievement'. In A. Duszak (ed.) *Culture and Styles of Academic Discourse* (pp. 63–87). Berlin: Mouton de Gruyter.

Farrell, L. (1997b) Making grades. *Australian Journal of Education* 41 (2), 134–149.

Farrell, L. (1998) Back to the future: School examinations, fairness, and the question of identity. *Australian Educational Researcher* 25 (2), 1–17.

Farrell, L. (2000) Ways of doing, ways of being: Language education and 'working' identities. *Language and Education* 14 (1), 18–36.

Gamaroff, R. (2000) Comment: ESL and linguistic apartheid. *ELT Journal* 54 (3), 297–298.

Gandhi, L. (1998) Postcolonialism and feminism. In L. Gandhi *Postcolonial Theory: A Critical Introduction* (pp. 81–101). St Leonards, NSW: Allen & Unwin.

Garcia, O. and Otheguy, R. (eds) (1989) *English across Cultures. Cultures across English: A Reader in Cross-cultural Communication*. Berlin: Mouton de Gruyter.

Gee, J.P. (1996) *Social Linguistics and Literacies: Ideology in Discourse* (2nd edn). London: Taylor and Francis.

Gee, J.P. (1999) *An Introduction to Discourse Analysis: Theory and Method*. London: Routledge.

Graversen, R. (2001) Imagining other places: Cosmopolitanism and exotic fantasies in multicultural cities. On WWW at http://www.anthrobase.com/Txt/G/Graversen_R_01.htm. Accessed 5 February 2005.

Graves, B. (1998a) Homi K. Bhabha: An overview. On WWW at http://www.scholars.nus.edu.sg/landow/post/poldiscourse/bhabha/bhabha1.html. Accessed 21January 2005.

Graves, B. (1998b) Homi K. Bhabha: The liminal negotiation of cultural difference. On WWW at http://www.postcolonialweb.org/poldiscourse/bhabha2.html. Accessed 21 January 2005.

Grossberg, L. (1996) History, politics and postmodernism. Stuart Hall and cultural studies. In D. Morley and K.H. Chen (eds) *Stuart Hall: Critical Dialogues in Cultural Studies* (pp. 151–173). London: Routledge.

Gupta, D. (2004) CLT in India: Context and methodology come together. *ELT Journal* 58 (3), 266–269.

Hall, S. (1992) Cultural Studies and its theoretical legacies. In L. Grossberg, C. Nelson and P. Treichler (eds) *Cultural Studies*. New York and London: Routledge.

Hall, S. (1996) Introduction: Who needs 'identity'? In S. Hall and P. Du. Gay (eds) *Questions of Cultural Identity* (pp. 1–17). London: Sage Publications.

Hall, S. (1997a) Cultural identity and diaspora. In K. Woodward (ed.) *Identity and Difference* (pp. 51–59). London: Sage Publications.

Hall, S. (ed.) (1997b) *Representation: Cultural Representations and Signifying Practices.* London: Sage Publications in association with the Open University.

Hall, S. and du Gay (eds) (1996) *Questions of Cultural Identity.* London: Sage Publications.

Hallward, P. (2001) *Absolutely Postcolonial: Writing between the Singular and the Specific.* Manchester: Manchester University Press.

Han, S.A. (2004) Effective environments for English language learning and teaching in Korea: A study of adult EFL learners' perceptions. Unpublished PhD thesis, Monash University, Australia.

Hashimoto, K. (2000) 'Internationalisation' is 'Japanisation': Japan's foreign language education and national identity. *Journal of Intercultural Studies* 21 (1), 39–51.

Hickling-Hudson, A., Matthews, J. and Woods, A. (2004) Education, postcolonialism and disruptions. In A. Hickling-Hudson, J. Matthews and A. Woods (eds) *Disrupting Preconceptions: Postcolonialism and Education* (pp. 1–16). Flaxton, QLD: Post Pressed.

Hiddleston, J. (2004) The specific plurality of Assia Djebar. *French Studies* LVIII (3), 371–384.

Holland, W. (1996) Mis/taken identity. In E. Vasta and S. Castles (eds) *The Teeth are Smiling: The Persistence of Racism in Multicultural Australia* (pp. 97–111). St Leonards, NSW: Allen & Unwin.

Holliday, A. (1994) *Appropriate Methodology and Social Contexts.* Cambridge: Cambridge University Press.

Holliday, A. (2005) *The Struggle to Teach English as an International Language.* Oxford: Oxford University Press.

hooks, b. (1994) *Teaching to Transgress: Education as the Practice of Freedom.* New York: Routledge.

Hu, G. (2005) 'CLT is best for China' – an untenable absolutist claim. *ELT Journal* 59 (1), 65–68.

Ingham, P.C. and Warren, M.R. (2003) Introduction. In P.C. Ingham and M.R. Warren (eds) *Postcolonial Moves: Medieval through Modern.* New York: Palgrave Macmillan.

Johnston, B. (2003) *Values in English Language Teaching.* Mahwah, NJ: Lawrence Erlbaum.

Kachru, B.B. (1986) *The Alchemy of English: The Spread, Functions, and Models of Non-native Englishes.* Oxford: Pergamon Press.

Kamler, B. (2001) *Relocating the Personal: A Critical Writing Pedagogy.* Albany, NY: State University of New York Press.

Kaplan, R.B. (1966) Cultural thought patterns in inter-cultural education. *Language Learning* 16 (1/2), 1–20.

Kawai, H. (2003) Nihon bunka to Kojin. In H. Kawai (ed.) *Kojin No Tankyu: Nihon Bunka No Nakade* (pp. 1–11). Tokyo: Nihon Hoso Kyokai Shuppankai.

Koczberski, G. and Curry, G.N. (2004) Divided communities and contested land-scapes: Mobility, development and shifting identities in migrant destination sites in Papua New Guinea. *Asia Pacific Viewpoint* 45 (3), 357–371.

Kramsch, C. (1993) *Context and Culture in Language Teaching*. Oxford: Oxford University Press.

Kramsch, C. (1998) *Language and Culture*. Oxford: Oxford University Press.

Kramsch, C. (2000) Second language acquisition, applied linguistics, and the teaching of foreign languages. *The Modern Language Journal* 84 (3), 311–326.

Kramsch, C. (2001) Language, culture, and voice in the teaching of English as a foreign language. *NovELTy: A Journal of English Language Teaching and Cultural Studies in Hungary* 8 (1), 4–21.

Kramsch, C. and Sullivan, P. (1996) Appropriate pedagogy. *ELT Journal* 50 (3), 199–212.

Krashen, S. (2006) *English Fever*. Taipei: Crane Publishing Company.

Kubota, R. (1998) Ideologies of English in Japan. *World Englishes* 17 (3), 295–306.

Lal, V. (2002) *Empire of Knowledge: Culture and Plurality in the Global Economy*. London: Pluto Press.

Lave, J. and Wenger, E. (1991) *Situated Learning: Legitimate Peripheral Participation*. Cambridge: Cambridge University Press.

Le Van Canh (2001) Language and Vietnamese pedagogical contexts. *Teacher's Edition* 7, 34–40.

Le Van Canh. (2004) From ideology to inquiry: Mediating Asian and Western values in ELT. *Teacher's Edition* 15, 28–35.

Le Xuan Hy, Howard, R., Nguyen Thao and Lilleleht, E. (2005) Vietnamese cultural and religious femininity: Implications for conflict management and synergy. Paper presented at the International Conference on Unity and Diversity in Religion and Culture, Seattle, 27–30 January.

L'Estrange, M. (2000) Learning is lost in the translation: Lots of Japanese study English. But how many could really be said to have mastered it? *Education Age* 26 July, 11.

Li, D. (1998) 'It's always more difficult than you plan and imagine': Teachers' perceived difficulties in introducing the Communicative Approach in South Korea. *TESOL Quarterly* 32 (4), 677–703.

Li, M. (2004) Culture and classroom communication: A case study of Asian students in New Zealand language schools. *Asian EFL Journal* 6 (1), Article 7. On WWW at http://www.asian-efl-journal.com/04_ml.php. Accessed 20 April 2007.

Liddicoat, A. (1997) Communicating within cultures, communicating across cultures, communication between cultures. In Z. Golebiowski and H. Borland (eds) *Academic Communication across Disciplines and Cultures* (Vol. 2) (pp. 12–23). Melbourne, VIC: Victoria University of Technology.

Lin, A.M.Y., Wang, W., Akamatsu, A. and Riazi, M. (2001) Absent voices: Appropriated language, expanded identities, and re-imagined storylines. Paper presented at the International Conference on Disrupting Preconceptions: Postcolonialism and Education, University of Queensland, Australia, 17–19 August.

Lin, G.C.S. (2002) Hong Kong and the globalisation of the Chinese diaspora: A geographical perspective. *Asia Pacific Viewpoint* 43 (1), 63–91.

Liu, D. (1998) Ethnocentrism in TESOL: Teacher education and the neglected needs of international TESOL students. *ELT Journal* 52 (1), 3–9.

Llurda, E. (2004) Non-native-speaker teachers and English as an International Language. *International Journal of Applied Linguistics* 14 (3), 314–323.

Mai Xuan Huy (1999) Thay do, thay giao, giao vien [Three words to describe teacher]. *Ngon Ngu Va Doi Song* [*Journal of Language and Life*] 3 (41), 25–26.

McArthur, T. (1998) *The English Languages*. New York: Cambridge University Press.

McArthur, T. (2003) *Oxford Guide to World English*. Oxford: Oxford University Press.

McDevitt, B. (2004) Negotiating the syllabus: A win–win situation. *ELT Journal* 58 (1), 3–9.

McKay, S. (2002) *Teaching English as an International Language*. Oxford: Oxford University Press.

McKay, S. (2003) Toward an appropriate EIL pedagogy: Re-examining common ELT assumptions. *International Journal of Applied Linguistics* 13 (1), 1–22.

Melchers, G. and Shaw, P. (2003) *World Englishes: An Introduction*. London: Arnold.

Miller, P.C. (2003) Review of *Values in English Language Teaching* by Bill Johnston. *TESL-EJ* 7 (2), 1–3. On WWW at http://www-writing.berkeley.edu/TESL-EJ/ej26/r3.html. Accessed 11 February 2005.

Mishan, F. (2007) Genesis of an organic, universal, online coursebook. Paper presented at the second International ELT Teaching Materials Symposium and Conference, Damai Lau, Perak, Malaysia, 5–9 February.

Mitchell, K. (1997a) Transnational discourse. Bringing geography back in. *Antipode* 29, 101–114.

Mitchell, K. (1997b) Transnational subjects: Constituting the cultural citizen in the era of Pacific Rim capital. In A. Ong and D. Onini (eds) *Ungrounded Empires: The Cultural Politics of Modern Chinese Transnationalism* (pp. 228–256). New York: Routledge.

Mitchell, W.J.T. (1995) Translator translated: Interview with cultural theorist Homi Bhabha. *Artforum* 33 (7), 80–84. On WWW at http://prelectur.standford.edu/lecturers/bhabha/interview.html. Accessed 21January 2005.

Modiano, M. (2001) Linguistic imperialism, cultural integrity, and EIL. *ELT Journal* 55 (4), 339–346.

Morgan, B. (2004) Teacher identity as pedagogy: Towards a field-internal conceptualisation in bilingual and second language education. *International Journal of Bilingual Education and Bilingualism* 7 (2/3), 172–188.

Ngugi wa Thiong'o (1993) The language of African literature. In P. Williams and L. Chrisman (eds) *Colonial Discourse and Postcolonial Theory: A Reader* (pp. 435–455). Hemel Hempstead: Harvester Wheatsheaf.

Nguyen Duc Dan (1993) Pham tru thu tu trong tam thuc nguoi Viet [The notion of order and position in Vietnamese culture]. In *Viet Nam: Nhung Van De Ngon Ngu Va Van Hoa* [*Vietnam: Issues in Language and Culture*] (pp. 47–48). Hanoi: Linguistic Society of Vietnam and Hanoi College for Foreign Languages.

Nguyen Duc Ton (1993) Nghien cuu dac trung van hoa dan toc qua ngon ngu va tu duy ngon ngu [Exploring national culture through language and language use]. In *Viet Nam: Nhung Van De Ngon Ngu Va Van Hoa* [*Vietnam: Issues in Language and Culture*] (pp. 17–21). Hanoi: Linguistic Society of Vietnam and College for Foreign Languages.

Nguyen, K.D. and McInnis, C. (2002) The possibility of using student evaluations in Vietnamese higher education. *Quality in Higher Education* 8 (2), 151–158.

Nguyen Lai (1993) Ve moi quan he giua ngon ngu va van hoa [Discussing the relationships between language and culture]. In *Viet Nam: Nhung Van De Ngon Ngu*

*Va Van Hoa* [*Vietnam: Issues in Language and Culture*] (pp. 5–8). Hanoi: Linguistic Society of Vietnam and College for Foreign Languages.

Nguyen Quoc Hung (2000) Vai tro nguoi thay trong phuong phap giang day tieng Anh [The role of the teacher in English language teaching methodologies]. *Ngon Ngu Va Doi Song* [*Journal of Language and Life*] 5 (55), 22–24.

Nguyen San (1999) *Moi Quan He Ngon Ngu Va Van Hoa* [*Ministerial-level Scientific Report Entitled 'The Relationships between Language and Culture'*]. Hanoi: Ministry of Education and Training.

Nguyen Trong Bau (1993) Tu dien hoc Viet Nam va van hoa dan toc [The study of Vietnamese dictionaries and national culture]. In *Viet Nam: Nhung Van De Ngon Ngu Va Van Hoa* [*Vietnam: Issues in Language and Culture*] (pp. 58–60). Hanoi: Linguistic Society of Vietnam and College for Foreign Languages.

Nunan, D. (1989) *Designing Tasks for the Communicative Classroom*. Cambridge: Cambridge University Press.

Nunan, D. (2003) The impact of English as a global language on educational policies and practices in the Asia-Pacific region. *TESOL Quarterly* 37 (4), 589–614.

O'Donnell, M.A. (2001) Becoming Hong Kong, razing Baoan, preserving Xin'an: An ethnographic account of urbanisation in the Shenzhen Special Economic Zone. *Cultural Studies* 15 (3/4), 419–443.

Paasi, A. (2002) Bounded spaces in the mobile world: Deconstructing 'regional identity'. TESG: *Journal of Economic and Social Geography* 93 (2), 137–148.

Pavlenko, A. (2003) 'I never knew I was a bilingual': Reimagining teacher identities in TESOL. *Journal of Language, Identity, and Education* 2 (4), 251–268.

Pennycook, A. (1994) *The Cultural Politics of English as an International Language*. New York: Longman.

Pennycook, A. (1998) *English and the Discourses of Colonialism*. London: Routledge.

Pennycook, A. (2001) *Critical Applied Linguistics: A Critical Introduction*. Mahwah, NJ: Lawrence Erlbaum.

Pennycook, A. and Coutand-Marin, S. (2004) Teaching English as a missionary language. *Discourse: Studies in the Cultural Politics of Education* 24 (3), 337–353.

Pham Hoa Hiep (2001) A second look at the question of the ownership of English. *Teacher's Edition* 7, 4–10.

Pham Hoa Hiep (2004) *Trained in the West, Teaching in the East: Vietnamese Teachers Returning from TESOL Courses Abroad*. Melbourne, VIC: University of Melbourne.

Pham Hoa Hiep (2005) Reader respond: University English classrooms in Vietnam. *ELT Journal* 59 (2), 336–338.

Phan Le Ha (1999) Different voices: Participants' comparisons of Vietnamese and English academic writing. Unpublished Master's thesis, Monash University, Australia.

Phan Le Ha (2000) Different voices: Participants' comparisons of Vietnamese and English academic writing. Paper presented at the LASU Conference, La Trobe University, Melbourne, Australia, November.

Phan Le Ha (2001) How do culturally situated notions of 'polite' forms influence the way Vietnamese postgraduate students write academic English in Australia? *Australian Journal of Education* 45 (3), 296–308.

Phan Le Ha (2004) University classrooms in Vietnam: Contesting the stereotypes. *ELT Journal* 58 (1), 50–57.

Phan Le Ha (2005) Toward a critical notion of appropriation of English as an international language. *Asian EFL Journal* 7 (3), 34–46. On WWW at http://www.asian-efl-journal.com/September_2005_EBook_editions.pdf. Accessed 16 October 2007.

Phan Le Ha (2006) Questioning the validity and appropriacy of presenting Communicative Language Teaching as 'the best' teaching method in TESOL teacher training courses. Paper presented at the sixth MICELT Conference, Melaka, Malaysia, 8–10 May.

Phan Le Ha (2007) Australian-trained Vietnamese teachers of English: Culture and identity formation. *Journal of Language, Culture and Curriculum* 20 (1), 20–35.

Phan Le Ha (forthcoming) Review of Holliday (2005). *Teacher's Edition*.

Phan Le Ha and Phan Van Que (2006) Vietnamese educational morality and the discursive construction of English language teacher identity. *Journal of Multicultural Discourses* 1 (2), 136–151.

Phan Le Ha and Song-Ae Han (2004) Two perspectives – Vietnamese and Korean – on English as an international language. Paper presented at the Faculty of Education Seminar, Monash University, Clayton, Australia, 15 September.

Phan Le Ha and Truong Bach Le (2007) Examining the foreignness of global EFL textbooks: Issues and proposals from the Vietnamese classroom. Paper presented at the second International ELT Teaching Materials Symposium and Conference, Damai Lau, Perak, Malaysia, 5–9 February.

Phan Ngoc (1998) *Ban Sac Van Hoa Viet Nam* [*Vietnamese Cultural Identity*]. Hanoi: The Culture-Information Press.

Phan Van Que, Duong Ky Duc and Phan Le Ha (forthcoming) *English in Different Cultures*. Hanoi: Hanoi National University Press.

Phillipson, R. (1992) *Linguistic Imperialism*. Oxford: Oxford University Press.

Pieterse, J. (2001) Hybridity, so what? The anti-hybridity backlash and the riddles of recognition. *Theory, Culture and Society* 18 (2/3), 219–245.

Quirk, R. (1985) The English language in a global context. In R. Quirk and H.G. Widdowson (eds) *English in the World: Teaching and Learning the Language and Literatures*. Cambridge: Cambridge University Press.

Quirk, R. (1987) The question of standards in the international use of English. In P. Lowenberg (ed.) *Language Spread and Language Policy: Issues, Implications, and Case Studies*. Washington DC: Georgetown University Press.

Rajagopalan, K. (2004) The concept of 'World English' and its implications for ELT. *ELT Journal* 58 (2), 111–117.

Ramanathan, V. (1999) 'English is here to stay': A critical look at institutional and educational practices in India. *TESOL Quarterly* 33 (2), 211–230.

Rao, Z. (2002) Chinese students' perceptions of communicative and non-communicative activities in EFL classroom. *System* 30 (1), 85–105.

Reed, G.G. (2001) Fastening and unfastening identities: Negotiating identity in Hawai'i. *Discourse: Studies in the Cultural Politics of Education* 22 (3), 327–339.

Ronowicz, E. and Yallop, C. (eds) (1999) *English: One Language, Different Cultures*. London: Cassell.

Rubdy, R. and Saraceni, M. (eds) (2006) *English in the World: Global Rules, Global Roles*. London: Continuum.

Said, E.W. (1978) *Orientalism: Western Conceptions of the Orient*. New York: Pantheon Books.

Sakui, K. (2004) Wearing two pairs of shoes: Language teaching in Japan. *ELT Journal* 58 (2), 155–163.

Seidlhofer, B. (2001) Closing a conceptual gap: The case for a description of English as a lingua franca. *International Journal of Applied Linguistics* 11 (2), 133–158.

Seidlhofer, B. (2003) A concept of international English and related issues: From 'real English' to 'realistic English'? On WWW at http://www.coe.int/t/dg4/linguistic/Source/SeidlhoferEN.pdf. Accessed 1 August 2004.

Sered, D. (1996) Orientalism. On WWW at http://www.english.emory.edu/Bahri/Orientalism.html. Accessed 23 January 2005.

Setiawan, A. (2006) The professional identity of non-native English teachers. Unpublished Master's thesis, Faculty of Education, Monash University, Australia.

Sharifian, F. and Palmer, G. (eds) (2007) *Applied Cultural Linguistics: Implications for Second Language Learning and Intercultural Communication*. Amsterdam and Philadelphia: John Benjamins Publishing Company.

Shulman, S. (1987) Knowledge and teaching: Foundations of the new reform. *Harvard Educational Review* 57 (1), 1–22.

Simon, R.I. (1995) Face to face with alterity: Postmodern Jewish identity and the eros of pedagogy. In J. Gallop (ed.) *Pedagogy: The Question of Impersonation* (pp. 90–105). Bloomington, IN: Indiana University Press.

Smith, L.E. (ed.) (1987) *Discourse across Cultures: Strategies in World Englishes*. New York: Prentice Hall.

Smith, M. (2002) Globalisation and local experience: Encounters with difference in a UK school. *The Sociological Review* 50 (1), 117–135.

Soter, A. (1988) The second language learner and cultural transfer in narration. In A.C. Purves (ed.) *Writing across Languages and Cultures: Issues in Contrastive Rhetoric* (Vol. 2) (pp. 177–205). Newbury Park, CA: Sage Publications.

Stratton, J. (1998) *Race Daze: Australia in Identity Crisis*. Sydney: Pluto Press.

Sullivan, P. (2000) Playfulness as mediation in communicative language teaching in a Vietnamese classroom. In J. Lantoff (ed.) *Sociocultural Theory and Second Language Learning* (pp. 116–131). Oxford: Oxford University Press.

Suzuki, T. (1999) *Nihonjin Wa Naze Eigo Ga Dekinainoka*. Tokyo: Iwanami Shinsho.

Tajfel, H. (1978) *Differentiation between Social Groups: Studies in the Social Psychology of Intergroup Relations*. London: Academic Press.

Tollefson, J.W. (1991) *Planning Language, Planning Inequality: Language Policy in the Community*. Harlow: Longman.

Tran Ngoc Them (1993) Di tim ngon ngu cua van hoa va dac trung van hoa cua ngon ngu [Searching for the language of culture and cultural characteristics of language]. In *Viet Nam: Nhung Van De Ngon Ngu Va Van Hoa [Vietnam: Issues in Language and Culture]* (pp. 9–16). Hanoi: Linguistic Society of Vietnam and College for Foreign Languages.

Tran Ngoc Them (1999) Tu nghi quyet trung uong 5, nghi ve ban sac van hoa dan toc Vietnam [Thinking about Vietnamese cultural and national identity]. Paper presented at the Vietnamese Culture Conference, Ho Chi Minh Political and National Institute, Ho Chi Minh City, Vietnam.

Tran Ngoc Them (2001a) Email exchange, 26 September.

Tran Ngoc Them (2001b) Email exchange, 27 September.

Tran Ngoc Them (2001c) *Tim Ve ban Sac Van Hoa Vietnam [Discovering the Identity of Vietnamese Culture]* (3rd edn). Ho Chi Minh City: Ho Chi Minh City Publications.

204 *Teaching English as an International Language*

Tran Quoc Vuong (2000) *Van Hoa Viet Nam: Tim Toi Va Suy Ngam* [*Exploring and Discussing Vietnamese Culture*]. Hanoi: The National Culture Publishing House and the Journal of Culture and Theatre Arts.
Varghese, M. (2004) Professional development for bilingual teachers in the United States: A site for articulating and contesting professional roles. In J. Brutt-Griffler and M. Varghese (eds) *Bilingualism and Language Pedagogy*. Clevedon: Multilingual Matters.
Varghese, M., Morgan, B., Johnston, B. and Johnson, K. (2005) Theorizing language teacher identity: Three perspectives and beyond. *Journal of Language, Identity, and Education* 4 (1), 21–44.
Verschueren, J. (1989) English as object and medium of (mis)understanding. In O. Garcia and R. Otheguy (eds) *English across Cultures. Cultures across English: A Reader in Cross-cultural Communication* (pp. 31–53). Berlin: Mouton de Gruyter.
Viete, R. and Phan Le Ha (2007) The growth of voice: Expanding possibilities for representing self in research writing. *English Teaching: Practice and Critique* 6 (2), 39–57.
Vu Ngoc Khanh (1993) Cu lieu van hoa dan gian va su phat trien van hoa Viet Nam [Folklore and the development of Vietnamese culture]. In *Viet Nam: Nhung Van De Ngon Ngu Va Van Hoa* [*Vietnam: Issues in Language and Culture*] (pp. 22–24). Hanoi: Linguistic Society of Vietnam and College for Foreign Languages.
Werbner, P. (2001) The limits of cultural hybridity: On ritual monsters, poetic licence and contested postcolonial purifications. *The Journal of the Royal Anthropological Institute (NS)* 7, 133–152.
White, R. (1997) Inventing Australia revisited. In W. Hudson and G. Bolton (eds) *Changing Australian History: Creating History* (pp. 12–22). Sydney: Allen & Unwin.
Widdowson, H.G. (1997) EIL, ESL, EFL: Global issues and local interests. *World Englishes* 16 (1), 135–146.
Widdowson, H.G. (1998) EIL: Squaring the circles. A reply. *World Englishes* 17 (3), 397–401.
Willis, K. and Yeoh, B. (2002) Gendering transnational communities: A comparison of Singaporean and British migrants in China. *GEOFORUM* 33, 553–565.
Windschuttle, K. (1999) Edward Said's 'Orientalism revisited'. *The New Criterion* 17 (5). On WWW at http://www.newcriterion.com/archive/17/jan99/said.htm. Accessed 7 February 2005.
Wodak, R., De Cillia, R. and Reisigl, M. (1999) *The Discursive Construction of National Identity*. Edinburgh: Edinburgh University Press.
Woodward, K. (ed.) (1997) *Identity and Difference*. London: Sage Publications.
Yeo, R. (2007) What I can't stand [article in Malaysian daily newspaper].
Yeoh, B.S.A., Willis, K. D. and Abdul Khader Fakhri, S.M. (2003) Introduction: Transnationalism and its edges. *Ethnic and Racial Studies* 26 (2), 207–217.
Yin, C.E.L.L. (2006) The perceptions of Malaysian parents on Malaysian English. Paper presented at the sixth Malaysia International Conference on English Language Teaching, Melaka, Malaysia, 8–10 May.